The Quietest Singing

The
Quietest Singing

Edited by

DARRELL H. Y. LUM

JOSEPH STANTON

ESTELLE ENOKI

STATE FOUNDATION ON CULTURE AND THE ARTS

HONOLULU, HAWAIʻI

List of Art Selections

The art selections that appear in this volume and on the cover are all works included in the Art in Public Places Collection of the State Foundation on Culture and the Arts and have been reproduced with the permission of the artist, Nora Yamanoha.

Mauna Loa Vigil (front cover)
monotype with chine collé, 1997
19⅞" x 16"

Scape II
etching, monotype, 1992
38¼" x 29¼"

Vivaldi Sojourn I
monotype, 1993
26¾" x 20¾"

Coffee with Mozart II
monotype, 1995
33¼" x 25¼"

All performances of *All I Asking for Is My Body*
are prohibited without the permission of the playwright.

Printed in the United States of America

00 01 02 03 04 05   5 4 3 2 1

ISBN 0–8248–2426–1

University of Hawai'i Press books are printed on
acid-free paper and meet the guidelines for permanence
and durability of the Council on Library Resources.

Distributed by
University of Hawai'i Press
2840 Kolowalu Street
Honolulu, Hawai'i 96822–1888

Contents

Acknowledgments

The editors wish to acknowledge the support of the following individuals and organizations: the National Endowment for the Arts, the State Foundation on Culture and the Arts Commission, SFCA Executive Director Holly Richards and Interim Executive Director Ronald K. Yamakawa, SFCA Acting Art in Public Places Manager Lisa Yoshihara and Collections Manager Malia Van Heukelem, the Information and Communication Services Division of the State Department of Accounting and General Services, the Hawai'i Literary Arts Council, State Comptroller Raymond H. Sato, and the Governors of the State of Hawai'i who have supported the Hawai'i Award for Literature since its inception in 1974.

Hawai'i Award for Literature

The Hawai'i Award for Literature was established in 1974 by the State Foundation on Culture and the Arts and the Hawai'i Literary Arts Council to recognize outstanding writers whose work is important to the people of Hawai'i. The award recipients over the past twenty-five years have made significant contributions to the literary and cultural history of the islands. We hope this book inspires you to explore other works by these authors.

O. A. Bushnell, 1974
Alfons Korn, 1975
Mary Pukui, 1976
Samuel Elbert, 1976
Leon Edel, 1977
Aldyth Morris, 1978
A. Grove Day, 1979
Gavan Daws, 1980
Marjorie Sinclair, 1981
Maxine Hong Kingston, 1982
Katharine Luomala, 1983
John Unterecker, 1984
John Dominis Holt, 1985
W. S. Merwin, 1986
Reuel Denney, 1987
Rubellite Kawena Johnson, 1988
Yoshiko Matsuda, 1990
Milton Murayama, 1991
Ian MacMillan, 1992
Cathy Song, 1993
Victoria Nalani Kneubuhl, 1994
Phyllis Hoge Thompson, 1995
Darrell H. Y. Lum, 1996
Eric Chock, 1996
Edward Sakamoto, 1997
Leialoha Apo Perkins, 1998
Tom Coffman, 1999

Introduction

This collection came into being because winners of the Hawai'i Award for Literature were asked to write works that in some way attend to voices in the community that are sometimes lost in the general noise. Sometimes the less heard voices are those of people whose economic situations have kept them at a disadvantage. Sometimes the voices come from those who refuse to be part of the mainstream out of personal choice or independent spirit. Sometimes the voices come from people who would like to become part of the mainstream if they could find out how. Sometimes the voices come from those who are challenged by illness. Sometimes the quietest singing comes from within people who are at a particular moment of crisis. As pieces arrived and this collection took shape the editors were often reminded that it is the human condition to be, in various ways and at various times in all of our lives, on the margins or beyond. We cannot decide through reading this collection exactly what it is that can put us on the edge of society's comforts, but we can learn much by carefully listening to these voices captured within the literary performances of award-winning writers. We can listen and we can hear.

JOSEPH STANTON

* * * * *

For the Hawai'i Award for Literature recipients, the task of their commission was to render the voice of Hawai'i's people living in some way apart from the mainstream. Through these selections, the reader experiences Hawai'i's rural environments, youth struggling for identity, families fighting political and economic oppression, individuals lacking access to educational opportunity, and cultural contrasts, including journeys into the spiritual significance of the land. For many of us who live in Hawai'i, these works tell of our own intergenerational experiences.

An inherent challenge for the writers was to explore, through the difficulties posed in their works, that which gives validity to our day-to-day existence. When the way is obstructed by the necessities and distractions of everyday survival, how is it possible to discover creative passion and intellect? The popular phrase that creativity begins on the edge is not quite accurate. One must first recognize the elements at hand. We must move past the edge to the metaphysical space between—this is where Cathy Song's "voice of the quietest singing" builds its strange and wondrous resonance. We hear it also in the call to an unseen suitor; sense it as we ride through the hollow of a wave; breathe in the green mountain fragrance of crushed leaves, overripened fruit, wet black earth. In such moments recognition begins, translation is made possible and creativity is just beyond.

ESTELLE ENOKI

* * * * *

This collection is inhabited by characters and voices which speak of our history: native Hawaiian, immigrant, literary. These are people who could very well be a relative, someone you work with, or someone you come into contact with everyday. They are voices of characters not ordinarily seen in literature: the immigrant woman struggling with her letter-writing, the weird guy next door who hoards stuff, the woman in church who goes sailing with her husband. Even Merwin's account of Koʻolau and Piʻilani feels familiar: a fugitive being hunted and nearly cornered. A scene from our history that has been played out in contemporary Hawaiʻi all too many times.

The collection is also a reminder of the responsibility that we have as island writers and island readers. Living in Hawaiʻi is a special privilege for those of us who are from immigrant stock or have come here from other places. And with this privilege comes the responsibility to listen to the land, to the people, to all the voices. The selections in this collection are as diverse as the authors. Each has contributed to our literary history through their own body of work. Eventually we must conclude that the quiet voices are not quiet at all. They are strong, powerful and eloquent. And they compel us to listen.

DARRELL H. Y. LUM

* * * * *

This collection features primarily new work and all the award recipients were invited to participate. We added a little twist to this collection and asked the writers to read and respond to some of the other pieces in the book. Their comments are included in the biographical notes and add a dimension which we think contributes to the understanding of the work. What was particularly gratifying was how the authors themselves responded to each other with their insights. It serves as a reminder that our understanding and appreciation of literature is deepened when it is shared. We hope you will share our enthusiasm.

Part One

The idea of local folks living by their wits, scraping out an existence is one of the themes in the first section. We visit with Eric Chock's characters in his poems. He lets us peer over the fence at his neighbor George, we feel the flush of embarrassment of the airline steward as he deals with a passionate passenger, and we laugh at his description of the funny and intimate idiosyncrasies of a true snack lover.

Ian MacMillan offers us a story which on one level can be interpreted as the triumph of art in helping the young artist to overcome his poverty and on another questions the relationship between the artist and the public as well as the notion of commissioning art.

Milton Murayama and Edward Sakamoto write of an earlier time, our plantation past. Both authors tell stories which seem to recall a simpler, pastoral time in our history but reveal a much more intricate and complex web of how the individual, the family, and the community interact in plantation Hawai'i. The stories they tell are layered; stories within the story. In fact in Sakamoto's story the reliability of a *benshi*, a silent movie narrator, is questioned. Who can you trust if you can't trust a professional storyteller? Everyone in the family and in the community seems to have a stake in the young girl's future. And the difficult decision causes us to consider if the story is really about the passing of an era. Murayama similarly gives us a different view of his classic novel, *All I Asking for Is My Body*, in his script. By including scenes from *Five Years on a Rock*, he gives us a different perspective on the Oyama family and creates a fresh and very different work.

Part Two

This section explores language and culture and brings us to a better understanding of the push and pull between language and experience. It opens with Phyllis Hoge's series of "Letter from Jian Hui" poems in the voice of a Chinese woman practicing her English. While we sympathize with her struggle with the language, the poems remind us of the struggle that all writers face with language as well as the particular sensitivity that people in Hawai'i have to language variation. The selections in this section, like the "Letter" poems focus on memory, family, and personal narratives. Rubellite Kawena Johnson's personal narrative traces her journey from San Diego to the islands in the south Pacific. Throughout her piece we marvel at the display of courage and faith in the face of personal tragedy. Maxine Hong Kingston's reflection on her son and his relationship to the ocean strikes a chord with every parent when they worry about the safety of their children. And Kingston recognizes the difficulty of the writing process as we witness her students' struggle to describe their experiences. Darrell H. Y. Lum's work—based in part on personal memories, mythology, and particle physics—takes some leaps in time and language. The pidgin narrator gets educated, grows old and yet retains a particular local sensibility. The mix of story, memory, language, and character takes us to a place where past and present, fact and fiction, voice and thought combine to contribute to our understanding of a particular moment in the narrator's life.

Part Three

The works in this section focus on the spiritual and metaphysical. They look at the past as well as the present and remind us that our lives have always been complex and conflicted. Victoria Nalani Kneubuhl's story "Ho'oulu Lāhui" looks both forward and back and suggests that the conflict over land and blood are timeless issues. Marjorie Sinclair takes us to a special place where the spiritual and the real intersect. In Hawai'i regardless of your background, respect for the land and a healthy respect of its spirit inhabitants are common in our folklore and our everyday lives.

W. S. Merwin's and Leialoha Apo Perkins' works play with the images of Hawaiians as warriors against images of Hawaiians as human beings with families and human concerns. Like many of the other works in this book, their selections tell tales of extraordinary people having ordinary, human concerns as well as ordinary people leading extraordinary lives. These two poets turn to the land for answers. Cathy Song ends the collection with a series of poems that are at once troubling and beautiful. The juxtaposition of images of compassion and abuse speak to the question, "How have we gotten to this point?"

This collection suggests that there are no easy answers. Yet the words of these writers assure us that there is hope. Always hope.

THE QUIETEST SINGING

PART ONE

Liar Liar

In the palm tree in the back yard, on one of the fronds, sat a gray heron, and the girls came running into the house to tell their mother, who sat with her face down inches from a Kailua street map, squinting through a magnifying glass, which threw a trembling, watery dot of light on the paper.

"Da heron inna tree!" Malia yelled.

"Doug, chase him out," his mother said, not looking up from the map. Doug stepped out, onto the rickety back porch and looked up. The heron walked slowly along the frond toward the coconuts, looking for baby mynahs to eat, its shoulders high and its long black beak angled downward. He wondered if he should let the heron eat one, and then decided against it and walked out under the tree clapping his hands. The heron flew off working its large wings in slow motion, its body lifting with each fluid downward flapping.

Back inside the house he looked at his two little sisters. They wore little white dresses and red patent leather shoes. Each had a ponytail, black hair done up with red scrunchies so that it went up like black fountains before hanging down their backs.

"You don't need to take the bus," his mother said, waving the magnifying glass before her. "It's about two miles to Keolu School, but you turn up a road before getting to the school." She looked at the map again, squinting through the glass, the dot of light shaking on the grid of streets.

"I know which road," he said.

"Da heron wen eat da babies?" Malia asked. Michelle stood next to her, eyes wide.

"No, he went away," he said, looking down at their four bright shoes.

"I seen um eat baby ducks," Malia said.

"Not," Michelle said.

"They do," he said. "I've seen that too."

"Fo real?" Michelle said.

"You sure you don't want the name of the street?" his mother asked.

"No, it's okay."

"And you're—"

"I decided to call it Our Redeemer Church."

"Where?"

"I'd say Kaneʻohe."

"That'll do. Do you have the flyer? I haven't seen it yet."

It was the one thing he could feel some pride about, he guessed. He went to the little table next to the couch and picked one up. He had drawn it himself, a picture of a church with bushes around it, and a perfect Camaro parked on one side. He handed the flyer to his mother.

She opened it on the table and leaned way down, and squinted at it through the magnifying glass. "Wow," she said. "It looks like its got to be real." Then she rose up and frowned, squinting. "Why the hot car?"

"I just thought it'd be nice to have one Camaro parked next to it," he said.

"But church people don't drive cars like that."

"Well, nobody'll notice."

"I suppose not," she said.

"Da heron eat kittens too?" Michelle asked.

"Probably."

"Why?"

"How many copies did you make?"

"Dey no let you make too many, but when Mrs. Hashimoto was out I took a little paper and did like thirty?"

"So that would make what?"

"Sixty?"

"'Kay," his mother said, the edge of the magnifying glass on her chin. "You say this is a fundraiser for a little playground behind the church, 'kay? The M and M's are two dollars, and—"

"Two? Who'll buy a box of M & M's for two dollars?"

"These are rich people," she said. "They don't care. Just go past the junky houses down off Keolu Drive and go up the hill to the big ones."

It would be a long walk, and he knew that the girls would start to bitch before they got halfway there. His mother leaned over the flyer again, squinting through the glass. "It's amazing," she said. "I mean, this looks like a professional job."

He stared out the window. The ace-in-the-hole was the girls. In their pretty dresses, and with their little bit of make-up around their eyes, the people in the big houses would not be able to resist. His mother rose up from the flyer. "I'm going to keep one," she said. Then she looked in the direction of the girls. "Come over here," she whispered. They both walked over to her and stood side by side, almost identical with their black hair and perfect little faces, magazine cover faces his mother had said. Although they might have been taken for twins, they were a year-and-a-half apart in age, six and seven-and-a-half.

"We gotta get going," he said, looking down at his shirt and jeans.

"Ohh I know," his mother said, leaning forward to squint at the girls. "My little babies," she said. "You're so pretty I can't believe it."

They giggled. "I like one playgroun' fo my church," Malia said.

"Yah, me too," Michelle said.

Liars, he thought. We're all liars.

"Now be careful," his mother said. "Look both ways before you cross the streets 'kay?"

He heard the mynahs squabbling outside, and went to the door. The heron was back, sitting on the frond, while mynahs and doves circled in a panic. He went out and shooed it away again while the girls watched.

It was hot outside, and they went along Kihapai Street to the corner where the liquor store his father used to go to was, and then across at the light, and across again so that they could walk along the canal that ran along Hamakua Drive. At the corner by the light stood a man in dirty clothes holding a sign on a piece of oily cardboard that said 'Homeless and broke, need a job.' He had seen the man before on different corners in Kailua, and once even saw someone give him a plate lunch out the window of a car. When the car moved off the man put the food down and kicked at it, then cursed because it was food and not money, and then held the sign up for the next car. And he always thought when he saw that man, 'this is what we're trying to avoid.' The vision of being kicked out of their house tortured him at night, and he imagined the four of them doing the same thing, his mother standing there squinting at people as they passed by, the girls standing there in their white dresses which would now be dirty. He would do anything, even rob a bank he imagined, to avoid ending up like that. Before the door-to-door scam they had tried everything else, Doug trying to hustle neighbors into allowing him to do yard work, collecting cans to recycle, and having garage sales. They never really worked that well because of the quality of the junk they offered, and because their little house was on a dead end street with hardly any parking.

The candy was in a bag whose strap dug into his shoulder. He had to walk slowly so that the girls could keep up, and he didn't like that, frequently sighed with frustration as they talked about what they passed: "I wen see ducks heah," Malia said, pointing at the dark water, and Michelle, "Dakine heron come heah an' eat um too?" "Yah, I guess. Heron flies 'ass why—can go anywheahs. Plus can eat big ducks too."

"Not. Fo real?"

"Yah, I seen um."

He stopped. "A heron can't eat a full-sized duck, just for your information, 'kay? Only little ones."

They went on, the girls whispering. "Puppies? Can eat um too?" "Yah, like gobble gobble, no puppy." This followed by a little gasp.

His father had left them. It was as simple as that. And he sent no money. And his mother was nearly blind. When she tried wearing her coke-bottle glasses she got a headache. There was no way they could keep the house, the rent for which kept going up, his mother told him. Just for now, it might be all right if they tried to raise money to stay there by doing things they wouldn't ordinarily do. That was how she put it, sounding like a teacher. It was Doug's idea to add a little believability to the scam by doing fliers, or official looking cards that they would show to the people. All you had to do was create an illusion that pleased or made sense to them.

The computers at school had all kinds of different fonts and things you could do to make them look real. It was his idea to use Our Redeemer Church in Kane'ohe, and he didn't know if there was a church called that in Kane'ohe or not, and he was fairly sure none of the people in the houses they went to knew either. It was easy enough—they would be watching football games or whatever, and some even looking over their shoulders at the TV screen would just pull their wallets out and pass the money out the door, not caring if they saw the flier or not. Two dollars for a box of M & M's was absurd, but he knew that no one would care. To people who had money, a couple bucks meant nothing.

By the time they made it to Keolu Drive the girls were beginning to slow down. He shifted the bag to his left shoulder, feeling the sweat pasting his shirt to the skin on his back. He looked at the girls. They weren't sweating, hadn't started to balk yet, or cry, which would ruin their make-up. His mother had put it on, working away with her face an inch from theirs, trying to make their eyes look bigger. He thought they looked a little too overdone sometimes, but it always worked. A door would open and there would be a gasp, then, "Ho da so cute!"

They got lucky—a large cloud came over, and a little breeze, and it cooled them. 'Iwas wheeled in the sky against the white underside of the cloud, and they looked at them as they walked, the stretched out W's of their form turning slowly in the wind.

"Dey ketch fish in mid-air," Malia said.

"What? Fish dat fly?" Michelle asked.

"No, I mean one gets one fish from da ocean and den da oddah steal um, den it drops, den anoddah flies down and picks um outta da air."

Michelle walked staring at the birds. "Da heron eat dakine too?"

"C'mon guys, the first house is just up ahead."

It was gray, past the older houses, and as he walked up the walk followed by the girls, he cleared his throat, getting his little speech ready. He knocked, and in about five seconds the door opened. The lady's face went into a mask of surprise. "My what pretty little girls!"

Eighty-four dollars. They even got to eat M & M's on the way home. The girls could barely drag themselves along, no longer whispering about what they saw as they walked. They were exhausted, as he was. Finally, approaching the house, he felt a little safer. He didn't like walking along with all that money in his pocket. Any kid could just come up and take it from him, and, at twelve and maybe even a little stunted, he knew he would never be able to fight his way past any intermediate school kid who decided he wanted candy or money.

Their house was small and not level—you could easily see it from the street, the white trim against the green tipping off horizontal in every window. That the landlord could charge seven hundred dollars a month for the little house with its huge mango tree and its dirt yard and its rusty fence and its rotted car parts and bricks and pails and junk all over the place—well, the car parts and junk were his father's—but that he could charge that much, made the eighty some dollars in his pocket seem like nothing. He would give the money to his mother and then go crash in his bed. They'd have to get ready and do the same thing tomorrow, pick out an area, see if there were enough fliers, make the girls up.

They went inside and he put the money on the table along with the bag and the remaining M & M's. His mother was on the phone. "—not able to come up with it until maybe next week?" There was a pause. It was probably the landlord, whom she negotiated with about every two weeks. "Thank you so much. We really appreciate it. Yes, thank you." He hated the sound of her voice, that begging, then too-thankful sound. He went to his room.

His real drawings were tacked up, and covered almost all of the wall space. He kept the rotted old drapes closed all day because he did not want the sun fading them. The best was a twenty-by-thirty rapidograph drawing of Akebono, looming above the viewer, muscles bulging, huge round opu shaded, wrestler's chi-chis above, his arms out and fists clenched. The rapidograph was an ink pen with a very fine point. His other pictures were of cars, superheroes, lions and sharks. The only two that were of other subjects were a portrait of the girls, which now hung in the living room, and a picture of their house, idealized a little in that he straightened it up and got rid of the junk in his execution of it. The picture of the girls, his mother told him, was her prize possession. He had done that one a year earlier.

He often dreamt of winning prizes with the pictures, but was afraid to take them to school, because the one time he tried that, with a picture of a shark, some kid had pencilled in little bubbles coming out of the shark's behind and a circle at his mouth with words inside: no mo' futless now!

He imagined someday showing the sumo picture to Akebono, and seeing the look on his face when he saw how good it was—Akebono had a sort of kind face, a real Hawaiian face, and he imagined giving the picture to Akebono, and then later watching TV when Akebono was in his office or something, and seeing the picture hanging on the wall behind his desk. He cultivated these illusions, he figured, as a means of convincing himself that the art was worth doing. But then he would get bored and stop imagining these things and snort, thinking that it never turned out that way—the world was made up differently. The reality of it was kids altering pictures, landlords demanding money, and people falling for his cheap little scam. When things went wrong, as they had for his family now for a long time, there was no real help. It was herons and baby mynahs, and the baby mynahs got no help. The strong ate the weak, and that was life. There was only one answer to it, to try to figure out how to be strong so as to avoid being eaten, and if it meant scamming rich haoles up in Kailua Heights or whatever the hell that area was called, then that's what he would do, although he hated it.

He did not like the feeling of the large wad of money in his pocket, and he did not like the fawning, oh da cute or oh my look at these elegant little beauties reactions of the ladies when they saw the girls, because the girls were made up and expecting that reaction. At times, too, he thought there was a real danger, that the girls might be abducted if they ended up in the wrong neighborhood, and he'd heard all about that, about child abuse and so on. One time when they were in Enchanted Lake at a suspiciously vacant looking house, which seemed to have little furniture and hardly anything planted outside, Malia said that she had to go to the bathroom, and then Michelle said she did too, and the lady ushered them into her house and left him standing there at the front door, and he had a sudden, horrible rush of dread settle over him—the lady had been waiting for the girls, to steal them and take them for her own because they were so pretty, and she was at the moment he stood there gagging them and stuffing them into some kind of canvas bags and with her husband carrying them out the back door and escaping over the fence. But they came back out, thanking the lady, who bought a box of M & M's for a fundraiser for the Ahuimanu Day-Care Center, for which he had a brochure and a one-dollar-fifty price for the candy. Now he thought of the Day-Care brochure as crude and amateurish. The church one was much better.

Sunday they got ready to go back to the same neighborhood, but farther up, where the houses sat on the hilltops overlooking the town and Kailua Bay. But his mother wondered if two dollars wasn't a little on the inefficient side, if maybe they shouldn't figure out something they could charge four or five dollars for. "There's that other new development, the one with the sort of moderately expensive tract houses? That would be younger families, and I thought that we might make shortbread cookies, the kind that you put a bunch in a bag and charge four dollars for?"

"I like make shawtbread cookies," Malia said.

"Me too," Michelle said.

"Is this Our Redeemer Church, too?" he asked.

"We only have twenty-five brochures left," she said, placing her hand on the little pile of them on the table. "That's fifty dollars if you unload them all. I think we need to take a day off and figure something else out."

"The Kailua Domestic Violence Awareness Project," he said. He could do a really scary domestic violence picture.

She thought, staring into the middle distance before her. "Close," she said. "But where is it located? What's the money for?"

"A shelter," he said.

"Is no dakine fo domestic abuse," Malia said.

"Dakine what?" Michelle said.

"Excuse," he said.

"It doesn't rhyme," his mother said. "I think the saying is 'no excuse for domestic violence'."

"Bettah when it rhyme," Malia said.

"But anyway," he said. They heard birds squabbling outside, and the girls ran to the door to look.

"Da heron is back!" Malia shouted.

He went outside. There on the palm tree it sat, shoulders hunched up high, looking like an old man or a cloaked vampire. He clapped his hands and it labored off toward the marsh. Then he went back in. "It won't work," he said. "It's too complicated. Try something else."

"Schools or churches," she said. "That's the only way. People believe schools and churches, but what can we charge four dollars for?" She leaned over the table and squinted at the brochure again, then picked up the magnifying glass and peered through it, the dot of light shimmering on the Camaro. "A new roof for this church," she said.

"That's about the same as a playground."

"And we have only twenty-five."

"I show them the brochure and take it back."

"Explain maybe that so many people have been so kind that you've nearly run out of brochures. It's what?" and she squinted at the clock on the wall.

"Eight-fifteen."

"We can go to Safeway—"

"Oh goody!" Michelle said.

"—and get the stuff to make cookies, and do the four-dollar thing."

"I don't think—"

"Let's just try it, " she said. "Let's give it a try."

"What about da heron?" Malia asked. When they shopped they shopped together, because his mother did not like to leave the girls alone in the house. They loved to go, because their job was to read the little price-per-ounce labels for their mother so they could get the most for their money. The only drawback to this was that his mother always took with her a grocery list with embarrassingly large lettering that anybody could see.

"The birds'll be all right," he said. "So will these cookies be done by like two or three?"

"Sure," she said.

"The late football game's on at three—that's a good time to be out."

The man with the sign was not at the corner, and he was glad about that because he did not want to give his mother any ideas. She knew about these men and sometimes mentioned them, saying how sad it was that they were in the fixes they were in, as if she were somehow much better off. That they were right on the edge of standing on a corner did not seem to occur to her when she mentioned them.

They walked the long block on Hamakua past the empty Foodland Store, where they used to shop, the girls' slippers slapping the pavement two steps to his one. "I wen dream about da heron las' night," Michelle said, her voice jerky because of the pace at which she walked. "He was looking eensai da window at me."

"How big was he?" Malia asked.

"Was ten feet tall," Michelle said. "Was huge."

"It's just a dream," he said.

"Did I forget my card?" his mother said.

"Here, lemme look," he said, and peered into her purse. It was there. "Nope, you got it." He looked back at Michelle. "I can make a picture of a huge heron with blood dripping off its beak for you. To hang in your room I mean."

Michelle stopped, her face a mask of awed horror. "I no like dat," she said.

"Doug," his mother said, "don't do that."

Safeway was not crowded, probably because the football games were on. He would ordinarily have watched them, but had given up on that because they had to be out selling candy. He no longer even complained about it to his mother.

First was the usual stuff: rice, milk, some vegetables, each of which involved a complicated communication system where the girls read off the per-ounce prices and his mother squinted at her billboard grocery list. While they were doing this he became aware that they were being watched by someone, a haole man and woman moving their cart along the aisles. Then he thought he recognized the woman, and suddenly became flushed with dread. He tried to remember— "'Ass fo'teen cents da ounce," Malia said. "Not," Michelle said. "Dis one fo da junks above." "Not, below," Malia said.

"Look," he said.

"You stupid!" Malia hissed.

The woman kept looking at them, and it was not because of the ridiculous grocery list. Then he remembered: she had asked what street Our Redeemer Church was on in Kaneʻohe, and he had said, 'Mahealani Lane, beyond the mall.' Instantly he had realized that it was a bad lie, and the woman had remained skeptical but bought M & M's anyway. She wondered why no phone number was on the brochure, and he had shrugged and said he didn't know, they just gave the brochures to him along with instructions.

When the girls had finally settled the per-ounce argument they moved the cart down the aisle and into another, out of sight of the couple. "Mom," he whispered, "somebody I sold candy to is watching us."

She looked at him, then around the store. "There's nothing they can do," she said. "What can they do?"

"I don't know," he said.

"I like buy crack seed," Malia said.

"Okay," she said, looking around again. "Where's the cracked seed?"

"Other side," he said. "Let's go there and get some now 'kay?"

They went on, and he kept looking back for the couple, and finally assumed that they had gone. His mother selected some special flour and a little bottle of vanilla, got a pound of butter, and they headed for the check-out. Just as they wheeled the cart into the line, he saw the couple again, in the line at the next register. He looked away, then picked up a *People* magazine and flipped through it, feigning a kind of studious scanning of the contents. As he did this he could feel her looking at him. The girls looked at a fashion magazine displayed lower on the wire rack. "I tink Cindy Crawford da mos' lovelies' of all," Malia said.

"Ho, me too," Michelle said.

"Our Redeemer Church," the lady said.

His mother looked in the lady's direction.

"Odd," the lady said in a voice of fake amazement. "We couldn't find Mahealani Lane."

His mother looked back down at her grocery list.

"Is there a reason we couldn't find Mahealani Lane?" the lady asked, louder.

"You must be mistaken," his mother said. Space opened up, and she moved the cart further into the lane.

"The M & M's were good," the lady said. Her husband didn't seem to like what she was saying, looked at her flatly, then away. "Quite expensive though I think," she went on. "By the way, where is Our Redeemer Church?"

"I think you must be—"

The lady cut his mother off. "It looks so pretty, just like a New England church. But then," she went on, her index finger on her chin, "this isn't New England now, is it?"

His mother turned and began placing things on the black belt, which moved in jerks as other things were taken off the far end and scanned. "This is far from New England, isn't it," the lady said. "This kind of thing wouldn't happen there, I believe."

He was so flushed with shame and fright that he could barely put the magazine back on the rack. His mother, on the other hand, looked angry. She kept putting things on the belt, a flat, tense took on her face.

"So what is it next week?" the lady asked. "Portuguese sausage? How much would that be?"

"Girls," his mother said, "put the magazine back and come through."

They did so, and the lady kept looking at them. He tried not to look at her, instead arranged the stuff on the belt, which moved enough so that he was able to turn and concentrate on the price readouts, and his mother fumbled in her purse for the red Safeway card. When they wheeled their cart out toward the door, his mother turned and looked in the lady's direction. He looked too, but they were now busy with their own groceries.

"Bitch," his mother said, loud enough that he winced.

Then they left. His mother did not speak, and he walked along with a heavy plastic bag in each hand. After walking a hundred yards he said, "We can't do this any more." The girls' slippers slapped double-time, and his mother did not speak.

When they got to the corner she stopped. The man was there with his sign, and she squinted at him from twenty feet away, making Doug nervous. Then she pulled up her purse and fumbled in it, stooping over to look inside, and drew out two dollars. "Give this to him," she said.

"Ma, are you crazy?"

"I said give it to him."

"No, look," he said. "We don't need to—"

Her face had become hard, and she said slowly, carefully pronouncing each word, "Give-him-the-money."

He put the bags down on the concrete, took the money and went over to the man. "Here," he said.

The man took the money. "Wah thank ya son," he said in a southern accent. "Prishate it."

When he got back to where his mother and the girls stood, his mother said, "Let's go—I've gotta make those cookies."

"I don't think we can do this any more," he said.

There her face broke a little, and she looked as if she might cry. "I'm making cookies, 'kay?" she said. "I'm taking this stuff home and making some goddamned cookies, do you understand?"

"Yeah."

"Mommy?" Malia said.

"Let's go," he said.

His mother had now calmed herself. "Come girls," she said softly. "Let's make cookies."

The girls claimed that they were the onoest cookies they had ever tasted, and he could tell it was to appease her. They too had seen something in the way she acted. She spent the entire day working on them, looking at them through the magnifying glass with a sort of flatness, a bummed-out objectivity, as if she were expecting to be out on the street the next day. She did not mention going out to sell candy or cookies or anything. Watching her and the girls working, he wondered about his mother—he had never seen her act that way, and he guessed that it showed the degree of her desperation. It scared him.

He went to his room after a while and listened to the pans being rattled and the girls asking questions, the sound of spoons being scraped in the bowl to get out the remainder of the dough. Maybe they could have another garage sale. He went into his little damp, moldy closet and looked in his junk boxes. Most of what was in them was pictures he had drawn, of cars and superheroes, and then an old baseball glove nobody in his right mind would pay a nickel for, an old Polaroid camera that probably didn't work, some comics nobody would want, a sun-bleached basketball, duct-taped swim fins and a mask with half-melted rubber. It was stupid to even look, because he had done it so many times before and sold everything of any value he had in the garage sales. Everything but his pictures anyway. He took the camera out, vaguely thinking that it might work. At least it had once.

In the middle of the night he was awake, staring into the blackness of his room trying to think of what they should do next. He wondered if there were any way that the lady could figure out where they lived and blow the whistle on them, or even if she already had. On the little dresser near his bed sat the old camera, its single eye reflecting some ashy light from one of the streetlights outside. They had eaten supper in near silence, the weight of that thing at the Safeway sitting on their shoulders, and his mother did not bring up selling candy at all. In any case he had to go to school the next morning, walk the girls to the elementary school by the park and then go the two hundred yards to the intermediate school. Sometimes in the evenings they went out on candy-selling jaunts, but closer to home, but now they had exhausted most of the neighborhoods near theirs. The camera's eye looked at him, and then, in a little rush of fear he was tense in his bed, remembering Michelle and her dream of the ten-foot heron. It was as if the heron were just outside his window now, long beak moving toward him. It was almost as if he could see its shape, the high shoulders, the stooped, vampire look, peering in at him and waiting with a lethal patience.

He left the girls at the elementary school, and passed by boys playing basketball at the park. He was too tired to join in. Throughout the day he kept envisioning the eye of the camera, and remembered it glinting at him in the middle of the night. Something hovered in his mind where the camera was concerned, and he was still thinking about it when he went back across the park and past the basketball and tennis courts to meet the girls before going home at three.

He hoped, as they approached the house, that his mother had stopped worrying about the Safeway thing, and would send them out to the neighborhoods near the beach with cookies. He had twenty-five of those brochures left, and there was no point in wasting them just because of some lady who saw through the scam.

But she mentioned nothing about the cookies. She sat at the table with her magnifying glass, but there was nothing for her to look at. The TV was off.

He sat down at the table across from her. "Well," he said. "Do we go out tonight?"

"No."

"I'll make a new flier for the weekend."

"No, you don't need to."

He sat and looked at her. She looked at her nails, not seeing them clearly, he knew. He looked up at the wall, where the two pictures were, the girls and the house. Then he remembered the camera.

"Why do we have a picture of our house in our house?" he asked.

She looked up, scowling, as if he had said something stupid. "Why? Well," she said, "why not? I like having a picture of the house in the house."

"But it's not the way it really looks."

"I like it," she said. "I like to look at it."

He wondered—if he had put all the crap and the off angles in, she'd not have liked it.

"I got an idea," he said. "Another scam."

"No more ideas, and I told you, I hate that word. It's a four-letter word."

"I need some money for a camera battery."

She held her hands out. "Broke," she said.

He got up. It was stupid but it might work. "Look," he said. "I gotta borrow the picture of our house."

"What for?"

He took it off the wall. Like all the ones he really liked, he had bound it carefully in acetate, so that it would be protected. It was a strange, even bizarre scam, but if he could play on people's—What? Self image? Or there was another word. Vanity, that was it. If he could play on people's vanity, he could get them to—There was another word they used for that. When an artist is hired to do something for somebody. Commissioned, that was it.

He went to his room and got the camera, and used a towel in the bathroom to clean it up. The batteries would come later. He tucked the house picture under his arm and carrying the camera, went to the front door. "I'm goin' out for awhile—I'll be back in an hour or so."

She shrugged, then sighed as if her opinion of what he was doing wasn't too positive.

To work a scam like this one, you had to find houses that showed the people's pride, like ones with mowed lawns, nice shrubbery and stuff like that. He walked into the edge of Kailua town, past the little fish store on the corner and then the Salvation Army, and then angled down a couple of blocks to go over to North Kalaheo Avenue where the rich people lived. When he found a good house, he walked up and knocked on the door. In a few seconds a man opened the door, an old man who had that why are you bothering me? look on his face.

"Hello, my name's Doug Cambra, and I'm canvassing the neighborhood looking for people who would like drawings of their houses, to hang inside their—"

"What?"

"See? This is a picture—"

The door closed.

The next house he tried brought the same results. And the one after that. Finally he went back home. So it was a stupid scam. It was worth a try anyway.

When he got home he walked in and almost tripped over the girls, who stood there with their fists on their hips. "Why you no take us wit' you?" Malia demanded.

"I—"

Michelle pushed at him. "You cannot sell candy unless we go. Mommy said!"

"Girls," his mother said.

"No ladies say oh da cute at you!" Michelle went on. "You get money hah? No I bet."

Later in the week his mother got some kind of state money he knew little about, and offered him five dollars for the battery. "You don't need to," he said.

"No," she said vaguely. "Go get the battery. In fact, take ten, because you need film too. I think it's probably expensive. Here, maybe you should take a twenty."

"I don't need it. It was a bad idea."

"That's all right," she said.

He went along with it, removed a twenty from her purse and put it in his pocket. He supposed it wouldn't be so bad to take an occasional picture, even if his mother couldn't see it. But she could, with her magnifying glass.

"Okay, I'll go to Longs."

The girls appeared at their bedroom door. He sighed and looked at the ceiling. He should have whispered that last sentence, because they always demanded to go when he went to a store.

The ladies at the Longs photo counter all knew the girls, and cooed over them whenever they were there. "Oh look da little cuties!"

The batteries and the film ate up almost all of the money, but the camera worked, or seemed ready to work, because its little red eye went on once the film was in. "The picture comes out the bottom," one of the counter ladies said. "You wait about thirty seconds for it to develop."

"'Kay."

"You don't touch the surface until it's done, 'kay?"

"'Kay."

He looked around. The girls were gone. "By the books," the lady said. He went around the rack and found them sitting on the floor flipping through a book. It was a book about pregnancy, apparently, because on each page there was a picture, done like a sophisticated cartoon, of a pregnant woman and her husband and daughter, and then Malia reached down and opened a little door in the page to reveal a baby inside the mother's stomach, at which both girls gasped and then looked at each other and giggled, as if they were allowed to see something they wouldn't ordinarily be allowed to see. "Da teddy beah's face changes," Michelle whispered, pointing. Each page had the bear with a different expression, jealousy, sadness, surprise. "Let's go," he said. "I like buy dis book," Malia said. "Can't. No money." Walking back home, listening to the rapid slapping of their slippers on the concrete, he looked again and again at the camera, thinking that there was something about a picture, a drawn picture, that was different from a photograph. He imagined that if the book the girls looked at were photographs, they would not have been as impressed with what they saw, because it was the imagination part of the picture that made them like it. That made sense—a drawn picture was more an illusion than reality, and if he could figure out how to make an illusion—He could not think of the word. Functional, that was it, then the scam would work. It needed a use.

It was stupid, but he decided to give it one more try. If you played on people's imaginations along with playing on their vanity, then it might work. You had to approach it like the heron. You had to be confident and sort of forward.

He showed his mother the red light on the camera. Then he said, "I'm gonna give this sc—This idea another try."

She shook her head.

"But I wanna borrow the picture of the girls."

"No," she said. She got up and went to the wall, moved in very close, and squinted at it.

"I'll bring it back. Besides, it's covered with acetate. Nothing'll happen to it."

"What do you need it for?"

"Look, I'll bring it back."

She thought a moment, then sat back down. "Okay, go ahead," she said.

"And I need the girls."

"Where are you going?"

"Over toward the beach. No long walks or anything. We'll be back in a couple hours."

She agreed to it. When the girls found out they were going, they got all excited and ended up at the table waiting for their make-up.

"You don't need it," he said.

"Why?" Michelle asked. "I no like go wit' no make-ups."

"I want you to look like you do in the picture."

"Why?"

There was no use in trying to explain. He got the picture of the girls and the picture of the house off the wall, and stopped. He put them on the table and went into his room and removed the tacks from the Akebono picture, and took it to the living room. "Okay," he said, "we're off."

On the way, the girls half-running behind him, he considered his approach. In fact, that was the problem the last time he tried: he had no approach. He might be an art student trying to raise money for a trip to—let's say California, where he had been invited to participate in a collective art project with other students his age, and plane fare had to be raised by the individual.

But he never got to make his pitch. At the first house they went to, a really rich-looking house on Dune Circle, he started to speak, and the woman look-ing down at what he held in his hands said, "We're not interested. Thank you," and she closed the door.

The next house was a face in a window next to the door. "No thank you," she said.

And the next. "Please leave us off your list okay? We give to United Way only."

It wouldn't work. He never even got the chance to give his pitch, which he had continued to refine as they went from house to house. He could qual-ify only if he raised half the plane fare, and the California Arts Foundation would raise the rest and include room and board.

"Dey so stink face," Malia said. "I like go home."

"Okay," he said. They went back across North Kalaheo and went into a cross-street toward home. He would try a couple more, but these weren't rich houses. They walked past one, though, that had a new van in the driveway, a second story, good-looking shrubs and a huge back yard. He turned and went in toward the door.

Just as he knocked he realized that it was a bad idea. Someone was yelling somewhere inside, a TV was blaring, and to his right was an inverted Hawai-ian flag in the window. To his left, near the driveway, a rotted blue tarp cov-ering something. Then there was more yelling.

He turned to leave just as the door opened. "What?" the man said. He wore blue jeans and no shirt and had tattoos on his arms. Behind him a woman yelled, "You poo yoah pants up and take dat goddam ting offa yoah head!"

The man looked back, then at the ceiling, rolling his head as if he might faint. "We get alla Potagee sausage we can handle," he said.

"Well, this is—"

The woman who had been yelling came to the door and peered around her husband's shoulder, which was tattooed with an eagle. She had wild-looking black hair with strands of gray in it. Her eyes went down to the girls. "Ohh," she said.

Doug cleared his throat, preparing his California Arts Foundation speech. A teenaged boy wearing no shirt, pants way down on his buttocks so that his white underpants showed, and a red rag on his head, came and stood behind the mother. She turned and saw the rag, then slapped him on the head. He laughed.

"'Kay," the man said, folding his arms.

He became tongue-tied, as if he could not will the California story out of his mouth.

"Pua girls." the mother said. "You look hot. You like one juice?"

"No thank you."

"No thank you."

"Of course you do—Jeff, get two Aloha Maids."

The boy went off.

Doug took a deep breath. "First let me show you these," he said, and handed the picture of the girls to the woman, the house to the man. He held the Akebono picture under his arm. "I would like to draw a picture of your house, as a sort of commission thing. It'll cost fifteen dollars."

The woman was looking at the picture of the girls, then at the girls, then at the picture. "Ho," she said.

"What dis foah?" the man asked.

The boy came back with the Aloha Maids, and the mother took them, opened them, and gave them to the girls.

"Thank you."

"Thank you."

"What?" the man said, "dis fo skoo?" The boy looked down at the picture Doug held.

"I like see," he said. Doug handed him the picture, and when he held it up and looked, his eyes went very wide. He pulled the rag off his head and wiped a couple of smudges off the acetate. "Dad, dis so cool. Try look. Rad yah?"

The father looked. "His shouldahs dat big? I tink he get too much muscle inna shouldahs."

"Not," the boy said.

Doug flushed. He knew the man was right—he had given Akebono the definition of a superhero. "Well," he said, "that's just an example of—"

"What's dis about a house?" the man asked.

He tried explaining what he wanted to do again, draw a picture of your house that you can hang inside. "And it's not for school," he said. He was becoming frustrated trying to make them listen. "I'm doing this because we live in a little rental, the one you're looking at in the picture, and my father left—" Malia gasped there. "—and my mother is almost blind. I'm doing this to raise rent money and food money. I want to figure out how to get enough money for her to get glasses that don't give her a headache. That's the story. That's why I'm here."

The man looked at him, then at the picture. The woman looked at the girls.

"I like buy dis," the boy said, holding up the Akebono picture.

"Oh, that was just to show—"

"How much fo dis?" the boy asked.

"You can draw my house?" the man said. "But da way I like you draw um? I mean dis one good."

"Any way you like. That house there is really not as pretty as the picture—it's way off, not level, and there's junk all over the yard."

The woman snorted. "Try look at ours," she said.

"Eh, I'm talkin' now," the man said.

"So talk awready," she said, then whispered, "babooze."

The man ignored her. "I want a pitcha of my house wit' dis in front," and he went and pulled the rotted tarp off a dusty, flat-tired Harley.

"Oh my God," the woman said. "I *hate* dat ting. You no put dat inna pitcha! Ugly damn ting."

Behind him one of the girls belched, too loud.

"Excuse me," Malia said.

"Dis manini pitcha," he said, holding the one of the house out. "I want one big big big li'dis," and he held his hands out. "Tchree feet."

"With the Harley in front," Doug said.

"Yah."

"No," the woman said. "Why you ruin a pitcha of my house wit'dat?"

"Buy yoah own den," he said.

She widened her eyes at him. "'Kay," she said, with a threatening sound in her voice, "'kay, mines is gonna be inna back yahd, not da front. You," she said to Doug, "come wit me. Bring da keikis too."

"I like dis pitcha," the boy said to his father.

"Den you cut da hedge and mow da goddam lawn 'kay?"

"Yah," he said. "No probs."

They followed the woman through a beautiful house, with really good-looking furniture, out into the back yard, where there were papaya trees, a tangerine tree, and a little fish pond. "I wan one from about heah," she said, looking back at the house. There were some rusty outdoor cooking things by the house, and a pile of dirt surrounded by two-by-fours and hollow tile bricks, and the steel teeth of a forklift.

"You want me to get rid of the dirt and wood and stuff?"

She sighed, so loud that it sounded like a tremendous relief to her. "God yes!" she said. "An' dat junk dea!" she almost shouted.

Now he was worried about the Akebono picture. He would have to get it back from the boy.

Back inside the house, the girls put their cans on a Formica kitchen table. "I have to go bat'room," Michelle said.

"Oh honey, come wit me. I show you wheah it is." She led Michelle off down a hall.

"Uh, I'll need my picture back," he said to the man. The man handed him the one of the house. "No, I mean the Akebono picture."

"How much you wan fo dat?"

"I—"

"'Kay, I gi' you fifty dollah fo dat 'kay?" He drew out his wallet and gave Doug a fifty-dollar bill. He stood staring at it, at the picture of Grant.

"But—"

The woman came back. "She so cute yah?" she said to her husband.

"You said fifteen fo dis," the man said. "But one big pitcha moa right?" He went to the corner and picked up a yardstick. "Les' see," he said, measuring the nine-by-twelve picture. "Jesus, dat cos' nine times fifteen."

"No, make it thirty."

The man scowled at him. "'Ass stupid. If I build one house dat way, den I outta business," he said. He pointed at the beige tiles on the floor. "One two tchree," he said, counting away from himself. "One two tchree," he went on, pointing across his feet. "Nine. Da pitcha big li'dat." He stared at the floor. Then they all stared at the floor, and Malia counted the tiles, and then produced a little gasp. Doug could see the man imagining the picture. "You le' me figgah dat out 'kay?" he said.

Michelle came back from the bathroom and stood next to Malia. "So pretty dis house," she whispered.

"I want mine big too," his wife said. "Hey, maybe biggah den his," and she giggled. The man was staring at the picture of the house.

"Me my braddah get one construction company 'kay?" the man said.

"'Kay."

"Get one weahouse Kaneʻohe, stupid junks onna wall, centahfolds an' stoffs—"

"Pilau crap dat," his wife said.

"Eh," he said. "I talkin' now."

"So—"

"Yeah yeah yeah," he said. "Can you do back hoes an' dakine bulldozahs and stuffs li'dat?"

"Yeah, anything."

"Dey all bus' up, dented and stuff. I wan' um look really new 'kay?" He stared at the picture again. "I geev um my braddah fo Christmas, so he can take dat crap offa office wall. Business really good, an' I get embarrass when client come an' look at um. I wan' some class, you know, like professional looks. Eh, maybe do one of da weahouse, too?"

"Sure, anything you need."

"How much?"

"No," he said. "You pay when I'm done, because you have to be satisfied."

"Dumb," the man said. "Heah, I put one down payment on um." He drew out his wallet, stared into the middle distance for a few seconds, and then said, "I give hundred fo' down." He counted out the twenties and handed them to Doug. Then he squinted at him. "You shuah you really do dis?"

"Yeah, right away. I can be finished in a week."

"Fo real?" the man said. "'Kay, I get one receipt slip, and you sign um."

The woman looked at, the ceiling and sighed. "Business," she whispered. "I do bookkeeping. Dri' me nuts."

Doug nodded, and the man came back. "Sign heah," he said.

His hand shook, badly, because he felt as if he were committing a crime and proving to the world these dishonest intentions by adding his signature, but he managed to do it. "'Kay, you no tell anybody you do da weahouse ting 'kay? Keep um secret 'ass why. When you come back wit' da house pitchas, we go Kane'ohe an' you take pitchas of da machines 'kay?"

"'Kay."

The man laughed and looked at his wife. "Dis blow his mine," he whispered. He looked again at Doug. "My choppah," he said, at which his wife growled and then sighed, "I wan' um new, no flats, shiny 'kay?"

"'Kay."

"Someting else," he said. "I show you." He went off into the living room.

"Pipes," she said.

"Huh?"

"He wants pipes, the chrome ones."

The man came back with a bike magazine. "I wan' dis heah," and he pointed. It was a chrome exhaust system that his Harley didn't have.

"Easy," he said. The man handed him the magazine.

"So, now you take pitchas? Come, I show you wheah I wan' dem from, an' den you take one of da bike 'kay?" Then he stopped. "An' plus," he said, "I tell you how fo do da excise tax 'kay? So you no get into trouble."

His mother didn't believe him until he showed her the money, which she squinted at for a long time, the money lying on the table between the two pictures. He stood there trying to think of what to do about it. Outside, the girls stood looking up at the palm tree talking about the heron and throwing crumbs of shortbread cookies to the mynahs. "But I lost the Akebono picture," he said. He flushed, his face hot. The one thing he didn't want to lose, and he lost it, became a victim of his own scam. The girls stomped up the steps and into the house.

"And the man's wife said she wants one too," his mother said.

"Da lady so nice," Malia said. "Oh she sweet."

"Yah," Michelle said. "She give us juice."

"So what do you do now?" his mother asked.

"I want to try to figure out how to get the picture back."

"You can't. You sold it."

Sold it, he thought. "But it's a strange scam, because it's—" He was confused. He would not get the Akebono picture back. "I need money to buy good paper, really big pieces. Here, let me show you the pictures." He took the Polaroids out of his pocket and handed them to her, and she looked at them through the magnifying glass.

"It's a nice house," she said. "What's the motorcycle for?"

"He wants it made new and put in front of the house. She wants one of the back, minus some junk that's there. Look, I have to go get the paper, so I need—"

She handed him two twenties. "Get the best paper they make. Buy another one of those pens. We can get you a better lamp."

"I don't need a better—"

"No, you'll ruin your eyes. Get a better lamp."

"Lamp is a four-letter word," Malia said.

He scratched his head, looking down at the money. "Work is a four-letter word," he said. He stared at the picture of the house that his mother liked so much, and shook his head in confusion.

"Don't worry about the Akebono picture," his mother said. "Can't you make another one?"

The Family

Michiko carried her 11-year-old sister Yuriko on her back, oppa, as Kumamoto Japanese would say, because the girl was too tired to walk very far. Yuriko was thin and frail. Dr. Hayashi in Holualoa said she had a dangerously enlarged heart, almost as large as a lung, and there was nothing he could do. Perhaps specialists in New York City might help. But that was impossible for a farming family in North Kona to consider in 1930. Actually the area in which they lived was called Keopu, a settlement where many of the farmers were from Kumamoto Prefecture.

Michiko brought Yuriko to their favorite spot in the coffee farm where Michiko would tell stories about lands beyond the sea. And Yuriko would say, "Someday I like go to all da places, Neesan. Okay? You going take me too?" Neesan was the Japanese term for eldest sister.

"Yes, Yuri-chan, you and me togedda. We going get so much fun."

They sat under the shade of a mango tree. Yuriko's calico cat, Keiki, pawed at a pile of dry leaves. "Wen da mangoes come ripe," said Michiko, "I going climb up da tree and drop da fruits to you, and you gotta catch um just like before."

Yuriko nodded. Michiko looked at her and brushed her fingers through Yuriko's hair, which was cut like a Kokeshi doll's.

The coffee season was over. Red coffee berries were washed, peeling off the skin, dried, and packed as beans in hundred-pound bags. The hard work was done, but not the hard times. The stock market crash in 1929 and the Depression hurt the farmers in Kona as coffee prices plunged dramatically. Some families gave up and moved to Oahu, taking menial city jobs. But not the Motoyamas.

At 65, Chuzo Motoyama said he was too old to leave the farm he had sweated over year after year: hoeing, planting, weeding, fertilizing, picking. He had leased the seven-acre farm from a Mr. Stillman years ago and had grown to love the land.

His wife, Fusae, was 47. The age difference is easily explained. The baishakunin, the matchmaker, lied in a letter to Fusae's father in Kikuchi, Kumamoto, saying that Chuzo was younger than he was, and he told Chuzo in Kona that Fusae was older than her real age. As it turned out, age didn't matter. In fact, it worked out well. Chuzo, because he was an older man, was patient, quiet, and self-sufficient in many ways. Unlike many of the men in Kona, Chuzo was less demanding of his wife. He always awoke early and cooked breakfast for the children while Fusae slept late.

The other children were Toshiko and Jun. Toshiko was fifteen and spent her week working and sleeping at the Thompson ranch, helping with housekeeping and cooking. On Sunday morning, Mr. Thompson would drive her back home. Monday she would walk back to the ranch. Jun was seventeen and was needed on the farm to help Chuzo and Michiko. In the offseason, he worked on the sugar plantation during harvest time.

Fusae enjoyed chatting with women friends while smoking her Bull Durhams. Rocking lightly on her haunches, she would deftly roll a cigarette and puff as she laughed and sang, with her friends clapping in rhythm. She did her share of the hard work in the coffee field when necessary, singing songs of her youth in Japan. She married late, by proxy, because she had to help care for younger siblings in Kikuchi. But when the time had come for her to settle down, she was shipped to Hawaii.

Now she believed it was time for Michiko, who was twenty. The baishakunin had his doubts. Once before Michiko declined to wed a bucktoothed farmer in Kohala, pleading with her father to save her from a dullard who picked his teeth with his dirt-crusted fingernails. Chuzo understood; Fusae didn't. But Chuzo was gently firm when he had to be, and Fusae didn't argue. Chuzo, after all, was descended from a samurai family, had served gallantly in the Army as a wartime messenger riding his white stallion across battlefields through artillery bombardment. After the Sino-Japanese War he married a woman whose wealthy father treated Chuzo like an ignorant peasant. Chuzo stoically absorbed the verbal punishment, but Chuzo's older brother, Suminori, was outraged and forced a divorce.

In a second marriage, Chuzo was a yoshi, a man who marries into a family without a son and assumes that family's name. It was an uneventful life, and Chuzo tolerated boredom without complaint. A fast-talking friend pestered him about going to Hawaii, that tropical paradise where they could earn a fortune and return home as heroes. It sounded too easy, Chuzo thought. But then his wife, Kasuko, tiring of her unassuming, meek husband, said he should seek his fortune across the ocean. So he told her he would return in two years. He departed but without his friend, who was frightened by stories of natives eating human flesh.

That's how it happened. But Chuzo toiled for years working first at a sugar plantation on Oahu and then leasing his own coffeeland. He wrote Kasuko that he couldn't return because he was too poor, so she should divorce him, which she did happily.

And now after more than twenty years of life together and four children,

Chuzo and Fusae walked to Holualoa to see the local Buddhist priest. They wore their Sunday best on a Monday. Michiko, Yuriko, and Jun watched them amble off. When Chuzo mentioned why they had come, he saw the priest's immobile face broaden into a smile. "You are the first Issei couple I will be marrying," he said and hurried them into the church before they changed their minds. Why they took so long to tie the knot on a personal basis, one can only guess. Returning home, the newly married couple said nothing to the children, and life went on as usual.

Later in the week, Fusae asked Jun to go to Kamuela to a small lake for koi. She needed the fish for its blood to give to Yuriko. A visitor from Honolulu, Kenji Kimura, said a koi's blood would give Yuriko strength. He had heard about this remedy from a deeply religious man from Tokyo who was a graduate of Waseda University. And if he was a Waseda man, he must not be a fool.

Kenji was a benshi, a narrator of Japanese silent movies, who traveled the island circuit, doing the voices for the silent films. Samurai or modern-day romance movies, male or female voices, Kenji could do them all. Sound movies, of course, was the rage in Honolulu, but people on the outside islands had to be content with the silents, at least for now.

People looked forward to Kenji's biannual visits. Families would walk as far as five miles to see a new movie at the Nakahara garage. This one was advertised as a samurai adventure, a chambara, which children enjoyed more than a love story.

Kenji always managed to stop at the Motoyamas, especially to see Yuriko. She reminded him of his baby sister who had died years ago in Hiroshima. He had seen Yuriko's health waning and hoped the koi blood would help. In the meantime he entertained Yuriko, putting a small towel on his head and prancing with mincing, dainty steps and speaking in falsetto. Yuriko smiled, showing her teeth, but she didn't have the energy to laugh out loud the way she used to before her heart began failing.

When Kenji finished, he rubbed his balding head with his left hand and bent down to kiss Yuriko's cheek. Tears welled up in his eyes, but he turned away so she wouldn't see his face. Michiko was touched by Kenji's gentle caring. He might have become a famous actor in Japan, but he had to leave Tokyo because he had injured a man in a bar fight and decided to leave on the next ship to Hawaii from Hiroshima. That's what he had told Chuzo and Fusae, and they assumed it was a true story. But nobody knew for sure. That wasn't important anyway; the thing that mattered was Kenji's kindness to children and old people. Michiko thought Kenji must have a dark side, but he never showed it. He was either eternally happy or a very good actor, indeed.

Chuzo invited Kenji to spend the night; Fusae would cook chicken hekka.

Kenji couldn't refuse. But somebody had to catch a chicken. Normally that would be Jun's job, but he was busy in Kamuela, so Michiko went out into the field. The chickens roamed freely, none lived in a coop. Eggs were laid in the grass, which the family picked up for breakfast. Michiko chased down a plump hen and brought it to Fusae, who expertly slit the throat of the squawking chicken. Fusae was not squeamish.

Dinner was good and satisfying, but Fusae was eager to hear the latest news or gossip, and Kenji obliged, regaling the family with stories about the bad boys and girls in Honolulu, yes, even Japanese girls. How shameful, Fusae said. Too many temptations, Kenji replied, temptations that he, of course, resisted, even if he was a bachelor. Michiko wondered about that. Kenji liked his sake too much, she thought, and sake always lowers one's inhibitions. She had seen too many men at wedding parties become boisterous, stumbling idiots; men such as farmer Nishi, normally a taciturn, serious man who turns into an uproariously drunken fool with sake in his belly.

The next day Jun returned home with his friend Masa and four koi. The boys dutifully brought the fish to Fusae, then politely excused themselves to gather outside with Michiko and Yuriko. Masa then described their adventure.

"Dempsey, da bakatare, he reach out da boat, and da whole ting huli ova. Da boat go upside down and we stay splashing around in da lake. I tought Dempsey was going ma-ke, you know, because he dunno how swim, eh. Ho, make me scared. Aeh, Dempsey, you tought you was one dead man, yeah."

Dempsey was Jun's nickname because he hated the name Jun, actually Jun-ichi. Non-Japanese children at school had kidded him, saying Jun was a girl's name, June. When they teased him about it, Jun, a stocky kid, always jumped on the offending boys and pummeled them in rage. Soon the nickname Dempsey caught on, in honor of boxing champion Jack Dempsey.

Jun didn't answer. Michiko covered her mouth with her hand, and Yuriko sat next to Jun, holding his hand.

"Jun, I happy you neva die," Yuriko said.

Masa continued, "I grab Dempsey by da shirt collar and swim to da shore. We lose da fish we wen' catch and hadda start all ova again. Humbug was."

Jun didn't tell Masa to shut up. Without Masa, he knew he would have had a difficult time catching the koi and bringing them back so soon. Masa's family owned a Model A Ford, and the family sometimes hired out as a taxi. But for the Motoyamas, this time there was no charge. They were neighbors, after all, and this was a sort of emergency.

Fusae cut off the head of a koi with her sharpest knife and tried to squeeze out a teaspoon of blood. This she gave to Yuriko to drink. Yuriko swallowed but grimaced. "Okasan, no ono," Yuriko said. But it was necessary, Fusae explained. when the koi were gone, Fusae was going to ask Jun to catch more. But Yuriko said she didn't want to drink any more koi blood. Besides, there didn't seem to be any positive effect. Yuriko continued to grow weaker.

The night for the movie came. Families streamed toward the Nakahara garage. So did the Motoyama family. They walked on the dirt and rock-strewn road with Chuzo leading the way. Jun carried Yuriko on his back. At the garage, Michiko counted as many as sixty men, women and children waiting to see the movie. A tent was erected and goza mats were laid out to welcome the families.

Kenji was heartened to see such a large turnout, and he dismissed talking pictures as only a fad. A benshi like himself will always be in demand, he thought. Nothing could replace a live narrator-actor who spoke and sang for all the characters male or female. Besides that, he also played the samisen.

The show went well. People cheered and applauded in all the right places. Yuriko sat in front of Michiko and sometimes leaned back against her. As the movie progressed, however, Yuriko wanted to lie on the mat and only listen to Kenji. She never did that before, and Michiko worried and couldn't enjoy the movie.

On the way home, Chuzo lit a kerosene lantern and Michiko carried Yuriko. Jun rushed ahead, slashing with his right arm like a samurai out to avenge his lord and master. He charged into the darkness and ran right into a large, black cow standing in the middle of the road. Jun was still sitting on the road dazed as Chuzo and the others approached. Fusae laughed.

"Nandai. Omoshiroi, no, kono bozu," she said. "Must be Ishikawa's cow," Chuzo said and he walked on. Jun stood up, brushed the dirt from the seat of his pants and dragged his feet behind everybody as they headed home.

Toshiko missed out on many family moments as she spent six days out of the week at the Thompson ranch. She was learning to cook American food from Mrs. Thompson, a sweet-natured mother of two boys, ages six and eight. She was grateful to Mrs. Thompson for teaching her so many useful things, but she missed her own family. Not that life in the Motoyama household was so exciting. Nights were quiet except when it rained. The totan roof raised a ruckus when rain pounded the metal covering. There was no radio and only lanterns to light the house. Occasionally Fusae would play hanafuda, the Japanese card game, with the children. But by eight o'clock it was time for bed.

In the offseason Michiko sewed dresses, shirts and trousers to sell. People liked the fit of her clothes, and she had more business than she could handle. But she was also sewing a special party dress for Yuriko. She had measured Yuriko carefully because she wanted a perfect fit. Yuriko was anxious to wear the dress as soon as possible. "Not ready yet?" Yuriko would ask.

Michiko smiled and shook her head. She hoped Yuriko would live long enough to wear the pretty white dress. Yuriko lay on a futon next to Michiko's sewing machine and softly sang her favorite Japanese children's song. This was on her good days, which were fewer and fewer.

Then one day Yuriko noticed that her cat, Keiki, was gone. This distressed her. Michiko asked Jun to find the cat. Fusae worried. She was a superstitious woman, and she believed Keiki had run away because he knew that his mistress, Yuriko, was going to die soon. She mentioned this to Michiko.

It's too soon for Yuri-chan to leave them, Michiko said. There are still so many things to do with her: songs to sing, stories to tell, new sights to see. Michiko also went out to find Keiki. She walked deep into the coffeeland yelling for Keiki. She was angry at the cat for deserting Yuri-chan now.

Jun explored another area and saw nothing. He gave up and went back into the house. Michiko continued on, knowing how much Keiki meant to Yuriko. She cursed aloud at the cat. She screamed his name in anger and frustration. By late afternoon, it seemed she had covered the whole farmland. In the distance she saw Jun running toward her, yelling her name. He reached her out of breath.

"Wat you doing?" Jun asked. "Where you was all dis time?"

"Wat?"

"Yuriko!" Jun said and began running home.

Michiko knew what he meant. She ran hard, passing a puffing Jun and racing into the house. Yuriko lay on her futon with Chuzo and Fusae seated beside her. The girl's eyes were dull and dark.

"Yuri-chan, talk to me," Michiko implored. "Please."

"Call Dr. Hayashi," Chuzo said.

Michiko jumped up and ran out, heading for the nearby Komo store to call the doctor. But the phone there wasn't working. What was there to do? Michiko decided to run all the way to Holualoa to the doctor's home, a distance of at least four miles. She set off quickly on the unpaved road. Running with her straw slippers hampered her, so she threw them off and raced barefoot. She ran and ran, past the Kobayashi farm, past Mrs. Honda pulling weeds by the roadside, past the Kurata children playing in the dirt. Six-year-old Yoshi ran behind her, crying out: "Where you going, Michi?" She powered ahead, and Yoshi stopped and, jumping up and down, yelled: "Run, Michi, run, run." The sharp rocks on the road cut her feet, but she felt no pain as she concentrated on Yuriko lying helpless on the futon.

Ahead was the Hayashi house. Michiko, gasping for breath, lunged forward and collapsed on the porch. She pounded at the bottom of the door until Dr. Hayashi came out.

"Yuriko!" Michiko cried.

Dr. Hayashi grabbed his medicine bag and carried Michiko to his automobile and drove off. When he saw Yuriko, he knew it was too late. Her heart just gave out, he said. He tried to console the Motoyamas with words of sympathy. Chuzo and Fusae bowed their thank-yous. Dr. Hayashi treated Michiko's feet and departed quietly, feeling a deep sadness in his own heart.

Chuzo silently mourned the death of his youngest daughter. Fusae wept while she washed Yuriko's body, thinking it was heartbreaking to have children die before their parents. Michiko was up the whole night, working to finish Yuriko's party dress. She blamed herself for not finishing the dress in time for Yuriko to wear while she was still alive. Now she would wear it in death.

That morning Chuzo went to call the priest. The reverend returned with Chuzo and prepared for the religious service the next day and the burial. Toshiko was summoned from the Thompson ranch. She and Michiko helped to clean the floor and furniture. The carpenter Wada went to work on a simple wooden coffin. Fusae asked Toshiko to make Yuriko look pretty. Toshiko had learned some makeup tips from Mrs. Thompson. She powdered Yuriko's face and added lipstick. She tried her best, hoping Yuriko would understand.

The next day people arrived, bowing, expressing sorrow, bearing white envelopes of koden. They sat politely on zabutons in the parlor. Some men waited outside smoking cigarettes.

Fusae surveyed the room, looking to see if everything was in order. Suddenly Keiki jumped in through an open window and dropped to the floor. Fusae was startled and frightened. Keiki knew Yuriko was going to die, so he ran away, but he returned for her funeral, Fusae thought. Another superstition gripped Fusae now. It's said that if an owner's cat jumped over the dead body, that body would sit up. It was a scary thought. She watched Keiki slowly advancing toward Yuriko's body. Fusae screamed "Keiki" as the cat bounded forward. Jun turned and lunged, grabbing Keiki just before it was about to leap over Yuriko's body. The cat yeowed in Jun's grasp, but Jun held firm. So it was never known if the superstition was true, and the body remained motionless.

After the funeral service several men carried the coffin to a site near the house for the burial.

Several days later, Mrs. Naito told Fusae she saw the spirit of Yuriko seated near Michiko during the service. Fusae told the family that night. Michiko wanted to believe, but Mrs. Naito tended to exaggerate stories. How could you believe a woman who babbles endlessly about the Japanese and Hawaiian spirits she sees on the island.

A month after Yuriko's death, the family received a letter from Fusae's older brother, Ichiro, in Stockton, California. He ran a small hotel for Japanese and wondered if Michiko would come and help. Later she could go south to Santa Ana and pick strawberries during the harvesting season. Fusae didn't object because she thought her brother might find a husband for Michiko. Chuzo was not one to say no to such an adventure after he himself had journeyed to Hawaii ages ago.

Michiko needed to think, so she walked to Kailua Beach, where the family had spent fun days when Yuriko was younger and healthier. Michiko stared out, looking beyond the sea. She heard the laughter of children, but there was no one else on the beach. Michiko walked away.

She stopped at their mailbox to check if the family had received any letters. There was one. From a family friend in Honolulu, Mrs. Kagawa. It was addressed to Fusae, so she walked to the house and gave it to her. Fusae opened the letter, looked at the Japanese characters and gave it to Chuzo. He was the only one in the family who could read Japanese. He read slowly and carefully, holding the letter at arm's length.

Mrs. Kagawa said the wealthy haole woman she worked for was looking for a sort of governess to help watch her ten-year-old daughter. She recommended Michiko because Mrs. Cook wanted a young Japanese woman for the job. Mrs. Kagawa made it clear that Mrs. Cook trusted her and Japanese people in general so that's why she asked her to help find someone.

That same afternoon the baishakunin, hesitant to ask again, walked over with a new proposal. Apparently a family in Hilo thought Michiko might make a good wife. The young man was clean (no picking at teeth except with toothpicks), hard-working and eager to start a family. Two choices, Fusae said to Michiko. How many women get two choices? Either go to Uncle Ichiro in Stockton or marry the young man in Hilo, a decent enough prospect. What more do you want? Don't expect too much out of life. Chuzo eyed Michiko. What do you think? he asked. Michiko showed no emotion.

Toshiko told Michiko she should work for the haole lady because she would learn so much working for haoles. Jun thought she should stay and help on the farm and never get married.

Michiko walked over to the mango tree carrying Keiki. She sat and petted the cat, which wiggled free and chased a gecko he had spotted. Michiko climbed up the tree and sat on a sturdy limb. She saw the stooped baishakunin leaving, trudging up the path to the main road. She picked a green mango and threw the fruit, watching it bounce out of sight.

Raindrops pelted the mango leaves. The sky was gray and soon a downpour was drenching the farmland. Michiko sat in the tree cold and wet, her dress clinging to her body. The rain was so heavy she couldn't see the family home anymore and she couldn't hear Fusae calling her.

All I Asking for Is My Body

A Play in Two Acts

Place: Puukolii, Maui, a sugar plantation camp, seven miles west of Lahaina

Time: 1940–1943

THE CAST OF CHARACTERS

Mrs. Oyama (43)
Kiyoshi Oyama (her son, 16)
Mr. Oyama (47)
Toshio Oyama (18)
Dalmatio, Kiyo's Filipino co-worker (doubles as Crapshooter and Boxer)
Mr. Yamada (doubles as Hiroshi and Big Bettor)
Michie Yamada (his daughter, 16)
Mr. Baker of the FBI (doubles as Referee and Crapshooter)

Taped Voices: Kiyo at ten, radio, crowd roar at fight, and radio on Dec. 7, 1941.

Set: A raised, raked square platform toward SR. It has a single railing at left. It becomes the veranda, the kitchen, the Single Men's quarters, boxing ring, and Schofield Barracks. The space to L of platform becomes the front yard where the boys spar, and the side yard between the two houses.

Props: Boxing gloves visible in a box on platform. Picks and shovels for Dalmatio and Kiyoshi, hoe for Father, leather gloves for Toshio, lunch pails in denim bags, denim work clothes. Jimmy DeForest's 5" x 8" *How to Box* pamphlets. Alarm clock. Radio. Small wooden table, bench, and 2 stools. Dice. Army blanket on which dice is rolled. Books in the chicken coop. Foot locker.

The play premiered at the Asian American Theatre in San Francisco in September 1989. Running time 90 minutes (including a 15 minute intermission).

ACT I

(Japanese children's song e.g., "Rain Song." Kiyo's memory warp. Dim lighting. Smoke. Mother, hair disheveled, in white hospital gown.)

KIYO'S 10-YEAR-OLD VOICE ON TAPE: Mother, when are you coming home?

MOTHER: *(turning pages of ledger)* Hmmm . . . I wonder when . . . When I left Japan, I promised my parents I'd be home in five years. *(pause)* It'll be twenty years in October. My little brother died last year, then my father died, then your father's mother. They say deaths happen in cycles of four's. . . . They say "A bad wife is 50 years of bad crops." That's how long the average life was long ago. I wasn't a bad wife, but a bad-luck wife. What did I do? I lie here and search and search my mind.

KIYO'S TAPED VOICE: You never did anything bad.

MOTHER: But some ancestor or close relative might have. Their *bachi* could be visited on me. *(Pause. She stops turning pages.)* We owe Aoki Store about $2000, Chatani Fish Market about $1000, the dentist $500, $300 in back rent. The others are smaller. They're all in here. You have to pay at least $2 a month to show them you're sincere. They say that if you don't pay off your debts by New Year's, you'll have a bad-luck year. *Shikata ga nai.* Father shouldn't have left the plantation. Fishing is so undependable. You could work all day and still lose money.

KIYO'S TAPED VOICE: Don't worry. Toshio and I will be working soon, and we'll pay off the debt in no time.

MOTHER: *(hands ledger to Kiyo)* Here, I'm giving this to you. Look after your little sisters. They like you. See to it that Toshio and father don't fight so much.

KIYO'S TAPED VOICE: Rest. Take care the body.

(Kiyo enters SR from behind platform returning from work, straw hat, lunch bag, canteen, shovel on shoulders. His narration is stream of consciousness, SOC.)

KIYO *(SOC):*

(Spot on him during Mother's talk of the debt) Take care the body. *(Simultaneous with his taped voice)*

Hospital, chloroform. The dispensary must've brought it back. The big debt, *bachi*, dying, the hospital stink. Yeah, must've been the dispensary. I gotta train harder. Move up the timetable: one year as an amateur, fighting in the main event after a year as a pro, for the world title after another year. Yeah, I gotta put some *Yamato damashi* into it. I gonna be the one. I hit harder, my hands faster. I hope Mama has something good for supper. Like red meat.

(*Blackout*)

Scene 1: Veranda, March 1940, 3:30 P.M. Hot.

(*Father enters SR, returning from work. He wears* palaka *shirt and pants, straw hat, and denim* tabi. *He has a denim lunch-pail bag and one-gallon canteen over one shoulder and a hoe on his other. His pants legs and* tabi *seem wet. Sits on veranda and begins to take off* tabi.)

FATHER: (*yells into house*) *Ohh-i, biru kure.*

(*Mother enters with beer.*)

MOTHER: *Okaeri nasai. Erakatta desho.* (*She gives him beer, takes his* tabi, *and hangs them on railing, picks up his lunch bag and exits.*)

(*Enter Tosh SL with lunch pail bag and canteen over shoulder, heavy work shoes and thick leather gloves in back pocket. He wears hat like Greek fisherman's cap, denim pants, and light-blue work shirt. His face is sooty. He pulls out dusty leather work gloves from back pocket and slaps them on veranda railing.*)

MOTHER: (*enters*) *Okaeri nasai.*
TOSH: Kiyo come home?
MOTHER: Not yet.
TOSH: (*taking off shoes, to himself*) Where the guy?

(*He strips to waist, takes off shoes, picks up* Jimmy DeForest's How to Box *pamphlet from box, and lays it open on veranda, picks out skip-rope from box on the veranda, and begins to skip rope, stopping every so often to shadow box, throwing different combinations. He does this continually while he talks.*)

(*Enter Dalmatio SL. He wears broad straw hat, light-blue shirt, denim pants, workshoes, and carries lunch pail bag, canteen and pick and shovel (tied together) on his shoulder. His pants bottoms are tied.*)

DALMATIO: Hello, Oyama.
FATHER/MOTHER: Herro, Dalmatio.

TOSH: *(skipping rope)* Hey, Dalmatio. Where my brother?

DALMATIO: I doan know. Maybe he got girl.

TOSH: You make $2 today?

DALMATIO: *(laughs)* You make $2, bye-n-bye the plantation cut down the price. You make $2?

TOSH: Sometime. When the *happai-ko* fast.

DALMATIO: So when you pight por money?

TOSH: Gotta win all-Hawaii championship first. Gotta beat your countryman, Jose Pasion. He *good* fighter.

DALMATIO: Then you go mainland?

TOSH: If I win.

DALMATIO: *(to parents)* Oyama, you boy, he geeb Pukoli beeg name.

FATHER: Bokusingu (boxing) no usu (use).

DALMATIO: *(about to leave)* Oh, Mama-san, you make me one more *ahina* pants?

MOTHER: Samu mayzya (measure)?

DALMATIO: One inch more big all right. *(Uses hands to indicate waist.)*

MOTHER: Toh (too) muchi *kaukau*, Dalmatio-san come *momona, ne?* *(Laughs)*

DALMATIO: No! No nuff *kaukau, pilikia.* Next Monday okay?

MOTHER: Nexto Monday okay.

DALMATIO: I come next Monday. Bye-bye. Hey, Tosh, good luck in Honolulu, eh? You beat Pasion and bring back the championship. *(Exits SR.)*

TOSH: See you, Dalmatio. *(To Mother while he skips rope or shadow boxes.)* Oh, I forgot. I need money to buy a sports coat. Cannot go to Honolulu without a sports coat. It's *hila-hila.* And I want store-bought pants.

MOTHER: My pants are no good?

TOSH: No, everybody wears store bought pants.

(Enter Kiyo SL in straw hat, dusty work clothes and shoes, pants tied down at bottom. He carries pick and shovel on shoulder, and lunch-pail bag, puts both down.)

KIYO: *Tada ima!*

MOTHER: *Okeri nasai. Erakatta desho.*

TOSH: Where you been?

KIYO: *(Sits on veranda and unties string from bottom of pants, and slaps dust off bottom with both hands.)* I took Philemon to the dispensary. A centipede been crawl up his leg and bite him. *(As he unties string of one pants leg and slaps off dust.)* His string came loose.

TOSH: *(to Kiyo)* You gotta girl?

KIYO: Naw. *(Strips and puts on gloves.)*

TOSH: *(putting on gloves)* What about Michie Yamada?

KIYO: I just borrow books.

TOSH: You better watch out. You get her pregnant, you finished. You'll die on the plantation.

(Enter Mr. Yamada SL. He wears same irrigation work clothes as Father. He holds white letter envelope in his hand, and bows excessively (short bows), obsequiously, and laughs haplessly. He bows to the boys, bows to Father, Mother. Boys nod.)

TOSH: Hey, your father-in-law.

KIYO: Shut up!

FATHER/MOTHER: *Konnichiwa,* Yamada-san.

YAMADA: *Kombanwa. (Handing father letter.) Tanomimasu. (Bows two quick short bows.)*

FATHER: *(takes letter. Nods.) Biru ikaga? (Calls into the house.)* Ooi! Takako! Miwa! *Biru motte koi! (Pause, listens.)* Hanae! *(To Mother.)* Where are the girls? *(Stands.)* Nemmind. *(To Yamada.) Naka ni hairo. (He waits for Yamada, who takes off zori and exits after him into house past the veranda.) Doh datta?*

(Brothers begin practicing during the above. The following is something they've done over and over. Kiyo throws a jab, Tosh parries to his left with his right palm, and throws a combination while pulling his punches: left to stomach and jaw, and right to head. Kiyo jabs again, and Tosh slips to his left and throws right to head. Mother goes to straighten slippers, slaps Tosh's leg to have him move off.)

TOSH: How come you bear more children than you can send to high school? *(This exchange is not shouted, but conversed in normal voice.)*

MOTHER: Huh, look at you! You've worked only two years, and you're talking big. Look at Minoru Tanaka, Hideo Shimada, Kenji Doi, and the others. They've been helping their parents for over ten years and they don't complain.

TOSH: They're dumb, that's why. They hate school. I like school.

MOTHER: Look at Kiyoshi, he hasn't had a year of high school, and he's not complaining.

TOSH: How come you forced me to quit? I could've boarded at Lahainaluna.

MOTHER: We had to keep the family together.

TOSH: How long do you expect me and Kiyo to help you?

MOTHER:	Your father helped grandfather for over ten years.
TOSH:	Grandfather was a thief.
MOTHER:	Don't you dare say that in front of your father!
TOSH:	He leeched on papa and Hilo and Honolulu uncles for all those years.
MOTHER:	Father didn't complain. He had *gaman.*
TOSH:	That's not *gaman.* That's being gutless.
MOTHER:	It's impossible to talk to you. You're a crybaby.
TOSH:	*(to Kiyo in pidgin, which the old folks don't understand)* Thass what the old man always said. I was no samurai. Thass why I been take up boxing. I got sick and tired of him hitting me all the time. *(They keep repeating the counters.)* You know, the old man, he shoulda quit fishing long ago. The stores shoulda refuse him credit and force him to quit. *(Yells toward Mother, knowing she doesn't understand. Mother ignores him.)* You know why they didn't? They figured his sons will pay up, thass why. And you know, papa is kind of lazy. Whenever the weather was bad, Mr. Komai threw his lunch bag over his shoulder, and went to work at the pineapple cannery. Papa, he loved to sit around, drink beer and talk story.
MOTHER:	You'll get your *bachi* some day. You'll have an unfilial son like you.
TOSH:	My *bachi* is now. What did I do to inherit a $6000 debt?
MOTHER:	Don't worry, we won't depend on you. We'll depend on Kiyoshi. *(Exits into house.)*
TOSH:	*(shouts at her)* I bet if we were in Japan, you'd sell the girls into prostitution and call it filial piety.

(Michie enters SL hurriedly during above exchange. Stops, embarrassed, wanting to go back.)

MICHIE:	Hi, Kiyoshi. *(Sheepish)*
KIYO:	Hi, Michie.

(Eye contact between Kiyo and Tosh. Tosh breaks out in smile, throws series of jabs in Kiyo's direction.)

MICHIE:	Is my father here?
KIYO:	*(irritably)* He inside.
MICHIE:	May I go in?
KIYO:	*(gruffly)* Go in.

(Michie slips off zoris and goes inside house.)

KIYO: *(angry)* Come on!

TOSH: You sure you can concentrate? Boxing and women doan mix. Damn Mama, she drive me crazy.

KIYO: Not all her fault. Papa happy-go-lucky, so she worry for both of them.

TOSH: He one loser.

(Enter Father and Yamada from house, followed by Michie and Mother, who holds bath bucket, and yukata and towel the size of hand towel folded on arm).

FATHER: *(to Yamada)* I'll have it ready tomorrow.

YAMADA: *Doh mo arigato. (Bobs head and bows to Mother and boys and exits SL hurriedly. Michie tarries, watching Kiyo.)* Michie!

MICHIE: *Osewa ni narimashita. (Exits behind her father.)*

TOSH: *(to Father)* You should charge them for every letter you write.

MOTHER: It's his duty. He gets paid in respect.

FATHER: *(to Tosh)* Oh, before I forget. I better pick some avocados to take to your uncle.

TOSH: *(still practicing parries. Irritably but not yelling.)* Cannot. I don't have the time.

FATHER: If that's the case, don't go.

MOTHER: *(to Father)* Why don't you pick the avocados on Sunday? Go take a bath before the bath water gets dirty. *(Hands bucket, yukata, and towel. Father takes them, puts on* geta *(wooden clogs) on veranda steps and exits SR. Mother exits into house backstage.)*

TOSH: *(stops. To Kiyo in pidgin.)* Shit! He think he sending me on *his* money! I been earn this trip with my fists! He not putting up a cent!

KIYO: I wonder if he no wash and jump into the bath like the other old futs?

TOSH: Yeah, all they do is rinse their balls. Go throw a straight right now.

(Kiyo throws a straight right to face, Tosh sidesteps to his right, and lands left to Kiyo's stomach. Tries second time.)

Jimmy Deforest says should be in one motion. How can you hit when you moving away?

KIYO: *(Kiyo goes to box on veranda and opens pamphlet.)* He says "as if" in one motion.

TOSH: Yeah, that make sense. *(They practice.)* Naw, thass too hard. Les try this. Try throw again. *(Kiyo throws straight right, Tosh slips to his left, and lands a straight right to Kiyo's stomach.)*

KIYO: Thass not in the book.

TOSH: (bangs gloves together) I jes invented a new counter! Again. (They do it again.)

KIYO: Thass dangerous.

TOSH: Not if you fast.

KIYO: You know, you telegraph your jab.

TOSH: (jabbing) Caw-mon! Everybody says I got a terrific jab.

KIYO: No, you go like this. (Demonstrates.)

TOSH: Nobody else can see it.

KIYO: But thass why I can stick you.

TOSH: Yeah, but how come I undefeated? You shoulda seen my jab against K.O. Toma.

KIYO: He a swarmer.

TOSH: First round, I circle right, jab, jab, clinch, bicycle, move, keep moving, jab, jab.

KIYO: His style made to order for you.

TOSH: Second round I sidestep, hook, sidestep, right cross, then down to the body and up to the head. Third round, the guy pooped! I can call my shots. I tattoo him with my combinations, (throws up-down-up combination), I floored him twice. I was picture book. The reporter from the *Maui Weekly*, he no even mention me before. He wanted to know how I learned to fight like that. All the plantation bosses, they come congratulate me. (Slowing down, angry.) Lots of guys in this hick town, they pulling for me to lose.

KIYO: How come?

TOSH: I tell em what I think, thass why.

KIYO: Like what?

TOSH: I call them "losers." They goin die on the plantation like the old futs. I tell them all they can brag about is filial piety. They good for nothing else.

KIYO: So when you goin turn pro?

TOSH: I gotta win the Territorial first, gotta build a following. Is gonna be hard. I hear these Honolulu guys, they train like pros. They no work. Shit, I work eight hours even on nights I fight. Les spar now. (Goes to box, and as he passes Kiyo, fans nose.) Phew! You been fut?

KIYO: (guiltily) Is the *kukai* ditch.

TOSH: (picks up alarm clock, winds it and sets it.) How come no stink yesterday?

KIYO: Maybe they been irrigate yesterday, thass why.

TOSH: (looking up the hill) Damn the lunas up the hill. They oughta come down here and see what their haole and Porogee shit smell like.

KIYO: They must think their shit no stink, eh?

TOSH: Let's spar. Try come in.

(Tosh is a stand up counter-puncher, Kiyo ducks and weaves trying to get inside, they have an exchange. Or improvise: Kiyo outjabbing Tosh, saying "Telegraph!", or feinting a right, and catching Tosh square on the face when Tosh counters with his "dangerous" slip to right against a right. Then Tosh gets mad and tries to beat up on Kiyo, etc.)

(Blackout)

Scene 2: Veranda. 8 P.M. A few days later.

(Single naked 40-watt naked bulb overhead. Extension wire to dome-shaped radio on front edge of veranda. Kiyo in Aloha shirt, shadow boxes on front lawn beside veranda. Dialogue with parents is in Standard English representing Japanese).

(Mother sits legs folded on cushion and sews, Father in tank top, legs on steps drinks beer, and smokes Bull Durham. Kiyo is in zori, on ground, nervous, throws a few combinations. Hawaiian music from radio, ca. 1940).

MOTHER: *(to Kiyo)* One boxer in the family is nafu. You're not like Toshio. He's like a rooster, he jumps up at everything. He's bound to be good in hitting others, *ne*, father. You're different. You're gentle, do you understand?

KIYO: Don't worry. I'm better than Toshio.

MOTHER: It's a fool's sport. Why don't you take up besuboru (baseball) or basuketto boru (basketball) like the others?

KIYO: We're not in it for the sport. *(Repeating parries.)*

MOTHER: What do you mean?

KIYO: We're going to turn professional.

MOTHER: Only fools become professional boxers. Talk to him, father.

KIYO: How else are going to pay off $6,000?

MOTHER: *Gaman, gambare.*

KIYO: It'll take twenty years.

MOTHER: Talk to him, Father.

FATHER: Back in Japan, the theatre groups used to beat their drums through our village, Ton-ton, ton-ton, ton-ton. It sounded like "Come, fools! Come, fools!" In boxing the fools are the ones in

	the ring. It's too bad they don't have professional *sumo* in Hawaii.
KIYO:	We're too small for *sumo* wrestling. Shhh, they're starting.
MOTHER:	I don't know if I can listen.
RADIO:	Aloha, ladies and gentlemen. Welcome to the territorial A.A.U. boxing finals. The winners will represent Hawaii in the nationals to be held in Boston, Massachusetts. This is the 7th fight of the evening. Coming up is Al Correa vs. Pete Yasui, light-weights. To recap the preceding fights. Tiger Handa of Honolulu decisioned Nobuo Kashima of Kauai; Maui champion Toshio Oyama was TKO'd in the second round by five-time territorial champ, Jose Pasion; Kenji Ito of the Big Island decisioned—

(Kiyo snaps off radio.)

MOTHER:	What happened?
KIYO:	He lost already.
MOTHER:	Was he hurt?
KIYO:	I don't know.
MOTHER:	Was he beaten badly?
KIYO:	I don't know. The announcer said, "Nakku outo (knock out)."
MOTHER:	Nakku outo!? Nakku outo!? Then he is hurt!
KIYO:	No, it's not an ordinary "nakku outo." It's a tekunikuru (technical) nakku outo.
MOTHER:	*(panicky)* What's a tekunikuru nakku outo?
KIYO:	He might have bumped heads and suffered a cut.
MOTHER:	But he's the one who lost. So he's the one who got injured.
KIYO:	We won't know until he comes home.
FATHER:	It's *hila-hila*. *(To Kiyo.)* How can he talk of turning professional when he can't win even one fight in Honolulu?
KIYO:	He might've bumped heads and suffered a cut.
FATHER:	He should quit.
KIYO:	No, he should train harder.
MOTHER:	Kiyoshi, why are you being so contrary? You father and I would cry if we had another son like Toshio.
KIYO:	He's not bad.
MOTHER:	He's unfilial, and that's bad.
KIYO:	Not all bad.
MOTHER:	How can you be unfilial, and not be all bad?
KIYO:	Minoru Tanaka is filial but he's a bully. Hideo Shimada is filial but a drunk—

FATHER: Midori Kaneshiro, she's only a woman, but she's remarkable. She began working at 14, and helped her family till she was 30. She sent all her younger brothers and sisters to high school. Not only that, she postponed her marriage for two years to help her family. Tamotsu Nakamura, he was no good. He got married as soon as he finished high school.

(Kiyo shrugs and exits SL.)

MOTHER: We could save some money if you cut down on your beer.
FATHER: It's only three, four bottles a day.
MOTHER: There's also money for tobacco.
FATHER: Bull Durham is only five cents! I'd feel like I'm being strangled without beer and tobacco. I put in eight hours a day under the baking sun!
MOTHER: Eight hours a day and you act like you've returned from battle with the prized head of the enemy.
FATHER: You're so stingy. No wonder you're always constipated.
MOTHER: You're getting to be more and more like grandfather. He loved to drink, put up a big face, and pretend he was rich.
FATHER: Don't worry, the beer wasn't wasted.
MOTHER: What do you mean?
FATHER: It turned into piss and irrigated the canefields.

(Blackout)

Dumb show under dim spot of Tosh returning from Honolulu.

(Father sits at veranda steps, smoking. Mother and Kiyo stand in yard. Tosh enters, puts down handbag, gives Mother box of pastries, his lei, kisses her cheek, as he picks up handbag to go in, he makes eye contact with Father. SLOW MOTION: Father slowly looks away. Tosh and the others rush into house.)

Scene 3: Supper Table, 5 P.M. A week later.

(Father in tank top and denim or khaki. Kiyo and Tosh in T-shirts or Aloha shirts, Mother in cotton print dress. Father sips from bottle of beer, while reading letter.)

MOTHER: It's terrible what they charge for *opakapaka*.
TOSH: I hate fish.
MOTHER: That's why I cooked you hamubaga (hamburger).
KIYO: I eat five bowls of rice, and I'm still hungry.

MOTHER: *(extends hand)* How about a sixth bowl. *(Kiyo hesitates.)* There's still lots of *miso* soup and *tofu*.

KIYO: Oh, all right. *(Gives her empty bowl with one hand, which Mother takes with both hands, ladles rice twice, the second scoop more a ritual, and gives it to him with both hands. He takes with one hand.)*

FATHER: Grandfather is working as an interpreter at the Canadian Consulate in Tokyo. *(Picks at fish with chopstick.)* If it wasn't for the big earthquake in 1923, he'd have a big store by now.

TOSH:

(Until now Tosh has always backed down, and avoided confrontation with Father. He'd complain to Mother about Father, but not directly to him. Father is still the seat of power. So in his presence, he makes asides and smolders. But he never pushes Father to the limit.)

It was his *bachi*.

MOTHER: Years of saving wiped out in minutes.

TOSH: *(more daring but under his breath)* You mean years of sponging.

FATHER: *(looks up irritably at Tosh)* He was about to call us back to Japan to help him.

KIYO: Is a good thing he didn't.

TOSH: You wrote the Japanese Consulate to cancel our Japanese citizenship? *(Father grunts without looking up from letter.)* Yes or no?

FATHER: I wrote.

MOTHER: *(to Kiyo)* Is that what you want? *(Kiyo nods.)* It'll make it difficult if you go to Japan.

KIYO: I don't want to go to Japan.

MOTHER: But it doesn't hurt to have both.

TOSH: It does. In case of war, Kiyo and me, we'll fight for America.

FATHER: It'll never happen.

TOSH: The Japanese say, "Piety to the parents, loyalty to the emperor." In our case the emperor is America.

KIYO: In America the first loyalty is to yourself.

MOTHER: Kiyoshi, what are you saying? Thinking of yourself first is selfishness.

KIYO: You can't survive unless you're selfish.

MOTHER: The family comes first. The first loyalty is to the family.

KIYO: I still say you have to be loyal to yourself. You have to think for yourself.

MOTHER: That's the way *haoles* think. That's why they have so many divorces.

FATHER: They even steal their brothers' wives.

TOSHIO: Which is worse, stealing a brother's wife or stealing from your own children? *(To mother)* How much of the debt have we paid up?

MOTHER: A hundred. Two hundred.

TOSHIO: That's all? I've worked over four years and that's all?

MOTHER: The plantation pays us barely enough to live on.

TOSHIO: Next year you better make Takako work in the canefields with the weeders.

MOTHER: She'll work a year and then go on to high school.

TOSH: *(raises voice slightly)* You force me to quit so you can send the girls?

MOTHER: Canefield girls marry canefield boys. High school girls, high school boys.

TOSH: *(Would explode at her if Father wasn't there. Now holds back, sounding nasal and apologetic.)* That's what I mean. She'll get married. She won't pay you back.

MOTHER: I don't want the girls to end up like me.

(Awkward pause)

TOSH: *(softening)* Educate the boys. Send Kiyo instead.

MOTHER: Kiyoshi can wait.

KIYO: Yeah, I can wait.

TOSH: I wanna hear you say that after they been squeeze twenty years out of you! *(Calmer)* Father, what do you say?

FATHER: Huh? *(Sending the girls to high school is Mother's idea and he doesn't want to get involved. Now he repeats argument Mother had put to him. Waves it off, wrist motion.)* The boys can catch up.

TOSH: *(voice higher)* Catch up twenty years!?

FATHER: *(waves it off like it was a trifle)* It won't take that long. *(Escapes back into letter.)*

TOSH: *(to Kiyo)* Shit! You all against me! *(Determined to force confrontation, but not raising his voice.)* I hear they fired grandfather from Puukolii Store because they caught him stealing.

MOTHER: *(under her breath)* Toshio!

FATHER: *(brushing him off)* That's a lie. He was fired because he extended credit to those the plantation had refused credit.

TOSH: That's not what the old timers say.

FATHER: Who?

TOSH: Miyabara, Yanagi.

MOTHER: You would listen to them instead of your father?

FATHER: *(unperturbed)* They lie.

TOSH:	I believe them.
FATHER:	*Nani!?*
TOSH:	I don't think as much of grandfather as you do. He works you for ten years and takes all the money with him to Japan.
MOTHER:	But we gave it to him.
TOSH:	He took it.
MOTHER:	He wept when he left. He said he couldn't ask for more filial children. He said we need not bring any gifts when we rejoined him. We can come with just the clothes on our backs. We did everything he asked. That's filial piety.
TOSH:	*(unable to restrain anger)* What about a little piety to the children!? Look at the *haoles!*
FATHER:	The *haoles* are wasteful and lazy.
MOTHER:	They're dirty, they don't take a bath every day.
TOSH:	They might be wasteful, lazy and dirty, but they don't sponge on their children!
MOTHER:	Every child must repay his parents.
TOSH:	How much!? How long!?
MOTHER:	Your father helped grandfather for over ten years.
TOSH:	*(to Kiyo)* Grandfather was a thief!
FATHER:	*(cocking jaw)* *Nani!?*
TOSH:	Grandfather was a sponge and a crook!
FATHER:	*Chikusho!* *(Jumps up.)*
TOSH:	I believe Miyabara and Yanagi! Anybody who steals from his children would steal from a store!

(Father swings backhanded at Tosh's head, Tosh backs off, Father throws a straight right to Tosh's head, Tosh slips to his left and throws a right to Father's stomach as he'd practiced with Kiyo. Father falls on his ass.)

MOTHER:	Father! Toshio! Stop it!
FATHER:	*(gasps)* Get out!
TOSH:	*(subdued, guilty. He hadn't intended it to go so far.)* It wasn't intentional.
FATHER:	Nemmind! Get out! *(Kiyo helps him back on the bench. Tosh sidles to doorway.)*
TOSH:	*(trying to explain)* You hit me first.
FATHER:	You're no son mine!
MOTHER:	Please stop! Both of you!
FATHER:	Get out! Don't come back!
MOTHER:	*(to Father)* You can't let him go yet. *(Facing Tosh)* Every child must repay his parents.

TOSH: How long?

FATHER: Get out!

TOSH: *(starts to leave, stops, more explanatory and nasal, restraining anger.)* You need me. I don't need you. But you treat me like dirt. I'd be happy to leave. I can work my way through high school and college and make something of myself.

FATHER: *(less vehemently)* Get out.

MOTHER: You can't let him go yet.

TOSH: Shit! *(Exits.)*

MOTHER: *(worriedly)* Are you hurt?

(Father pushes her away, rubbing his stomach.)

MOTHER: *(picking up tea pot)* What about *chazuke?*

FATHER: *Biru kure. (Mother exits.)*

(Kiyo's memory warp. Music as in opening hospital scene, light change. Spot on Kiyo upstage. Father moves downstage in his own spot.)

KIYO *(SOC):* Poor guy. They used to call him the *onaga* king.

FATHER: *(rocking side to side slowly as if he's on his sampan)* Fish are like people. They live in communities in the valleys. So you have to be precise in where you drop your lines. A few feet off and your lines drop on the ridges instead of the valleys and you don't get a single bite. I always line the top of the Lahaina smokestack with a spot on the mountaintop.

    I bait all ten hooks and drop the line over the side. Then I roll a Bull Durham and smoke it to the end before hauling up the line. I can tell immediately how many bites I have. The *onaga* swim upwards, and lighten your pull. The more fish, the lighter the load. Their milky white guts pop out of their mouths like little balloons. That's why they made the best *sashimi.* Their flesh is firm from being down 70 fathoms. They call me the *onaga* king.

MOTHER: *(back to normal lighting, Mother enters and hands beer)* Ne, father, we can't let him go yet.

(Blackout)

KIYO *(SOC):* *(shines yellow flashlight)* Why I always have to be peace-maker? Why they no can get along? *(Walks, looks around and up.)* Night time different world. Dark forest. Cool breeze in the eucalyptus. Stars galore. Damn Tosh, why he take it out on them just because he got beat? Where can he go this time of night? Single Men's Quarters the only place.

Scene 4: Single Men's Quarters. A few hours later.

(Tosh in zori *sits on railing on veranda, watching crap game. Farther off four men shooting crap on veranda floor, talking quietly as heard from afar. Exchange done swiftly.)*

HIROSHI: *(rolls)* Seven right. Shoot it.

1ST CRAPSHOOTER: I cover 10.

2ND CRAPSHOOTER: Here 5. Shoot, you covered.

HIROSHI: *(rolls)* Four my point. Little Joe. Who give me two to one? *(He looks up as Kiyo enters and sits next to Tosh.)* Hi, Kiyo.

KIYO: Hey, Hiroshi. How you get here?

HIROSHI: My father's cab. *(He rattles dice and rolls.)*

KIYO: *(to Tosh)* My classmate back at Lahaina. *(Leans on railing beside Tosh.)*

TOSH: Funny kind the way he roll.

KIYO: *(They watch him roll several times.)* Yeah, the way he pick up the dice. Extra motion like telegraphing a jab.

TOSH: *(after watching a moment)* Mama been send you?

KIYO: Yeah.

TOSH: You shoulda been *chonan.*

KIYO: Thass what you get for getting born first.

TOSH: No, they like you more. You their golden boy. You can do no wrong. Me, everything I do is wrong.

KIYO: Listen the way he shake the dice. Sound different. Like only one face banging one face. Like the dice not moving. *(They listen.)*

TOSH: He cleaning them up.

KIYO: How come you keep provoking the old man?

TOSH: *(loudly)* Me provoke him!? *(Lowers voice.)* What about the 6 G's!? What about forcing me to quit high school! He skinning me alive, and he expects me to *gaman* and take it.

KIYO: Lots of number one sons doing it. They don't crab.

TOSH: Bullshit! They crab to me, they crab to their brothers, but they doan have the guts to crab to the old futs.

KIYO: How come you crab so much?

TOSH: Shit! All I asking for is my body! I doan wanna die on the plantation like these dumb dodoes! Shit, Mama, she treats him like he was a feudal lord. "It's pitiful for father," she says, "we shouldn't make him feel bad." Shit, why shouldn't he feel bad!? He the one on top. He the guy responsible.

KIYO: Why don't you talk to him plain sometimes? You punch when you talk.

TOSH:	You know why you can talk to him? I been soften him up, thass why. Yeah, he hit you if it wasn't for me.
KIYO:	Papa never been hit me once.
TOSH:	You his favorite, thass why!
KIYO:	Look the way the dice roll. They no flip on their sides, they roll like wheels. *(Both watch.)*
1ST:	Boy, you lucky, Hiroshi. You bust me.
TOSH:	The guy a crook. These guys no can see it.
KIYO:	Maybe you should come live over here, Single Men's Quarters.
TOSH:	You think Mama let me? Shit, it's $5 more for rent.
KIYO:	You want me to ask them? It's worth five bucks for a little peace and quiet.
TOSH:	Which side you on!?
KIYO:	*(shrugs)* Neither.
TOSH:	You against me if you not for me!
KIYO:	*(shrugs)* I not against you, I not against them. I just want some peace and quiet.
TOSH:	Thass what the old man wants. He sucking my blood, and he wants peace and quiet. You in his corner, no try kid me.
KIYO:	I not for him and I not for you.
TOSH:	You gotta choose. A guy a friend or enemy.
KIYO:	So who me? Friend, enemy, or just a sparring partner?
TOSH:	You Mr. Nice Guy.
KIYO:	Yeah!? Who else you got to talk to?
TOSH:	I went to see Takemoto *sensei.* I asked him if ten years of filial piety was enough.
KIYO:	What'd he say.
TOSH:	He said, yeah, since this Hawaii and not Japan, ten years should be plenty. *(Pause)* Papa, he been do his big thing already. He was filial number one son, so he figure it's his turn to sit back and catch all the gravy. All this shit about *chonan* make sense only if the old man got property. He leave everything to the oldest son. In return the *chonan* look after him and his family. But shit, the old man, he doan have a pot to piss in! He came here as a *hanawai* man, and he gonna die as a *hanawai* man! I doan think it bother him if we all die on the plantation as long as we give him lotsa face! He likes it here! He can act the big shot! In Lahaina he was nobody! He got no ambition! Shit, I get so mad sometimes, I wanna kill them!
KIYO:	*(fed up)* You goin' home? Makes no difference to me. *(Exits.)*
TOSH:	*(watches him leave, stands)* Shit, I get choice? *(Exits.)*

(Blackout)

(As soon as BLACKOUT, *taped crowd noise at fight, sound of* BELL *simultaneously, followed by haole radio announcer voice.)*

TAPED RADIO ANNOUNCER: *(delivered high-pitched, excited, and fast)* That's the bell ending the second round! What a fight! What a fight! Each fighter has rocked the other, and traded blows like gladiators! Everybody said Kiyoshi Oyama would knock out Napoleon Reyes by the second around as he's done all his previous eight opponents! But Reyes has taken his best shots, and hammered Oyama on the ropes! Toshio Oyama, who repeated tonight as Maui's middle-weight *(depends on the weight of the actor playing Tosh)* champ in his brother's corner . . .

Scene 5: Corner of boxing ring. March 1941.

(Lights reveal Kiyo on stool, in his corner of the ring. He is confused and disheveled, is bare foot, wears 8-oz gloves. Tosh is his second, wiping his face with white towel, rubbing him down while he exhorts. Caucasian referee in dress shirt and bow tie. Another fighter waits in the dark.)

TOSH: *(yelling over crowd noise)* You gotta keep moving!

KIYO: My legs shot!

TOSH: You shoulda run with me!

KIYO: All he got is condition!

TOSH: See if you can slow him down! Set him up for your left hook!

KIYO: I been give him my best shot already! He get iron jaw!

TOSH: Keep jabbing! Circle right!

KIYO: Bastard! He no can even throw a decent punch!

TOSH: He a brawler! His style made to order for me! *(Bell sounds)* *(Picks up stool and backs out.)* Stay outside, jab!

(Tosh exits ring with stool. Boxers fight in 3/4 to 1/2 speed, Reyes is a swarmer. Kiyo is a one-punch fighter without conditioning. Both are exhausted and weak-kneed. Kiyo keeps landing left hooks and clinching. Reyes fights like a street fighter, raining blows from every angle, shaking off Kiyo's left hooks like they're taps. Kiyo decides to slug it out, catches Reyes with a left hook that stings him.
SLOW MOTION: *Crowd noise stops,* TOM-TOM, TOM-TOM OF TAIKO DRUMS. *Reyes floors Kiyo, he tries to get up, and falls back, Referee pushes Reyes to neutral corner, and begins* COUNT BACK TO NORMAL TIME.*)*

TOSH: *(during above before the* SLOW MOTION. *Yells above the crowd noise)*

Circle right! Circle right! Stick um! One more! Move! To your right! Clinch! Hold 'im! Bicycle! Kiyo! Bicycle! No! No! No! No slug! No slug! Clinch! Clinch! Duck! No slug! Yeah! Stick um! Again! Move! Move! No slug! No slug! Hold um! Clinch!

REFEREE: One, two, three, four—
TOSH: *(over din of crowd, hoarse)* Take the count! Take the count!
REFEREE: Five, six, seven—

(Kiyo looks about, not knowing where he is.)

TOSH: No get up! No get up! *(Raises towel to throw into ring, stops.)*
REFEREE: Eight, nine, ten!

(Blackout as Reyes leaps.)

Scene 6: June 1941. Front yard. 4 P.M.

TOSH: Hey, Kiyo! Kiyo!
KIYO: *(enters SL)* What? *(He wears sweat-stained sweat shirt and pants. He shadow boxes.)*
TOSH: Come over here. I got something to show you. *(Kiyo keeps shadow boxing.)*

(Kiyo keeps shadow boxing.)

             Hey, no go punish yourself. You go stale if you doan lay off once in a while.
KIYO: The Bulaheads, they brag about *Yamato damashi!* It don't work with me! Shit, I need red meat! *Tofu* not enough!
TOSH: *(hands him letter)* Sad Sam been write me.
KIYO: Sad Sam Nakata? *(Reads)* Hey, he wants you to turn pro in a year! Is about time we got a break!
TOSH: I doan know if I going.
KIYO: Why not?
TOSH: The old futs, they make me feel like hell.
KIYO: Go, I'll stay. Is better than ten more years in this dump. *(Tosh doesn't answer.)* You think your girl . . . You think Fumiko will say "doan go"?
TOSH: Naw, she'll say is up to me.
KIYO: So what's the problem?
TOSH: They'll say I ran away.
KIYO: Who, the old folks?
TOSH: Yeah, and the whole camp.

KIYO: What you care what they say? You no can let them run your life.

TOSH: Yeah, thass right. Go write Sad Sam for me.

KIYO: When you going?

TOSH: Coupla months.

KIYO: Hey, maybe I can join you bumbye. *(Throws combination)* The Oyama brothers. We make 6 G's in no time.

TOSH: Naw, maybe I better not.

KIYO: Sad Sam not going ask you a second time.

TOSH: You think I should go, huh?

KIYO: Why else we been training?

TOSH: You sure you doan mind holding the bag?

KIYO: No! I thought was understood. Whoever get the first break, the other guy goin support him.

TOSH: Naw, I doan think so.

KIYO: I guess is just as well. You a counter-puncher. You not goin draw as a pro.

TOSH: You talking pretty big for somebody who got KO'd.

KIYO: You got KO'd too!

TOSH: Yeah, but mine was all to the body. My legs been give way. Besides, I been beat Jose Pasion this last time. I knocked him down twice. I win if I dint get a cut.

KIYO: I goin get my man next time too. All I need is my legs. Same as you.

TOSH: *(takes letter from Kiyo)* You doan know what it's like being number one son.

KIYO: Most of them are bullies.

TOSH: No, I thinking about Mama.

KIYO: You think she goin let you go? Why you always asking for the impossible? Shit, if was me, I do it first and ask later.

TOSH: They been give her a rough time. Grandma was a big miser. She been ride Mama like one slave driver. I doan wanna leave her holding the bag again. I pity her.

KIYO: *(under his breath)* Shit. What about the debt?

TOSH: *(calls into house)* Mama! *(Mother enters onto the veranda.)*

MOTHER: Nani? *(Steps into slippers on step.)*

TOSH: *(gives her letter)* Nakata-san, the big boxing manager in Honolulu, wrote me. He wants me to join his stable and turn professional.

MOTHER: You should refuse. You'll get hurt.

TOSH: I'm refusing because of you and papa. I'm refusing because I'm filial.

MOTHER: Professional boxers are good for nothing else afterwards.

TOSH: *(almost pleading)* Here, I'm sacrificing myself for you, and you can't even say, "Thank you."

MOTHER: *Arigato gozaimasu. (Ironic, bowing low. Except for Mother, the others don't bow, they nod.)* But it's also for your own good.

KIYO: You should let him go. How else are we going to pay off the debt?

MOTHER: What good is money if your head gets *gota-gota*.

TOSH: Aren't you going to praise me for being filial?

MOTHER: You filial? Hmmm. A filial son wouldn't have gone to Takemoto *sensei* to talk about our debt. You shamed your father.

TOSH: That was a year ago. I wanted an outside opinion. Were ten years of filial piety enough? I wanted to know, because at this rate, it's going to take twenty years.

MOTHER: Family business is family business.

TOSH: You're always defending father. He didn't even protect you when grandmother was so mean to you.

MOTHER: He had to be a filial son first . . . like Minoru Tanaka, Hideo Shima—

TOSH: They're ghosts! They've been used up! They hate it, but they don't have the courage to fight back!

MOTHER: It's not courage. It's selfishness. Besides, you talk big of helping us. Your boxing eats away a lot of what you earn.

TOSH: Like what!?

MOTHER: Your trips, new clothes, time off from work, spending money, special food.

TOSH: Tell me, does it cost any more than sending Takako and Miwa to high school!? What about *their* new clothes? What about their $10 a month for car fare!? What about the expenses for books and things!? And they're not even going to pay you back! They'll get married!

MOTHER: Don't worry, we won't depend on you, we'll depend on Kiyoshi.

TOSH: *(explodes, hands letter to Kiyo)* Go write Sad Sam. Tell him I coming. I go *pupule* if I stay here! *(Exits)*

MOTHER: What did he say?

KIYO: He's leaving for Honolulu.

(Blackout)

End of ACT I

ACT II

(Lilting Hawaiian music on radio during Intermission)

RADIO ANNOUNCER: *(Announcer is hysterical, trying to convince an incredulous population)* We interrupt this program with a bulletin! Pearl Harbor has been attacked! I repeat Pearl Harbor has been attacked! This is no maneuver! This is the real McCoy! This island is under attack! I repeat, this island is under attack! Besides Pearl Harbor, sporadic attacks have been made on Honolulu! The black puffs of anti-aircraft fire over the city are for real! Stay in your homes! Stay out of the streets! I repeat, this is no maneuver! This is the real McCoy! The markings of the rising sun have been sighted on the wings of the attacking planes! *(Calmer)* All National Guardsmen, report to the Armory. All ROTC students, report to your schools. *(High-pitched again)* This island is under attack! I repeat, this is not just another maneuver! This is the real McCoy . . . !

Scene 7: Veranda. A week after Pearl Harbor. Sunday afternoon. Dec. 14.

(Tosh hair disheveled, holds a bottle of beer, half empty, and sits on steps. Kiyo enters from his roadwork, is surprised at his drinking.)

KIYO: Hey, you gotta keep in shape.

TOSH: What for? Boxing *pau*. The war's gonna last forever.

KIYO: They goin lift martial law some time.

TOSH: Yeah, after they send us to Molokai. They freeze us to the plantation. They say only three Bulaheads can hang out at one time. *(Watches Kiyo shadow boxing.)* You wasting your time.

KIYO: How can they bomb Pearl Harbor while they talking peace in Washington? A samurai not two-faced, a samurai never go back on his word, they teach us.

TOSH: Bullshit!

KIYO: They all lies? How come I swallow all that crap? I must be dumb. I used to be kinda proud being a Bulahead.

TOSH: I smart I flunk Japanee school. Hey, I wonder why they never been grab Takemoto *sensei*.

KIYO: Maybe because he a Christian. The been grab the Buddhists right away.

(Mother enters.)

MOTHER: *Maah*, are you drinking beer now?

TOSH: I need something for my headache.

MOTHER: I just heard they pulled in Mr. Hamaguchi.

TOSH: You mean the old man who works for Puukolii Store? Why?

MOTHER: He was the Japanese consular representative for Puukolii. They didn't give him a chance to pack.

TOSH: Wasn't papa the representative in Lahaina?

(Mother nods.)

(Enter Michie SL, agitated.)

MICHIE: A haole man! His car is at the language school!

TOSH: *(to Mother)* You better get papa ready. Give him a clean shirt. And pack his things.

MOTHER: Hai, hai. *(Exits backstage into house.)*

MICHIE: No, he's coming for my father because he goes around bragging Japan's going to win the war.

KIYO: They not goin' grab him for that.

MICHIE: What? You think they pulling in Takemoto *sensei?*

KIYO: If they grab him, they grab my father for sure.

MICHIE: Do you think the Japanese Army will invade Puukolii?

KIYO: I hope not.

TOSH: Nobody wants a stink place like this.

MICHIE: He coming! I gotta go! *(Exits)*

TOSH: *(calling into house)* Papa! Mama!

(Father enters buttoning long-sleeve white shirt. Mother follows behind with suitcase. At the same time Paul Baker strides toward the veranda, holding some papers.)

BAKER: *(to Tosh)* Are you Mr. Oyama? *(Tosh shakes head.)*

FATHER: I am Oyama.

BAKER: I'm Paul Baker of the FBI. You're Mrs. Oyama, your sons. I wonder if I can have a few words with you. *(Scans papers)* You came to Hawaii in . . .

FATHER: 1910.

BAKER: You went to Lahaina and became a fisherman in 1921.

FATHER: *Hai.*

BAKER: Then you quit and came back here in 1937. Why did you quit fishing?

FATHER:	No nuff fish. Toh muchi baby. *Pilikia.*
BAKER:	You had a large boat.
FATHER:	Thirty two feeto. One hossu power, four knots.
BAKER:	You could go out to the open sea beyond sight of land?
FATHER:	Go sea, *hai.*

(Tosh steps forward.)

TOSH:	No, no. *Riku ga mien hodo oki ni itta?*
FATHER:	No can. No can. If go, no come back.
BAKER:	Why not?
FATHER:	Get lost.
TOSH:	He doan have compass.
BAKER:	You worked for the Japanese Consulate while in Lahaina?
FATHER:	*Hai.*
BAKER:	How much did they pay you?
FATHER:	Hmmm . . . $3, $5 monsu (month).
BAKER:	What did you do for them?
FATHER:	I repoto (report) somebody die, baby born.
BAKER:	What else?
FATHER:	*Dasu oru* (That's all).
BAKER:	You could find nothing else to report?

(Father looks helplessly at Tosh.)

TOSH:	*Hoka ni tsutaeru mono nakatta?*
FATHER:	No. No. Only baby born. Orudo (old) people *ma-ke* (die).
BAKER:	You go Honolulu?
FATHER:	Only one taimsu (time) when boat come. Japan boat. Big boat. 1910.
MOTHER:	*(stage whisper)* Papa! Papa! *(Holding up two fingers) Ni doh!*
FATHER:	No, tsu (two) taimsu, when wife come 1915.
BAKER:	Why did you withdraw $7,000 from the Bank of Hawaii?
FATHER:	I reado newspapa. Nobemba. Gobermento taku oru Japanee moni (money). So I taku outo. Japan Clubu.
BAKER:	On whose authority?
FATHER:	*(looks at Tosh)* Huh?
TOSH:	*(stumped by Japanese for "authority") Da re ga yuuta?* (Who told you?)
KIYO:	*(steps up) Da re no kenri de?* (On whose authority?)
MOTHER:	*Da re no kenri de?*
FATHER:	No can? Why dey no stop if no can.

BAKER: *(slowly)* Where is money now?

FATHER: I bringu homu, keepu insai chicken housu. I asku Toshimi
            Omura, *nisei*, put under him namu. Decemba *sebun*, in chicken
            housu. I talku membas. Fai (gives high five) hundredo dolla,
            gibu Redo Kurosu (Red Cross), okay? So gibu Redo Kurosu
            (high five) fai hundredo dolla.

BAKER: What happened to the rest of it?

FATHER: Membas keep. Sebunty dolla, one memba.

BAKER: How did you get $7000?

FATHER: Oba tarty year. Ebery monsu, quarter *(takes quarter out of pocket,
            and shows him)* Now onri (only) ninety membas. Befo three hun-
            dredo membas. Befo onri quarter. Now one dolla.

BAKER: You are the president of the Japanese Club?

FATHER: *Hai.* Fibu *(holds up five fingers)* year.

BAKER: *(wants a direct answer from Father without sons interpreting)* Amer-
            ica, Japan, which side you want win?

FATHER: America, Japan *aikane* oru rai (all right).

BAKER: If Japan Army come Puukolii, you shoot?

FATHER: *Hai*, I shoot.

BAKER: What if other side your cousin?

FATHER: How can tell cousin? *Hai*, I shoot.

BAKER: Are your sons Japanese citizens?

FATHER: No Japanee, only American.

BAKER: Did you cancel their Japanese citizenship?

FATHER: *Hai.* Stop all Japanee.

TOSH: We been apply for cancellation last year. We Americans.

BAKER: You have the cancellation papers and the Red Cross receipt?

FATHER: *Hai, hai! (Runs into house.)*

BAKER: *(sees boxing gloves, etc. in box)* Who's the boxer?

TOSH/KIYO: *(simultaneous)* Me.

BAKER: Both of you?

KIYO: He quit.

TOSH: I never said that.

(Father runs out with papers, hands them to Baker.)

BAKER: Okay, papa-san. Thank you for your time. *(Exits. Father and
            Mother bow, Mother holds her deeper bow longer.)*

TOSH: *(to Father)* You're lucky I told you to cancel our Japanese citi-
            zenship *(Father walks in a daze toward chicken coop SR. To Mother.)*
            He's not even going to thank me.

MOTHER: *(bows deeply)* Domo arigato gozaimasu. *(Sincere.)*

TOSH:	I want him to thank me.
MOTHER:	*(shorter bow)* I thank you for him. You saved us.
TOSH:	*(to Kiyo)* Good thing the mongoose dint eat the 7 G's. We be 13 G's in the hole. I goin to Fumi's house. See if she okay. *(Exits.)*
MOTHER:	I'm so relieved! *(Bows to Kiyo)* Domo, domo . . . *(Carries suitcase into house.)*

(Kiyo walks to chicken coop where Father sits among his stacks of Japanese soft-cover books. He is thumbing through one.)

KIYO:	What are you doing?
FATHER:	Toshio said to hide my books so I brought them here. I'm try-ing to decide which to burn. Most of the novels I read only once anyway.
KIYO:	You don't have to burn any of them. They won't arrest you for books. Besides, the danger is past.
FATHER:	He won't come back?
KIYO:	I don't think so. So you hid the $7,000 here for two weeks?
FATHER:	Three weeks. Toshimi Omura just couldn't get a day off during the week to go to the bank.
KIYO:	You did the members of the Japanese Club a great favor. *(Father laughs embarrassedly. Pause.)* Father, why didn't you quit fishing before the debt got so large?
FATHER:	It happened so suddenly. You remember when mother got so sick, she had to spend three months in the hospital? I had to stay home for three months to cook and launder and fix the bath for all of you.
KIYO:	But you don't go $6000 in debt in three months.
FATHER:	No.
KIYO:	So?
FATHER:	Quitting meant returning to the plantation. You've seen how miserable plantation work is. In the old days we worked ten hours a day, six days a week. We did the same work as the Por-tuguese and Chinese and got paid less. My younger brother, Azumi—your uncle in Honolulu—he was a steam plow opera-tor. He stayed home with fever one day, and the *luna* came for him with a whip. He collapsed in the field, and they carried him home. When he recovered, he walked like an old man. "I can't stay here," he said, "they'll work me till they kill me." Mother made him rice balls wrapped in seaweed for his lunch, and he left early when we left for work, and we never saw him again. Today it's only eight hours a day, but my feet are in sewage

water all day. When the cane is short, you breathe dust, the sun bakes you. When it's tall, you have to wear a thick shirt, and roast. Quitting fishing meant admitting failure, being laughed at, people saying, "He couldn't escape the plantation after all." *(Walks toward veranda during last part of speech.)*

KIYO: You could declare bankruptcy.

FATHER: Bankruptcy? *(Turns, then keeps walking.)* It's *hila-hila*. Only *haoles* do such a thing.

KIYO: What can be more *hila-hila* than Pearl Harbor!?

FATHER: *(doesn't hear or ignores questions, and walks onto veranda.)* All my creditors are lifelong friends. They don't charge me any interest. We trust each other. I wouldn't be able to face them if I declared bankruptcy. I'd have to move somewhere far away. I just can't start life all over again. I'm too old.

(Music and change of lighting for memory warp. Father picks up wooden clappers from veranda.)

KIYO *(SOC):* He used to be so proud. I loved watching him announcing the sumo matches.

FATHER:

(Strikes wooden clappers and moves to one side on raked stage, sing-songs his announcement, then clapping moves over to other side and sing-songs name of wrestler on West. Then repeats the names kabuki-style.)

Nnnn-higashiiiii, Konomi-yama, Konooomiii-yama. ("On the East is Konomi-yama" saunters to opposite side, clapping.) Nii-shiiii Takan-omori, Takaaaano moriii ("On the West is Takano-mori.")

(Thrusts right hand east and then west, using nasal high-pitch kabuki-type intonation.)

Higashi wa Konomi-yama, Nishi wa Takano-mori!

(Blackout)

Scene 8: Veranda. Sunday afternoon. Spring 1942.

TOSH: *(entering with rain-wet umbrella)* What you doing?

KIYO: *(studies dice with paper and pencil)* I figured um out. Why Hiroshi never lose. If you can roll um so they doan flip over, you can kill four numbas. See if you bury 6 and 1, and 6 and 1 on the first roll, you no can crap out. No 2, 3, or 12. If you get a point, any point. Take 4 or 10. If you bury 1 and 6, and 3 and 4, you can get a 7 only two ways, and a 4 or 10 two ways. So it's 50/50. The real odds is 2 to 1. What I no can figure out is how he make um no flip over.

TOSH: *(takes dice and rolls on floor as he says)* So you goin' be a crap-shooter now.

KIYO: Naw, just curious. Everybody says Hiroshi a terrific gambler. He a crook.

TOSH: 'Ass what I told you. *(Rolls again.)* I knew right away.

KIYO: Yeah, but you dint know why.

TOSH: *(gives dice back)* Where the old futs?

KIYO: Papa, he had on his white shirt. Match-making . . . *(Shrugs)* I doan know. Mama, she cleaning the pig pen.

TOSH: Fumiko and me, we wanna get married. I wanna ask them.

KIYO: She pregnant?

TOSH: Wachu take me for?

KIYO: *(nods several times)* So you gonna die on the plantation like the dumb dodoes?

TOSH: I not goin start a family yet. I goin take a correspondence course. Fumi goin help me. Shit, I no can concentrate living here.

KIYO: You only twenty.

TOSH: Same age as papa when he got married.

KIYO: Thass different. They got papa a wife because they wanted a maid to help grandma with the tofu and pigs. You guys goin come live here?

TOSH: Cannot. Fumi works at the hospital in Lahaina, and I goin go haul bagasse from the mill 6 P.M. to 6 A.M., seven days a week, so we gotta live in Lahaina.

KIYO: What about the debt?

TOSH: We been talk it over. We give them all of Fumi's pay for a year, and one third of mine till all paid up. I gonna be working twelve hours so I gonna be making one and a half times what I making now.

KIYO: So you find a house already?

TOSH: Not yet.

KIYO: You know why they get so many kids here in Puukolii? Nothing to do at night, as why. Is gonna be the same in Lahaina with the blackout and curfew.

TOSH: *(raising voice for first time)* I told you! We not gonna start a family yet!

KIYO: But once you get stuck, you're finished. 'Ass what you said.

TOSH:	'Ass not what I said. Anyway, Fumi goin' help me! If I stay here, I not goin' amount to nothing! I goin' take a correspondence course.
KIYO:	You no can study by yourself?
TOSH:	Not here!
KIYO:	I can.
TOSH:	You bookworm, 'ass why!
KIYO:	No, I get more *gaman.* You know, if they send us to Molokai or the mainland camps, be easy, eh, if you already get a wife?
TOSH:	Wassa matter with you? You doan like Fumi or what!?
KIYO:	She okay.
TOSH:	So whas bothering you? You scared I goin' leave you holding the bag? You think I that kinda guy?
KIYO:	I jes doan wanna see you end up one dumb dodo.
TOSH:	I told you! We not goin start a family right away! She goin help me. She was one honor student at Lahainaluna. *(Exiting.)* Shit! I thought you my friend!

(Blackout)

Scene 9: Backyard. About 10:30 P.M. January 1943.

(Kiyo returns from walk in the canefield with flashlight covered with blue cellophane to conform to blackout regulations. He sits in backyard.)

MICHIE:	*(returning from outhouse with blue flashlight, sings softly)* Aitah sah, mita sah ni, kowasah wo wasure . . .
KIYO:	*(whispers)* Michie.
MICHIE:	*(shines flashlight at him)* Oh, you scared me! Were you in the *benjo?*
KIYO:	I went for a walk.
MICHIE:	Where?
KIYO:	In the canefield.
MICHIE:	You're not scared walking past the graveyard?
KIYO:	Naw.
MICHIE:	You'll get arrested for breaking curfew.
KIYO:	By who? Ghosts?
MICHIE:	Is it part of your boxing training?
KIYO:	Naw, lots of nights I just gotta walk and walk.
MICHIE:	How come?
KIYO:	I feel like everything inside ready to bust out. I gotta make up my mind.

MICHIE: You're thinking of joining the Army?
KIYO: Yeah.
MICHIE: My father says they'll put you all in one unit so that they can kill
           you off.
KIYO: Is our chance to prove we loyal. I rather fight Japan than the
           Nazis though. Naw . . . I gotta think about our debt. You know
           my dumb dodo brother? His wife expecting.
MICHIE: What's wrong with that?
KIYO: He used to brag he not goin get stuck on the plantation! He jes
           giving up! I not gonna be like that. *(Pause)* You know my family
           $6000 in debt?
MICHIE: Not.
KIYO: Thass why we moved here.
MICHIE: I'm glad you folks moved next door though. My father was so
           embarrassed going to Takemoto *sensei* to get his letters written.
           Your father has a beautiful hand. *(Pause)* I offered to write my
           father's letter. Do you know what he said, "Don't be a *baka!*
           Yours is a woman's hand!" *(Pause, looking up)* I'm flying away as
           soon as I can.
KIYO: Where to?
MICHIE: *(points)* To that star.
KIYO: Is a long way.
MICHIE: The farther the better.
KIYO: I feel like that too.
MICHIE: So are you going to volunteer?
KIYO: I think so.
MICHIE: What do your parents say?
KIYO: My mother worry about the debt. But I'll be making the same
           $50 a month. I'll send them $40. They get $10,000 if I die.
MICHIE: Hey, no talk like that! *Bachi! (Pause.)* Do you want to borrow
           more books? You may keep them.
KIYO: Naw.
MICHIE: *(begins to leave, sings) Aitah sah, mita sah ni, kowasah wo wasure . . .*
KIYO: How come you doan sing in the toilet no more?
MICHIE: I didn't know you were sitting there listening!
KIYO: I dint wanna embarrass you. I even held back my futs.
MICHIE: You could've cleared your throat or something.
KIYO: I did once, but you sing so loud . . . You know I been see you
           naked?
MICHIE: No.
KIYO: At the bathhouse.
MICHIE: No.

KIYO: The hole in the wall.

MICHIE: *(comes back at him)* Is that why all you sit outside and watch us going in!? You pretend you're talking story! You're terrible!

KIYO: Not me! It was the only time I peeped! Honest! I was alone, thass why.

MICHIE: The next time, I'm going to poke you in the eye. *(She jabs right finger at his chest, he catches her wrist with left hand.)*

KIYO: Come, I teach you to dance. Waltz the easiest. Follow my feet. *(They turn off flashlight, he holds it in his right, she in her left.)* One-two-three, one-two-three, one-two-three. *(They dance.)* One-two-three, one-two-three, there, you getting it! *(Holds her tighter, and tries to kiss her.)*

MICHIE: *(spins free, giggling, sits)* How did you like Charles Dickens?

KIYO: I like Oliver Twist.

MICHIE: Isn't it surprising to learn many *haoles* are poor like us? How did you like Silas Marner?

KIYO: They get misers like him?

MICHIE: Oh, yes.

KIYO: Like who? Your father? *(He peck kisses her, she pushes off playfully.)*

MICHIE: Why don't you dance by yourself. I'll watch. *(Stands, shining flashlight at his feet.)*

KIYO: One-two-three, one-two-three. Is hard dancing alone.

MICHIE: I learn more by watching you.

KIYO: Les go behind the pig pen.

MICHIE: Why?

KIYO: Somebody might come.

MICHIE: I don't like sneaking around.

KIYO: Everybody do it.

MICHIE: Everybody *does*. "Everybody" is a singular noun.

KIYO: Yeah, I know.

MICHIE: It doesn't take any more effort to say it correctly.

KIYO: The guys razz me, "You think you haole, or wat!? . . . You must think you shit ice cream!"

MICHIE: You're afraid of what they'll say? Of course, it wouldn't matter if you're planning to spend the rest of your life on the plantation.

KIYO: I goin' in the Army.

MICHIE: I'm talking of when you come back

KIYO: *(over enunciates)* No, I'm getting out on my first opportunity.

MICHIE: Why don't you punch the bag anymore? I used to love its sound.

YAMADA: *(voice off-stage)* Michie! Are you all right!? How long are you

	going to stay in the *benjo!?* *(A pause.)* Michie!? Can you hear me!?
KIYO:	You better go.
MICHIE:	It's so stuffy inside with the blackout.
YAMADA:	*(voice off-stage)* Michie!!
MICHIE:	I'm coming! *(To Kiyo)* The farthest I can run off to is the out-house.
YAMADA:	*(voice off-stage) Bakayaro!* I'm calling you for the last time!
MICHIE:	I'm coming! Bye.
YAMADA:	*(voice off-stage)* What were you doing!?
MICHIE:	I was practicing a song.

(Blackout)

Dumb show of Kiyo leaving for the Army.

(Father sits on railing on veranda, he keeps taking sembetsu *money out of small white letter envelopes, and gives money to Mother who puts it in large white letter envelope, and notes in her ledger who it's from and how much. A* sennin bari, *a "strip of white cloth, embellished with 1,000 stitches (French knots) sewn with red thread by 1,000 women," is draped on the railing. Mother also carries a red apple in her apron pocket.)*

(Kiyo enters in Aloha shirt, shoes, and travelling bag.)

(Mother goes to him, and wraps sennin bari *around his waist. She gives him envelope of money, he refuses, she takes money out of envelope, and forces wad into his hand. She moves off, then remembers the apple. He takes apple, and begins to put it in his bag, she stops him, and tells him to eat it. He takes a bite, and she hugs him impulsively, their first embrace. SLOW MOTION as he catches Father's eye. He sitting on railing, nods in SLOW MOTION. Mother steps back in normal speed.)*

KIYO *(SOC):* Eat something round. Go and return roundly. Make you come home safe. *(Takes off sash.)* A thousand-stitch belly band. Protect you against bullets, she says. *(Pause.)* What if it don't stop the *bachi?* *(Digs money out of pocket.)* How she goin to pay back all this gift money? What I goin do with all this dough?

Scene 10: Schofield Barracks. *(Crap game overlaps above SOC)*

1ST CRAPSHOOTER:	Okay, let it ride, shoot 200.
2ND CRAPSHOOTER:	Shoot, you're covered.
1ST:	*(rolls)* Five, the point. *(Picks up dice, and rolls.)* Phoebe!

2ND:	Seven! *(Laughs)* Short life! *(Picks up money in pot.)*
1ST:	You lucky bastard! I quit!
2ND:	Come on, no be a sore loser! *(Moves dice in front of Kiyo, who's just joined the game.)* How about you, country boy?
KIYO:	*(tosses money onto blanket)* Shoot 200.
2ND:	Shoot, I got you covered.
KIYO:	

(Fiddles with dice, to make them easier to pick up. He picks them up in wrong combination, and deliberately, pops one out when he shakes them. He bumbles, acts as if dice were hot potatoes. Picks them up correctly. He is a novice at pad-rolling and cheating. He's nervous he'll get caught. He also has stage fright.)

	Gimme a natural! *(Rolls. A slight pause after each roll.)* Seven right! Shoot it!
2ND:	I catch 200. *(To 1ST)* How about it, sore loser?
1ST:	Here's 200.
2ND:	Atta boy! Join the action.
KIYO:	*(fiddles with dice, picks them up)* One more time, baby! *(Rolls.)* Seven right! Shoot 800.
2ND:	Here's 400. No way he goin throw three passes.
1ST:	Okay, I catch 400.
KIYO:	*(he fiddles with dice again. Picks them up, and begins a long back swing, and stops. Looks back to his right, where Big Bettor stands. Big Bettor watches intrusively, but does not bet.)* Hey, how about some room?
2ND:	Yeah, give him some room.
KIYO:	*(Big Bettor backs off. Kiyo goes into long back swing and rolls with a follow through.)* Give me one more natural!
BIG BETTOR:	Ten's the point!
KIYO:	*(picks up dice in combination, and rolls)* Tennessee!
2ND:	*(simultaneously)* Crap, you bastard!
KIYO:	*(rolls again)* Give it to me the hard way!
1ST:	*(simultaneously)* Seven!
KIYO:	Ten, right! Shoot it.
2ND:	You musta step on dog shit! I catch 1200.
1ST:	Here's 400. Shoot! You're covered!
KIYO:	*(picks up dice right the first time, and shakes them, gaining confidence.)* Everybody happy!?
1ST:	How about more music!?
KIYO:	*(shaking dice harder)* Enough music!?
1ST:	Shake um hard!

(Kiyo agitated, afraid he's been caught. Drops dice and fiddles with them.)

2 ND: Hey, come on, no fool around! Just pick um up and shoot!

KIYO: *(picks up dice, and shakes hand vigorously)* Enough music?

2 ND: Shoot already!

KIYO: *(rolls)* Gimme another natural!

BIG BETTOR: Four the point!

KIYO: *(picks up dice right first time, and shakes them)* Thass the mate. *(Rolls)* Come to me, Josephine!

2 ND: *(simultaneously)* Crap!

I ST: Seven!

BIG BETTOR: Phoebe!

KIYO: *(picks up dice again, and rolls)* Three and one!

2 ND: *(simultaneously)* Crap, you bastard!

BIG BETTOR: Eight!

KIYO: *(gaining more confidence in picking up dice and rolling)* Give it to me the hard way! Two and two!

2 ND: *(simultaneously)* Seven!

I ST: Six and one!

KIYO: Four right! Shoot it!

BIG BETTOR: How much in the pot?

KIYO: 3000 *(as he drags and pockets 200.)*

BIG BETTOR: I catch 'um all. Shoot, I got you covered.

I ST: How about 100 more.

KIYO: You got it. *(Throws down 100.)*

BIG BETTOR: How much more you got?

KIYO: 100.

BIG BETTOR: *(tosses in 100)* No be *manini*. Go for broke.

KIYO: *(tossing in money)* Yeah, go for broke. All I got to lose is 200 bucks. *(Full of confidence.)* Okay, okay, this is it, now or never! (Kneeling, takes a long back swing and guides the dice with follow-through.) Gimme a natural, baby!

BIG BETTOR: *(just as Kiyo's hand moves forward)* No dice! No dice! Hey, no roll like that, eh? *(Grabs dice before they come to a stop.)*

KIYO: What?

BIG BETTOR: *(hands dice to Kiyo)* Go bang the wall. No. Go bang the footlocker.

KIYO: *(turns hyper)* "Bang the foot locker, bang the foot locker," the man says!

(1st crapshooter and 2nd crapshooter bring footlocker downstage. Big Bettor piles the money on it. Kiyo is downstage.)

Give um the old one-two! Set um up for the old left hook. *(Throws left hook.)* One big bang on the big box! *(Tosses dice in air and picks them up and shakes them every which way, real loud.)* Enough music?

BIG BETTOR: *(impatiently)* Shoot, I got you covered!

(Kiyo rattles dice furiously, bends head momentarily in silent prayer.)

Shoot, you focka, I got you covered.

1ST: *(laughs)* Hey, thass what the rubber been say to the dick!

KIYO: Gimme a natural! *(Slams dice underhand as if pitching softball. He jumps back to get out of the way of rebounding dice, one of which is spinning. Following done in overlaps.)*

1ST: *(glancing at stationary die)* One!

2ND: Crap!

BIG BETTOR: Snake eyes!

KIYO: Six! Yeowwww! *(Gathering money in his hands.)*

(Blackout)

(Spot on Kiyo sitting on foot locker writing letter.)

2ND: Hey, country boy, you know what I been hear.

KIYO: *(looks up)* What?

2ND: I hear you never been gamble before. The guys from your home town been tell me. Pupupipi.

KIYO: Puukolii.

2ND: Yeah, they tell me you never been gamble. No drink, no play with girls, real quiet type.

KIYO: Thass right.

2ND: Caw-mon!

KIYO: That was long time ago.

(2ND disappears. Spot on Tosh, reading Kiyo's letter.)

KIYO: *(facing audience, but as if talking to Tosh.)*

Dear Number One Son,

Here's 6000 bucks. Go pay all the bills. Go do it yourself. Don't give it to the old folks. They might use it to send the girls to college.

I manufactured half of the luck, but half was honest. I think I finally busted the Oyama jinx. I told you I was gonna be the one!

Yeah, like my left hook was so good it took me all the way to the top.

Anyway, our luck goin turn around. *Bachi* is dead. See you after the War *(half salutes.)*

Say, hello to Fumi, eh? And no go be a dumb dodo. Take care the body.

TOSH: *(simultaneously)* Take care the body. The Champ, Kiyo.

(Kiyo raises both clenched fists as when he scored knockouts.)

(Blackout)

End of Play

For George, Our Neighbor

Because he would sit for hours on a rusty dinette chair right at the
bottom of his front steps, facing our picture window, smoking and
reading his paper, or just staring through his smoke

Because our landlady, his niece, grew up there, we shared his mailbox
at the end of the lane

Because sometimes our mail would be late a day or two, or we'd get
a bunch at one time, or on Sundays, and then none for two days,
or sometimes we'd expect mail that never came

Because from when we first moved there he was always generous,
like with his push cart which he insisted I use to drag our garbage
down the lane to the street even though its plastic wheels rattled and
scraped the crumbling asphalt so loud the vibrations could be heard
five houses away and everyone would look out their windows at me,
so finally I stopped using it and just carried our plastic bags by hand
in the dark in my pajamas

Because he one day offered me his pole saw so I could cut the mango
tree which actually was hanging over his roof, causing his gutters to
clog with mango flowers and leaves

Because the landlady had grown up there you would think they had it
all worked out years before, the two mango trees literally splitting the
fence between their properties

Because he just walked over once and handed me his old bamboo
mango picker, which made me cringe when I picked a mango and
heard it crack

Because he never ate the mangoes we gave him, but always gave them to the Wongs next door on the other side

Because he liked to play with the Wong's children, especially baby Matthew, and sometimes Popo Wong could be seen entering his kitchen door with food in her hands after calling out Un-co Jodge Un-co Jodge in her Hong Kong accent and hearing no reply

Because when we would talk to him or drop off his mail on his chair you could look in the screen door and see that his house was completely filled with junk with just enough room for him to walk past the doorway: dusty newspapers, magazines, books, reel-to-reel and 8-track tapes, Guy Lombardo records, cans of catfood, 25 pound bags of rice, empty aquariums, license plates from the 40s, piled to the ceilings and the darkness

Because when a prowler entered our kitchen door and I told him about it he just looked at me blank-faced and said oh he had never heard of anything like that in this neighborhood, which is only one and a half blocks from public housing

Because of this, and of course the cats, we considered getting a dog

Because he at one time had around him over 25 cats that had mange and fleas or were half blind or limped from being bitten in cat fights, and most of the kittens never survived, and worst of all, always had diarrhea from never being taken for their shots even though, being a senior citizen, the Humane Society would do it for him for free—and so they were always pooping all yellow and soft in front of our dining room window or my study where I'd sit in the afternoons, the heat percolating the fresh batter

When I complained to him about the cat-shit minefield my yard had become he told me with a smile that it was just as bad for him, and pointed to the flies rising around us from the small stinking plot of flowers he kept in his asphalt front yard

It became an accepted ritual for me everyday when I came home from school to walk around the yard with a shovel and scoop up the cat shit and hose down the grass and garden

I spent ten dollars a pound on cat repellent which kept them away from the front, but then they'd go to the back, or wherever I hadn't spread it around, and pretty soon I was going broke trying to keep the whole yard covered at all times and we couldn't stand the smell either and so finally I stopped

There were times I admit I actually threw the yellowy goop over the fence back to his side when I was particularly irritated

I considered buying a BB gun but ended up getting a cheap slingshot and actually started sniping cats from my front door to keep them away, never really hitting one solid, that I know of

Because the Humane Society came and took away a whole bunch of cats one day, and he probably thought it was me but it wasn't, it was probably his neighbors on the other side, the Wongs who, I was told, had called once even before we moved there

Because he never used the 25 pound bag of kitty litter I one day bought and plunked down on his muddy front steps, so it sat there for over a year among old newspapers, shoes, garden tools, probably too heavy for him to move

Because he hardly said much to me ever, and even less after that

Because we were told there were always dogs, big dogs, with whoever had lived in our house, we finally got one from the Humane Society, but he was only *part* German Shepherd and turned out to be a smaller dog who still let some cats dig and shit at our window, in our hedge, in the basil and mint, and who we could see played with one kitten when we weren't home until we drove right up to our gate, and then we could see him growl and chase it away, that actor

Because it became almost an accepted ritual for me to get up early each morning to let out our dog to chase his cats away from their morning shit routine

Because I could blame him for my giving up on having a nice garden, or the mint having died, or Daro's pua keni keni which was dug up at the roots

Because when I came home once and our dog was loose, I accused him of cutting the dog's rope which I tied him to the tree with, the dog that is

Because he started buying big bags of bird seed and started scattering it in the driveway, always in the same two parallel lines about four or five feet long, near the cat dishes and the flowers, always in the early evening, even if that was when we always drove out to exercise at the park and ran over the lines with our tires when we turned our car around at the deadend of our narrow lane

Because he started having several hundred spotted mountain doves and small zebra doves and brown sparrows and over fifty java sparrows with their striking grey and black and white bodies and bright red-orange beaks swarming over the driveway and our mango trees and our fences and gazebo and shitting all over everything, and we would drive through a flurry of wings everyday when we came home

Because he had hundreds of birds in his yard the cats were eating more regularly

Because we had hundreds of birds in our yard, our dog became a good bird catcher, but never ate them and so our yard became littered with dead dove carcasses rotting in the ilima hedge after I threw them off the lawn and driveway

Because one day our gate was open by accident and our other neighbor from across the lane was going jogging and our dog growled and chased him right past George in his chair up to George's front door and nipped him, and George looked under the man's short jogging shorts and saw the red mark on his butt and laughed in his quiet old man's almost private laugh

Because one hot summer day he walked through our gate and trimmed our thick ilima hedge three feet down so he could see right in our window, my wife and I walking around in our underwear, and so we had to always keep our curtains closed

Because he would sit in his chair till 1 A.M. burning something in a coffee can or plastic container till it melted, black smoke making black shadows in the night, bringing us to our window curtains with its black smell, and there were three or four of these sooty twisted sculptures near his chair

Because after the smoke disappeared he would drive his white Oldsmobile to who knows where

Because he shocked me one day by walking up to our gate as I was hanging laundry in my garage, telling me to turn the pockets of my jeans inside out, they would dry faster that way, and then went back to his chair

Because on the day after Labor Day 1991 when we built our gazebo and I smashed my thumb with the hammer, he showed up with our mail with a big gauze bandage around his forefinger

Because a few weeks later it was getting worse and my wife, a nurse, looked at it and told him he needed to see a doctor, it was getting gangrene and they might have to cut it off, which they did

Because he kept a graveyard for his cats in the back, right outside my study desk window, handpainted yellow stones with dark blue letters: SCHWARTZ 10-10-89 and SPUD 10-17-89 and FLUFFY 11-16-89 and CRISTAL 12-9-89 and without dates BIRDIE and SNOW PUFFS 2 KITTENS and TIGGERS 3 KITTENS and TIGGER'S KITTEN all in a row in a nice little brick-edged garden plot along the fence where you'd expect some green onions or flowers (and one of the kittens I think our dog Kriya ran out and bit in the neck one day and probably killed)

Because he one day in 1991 took a pick and started digging another hole and after a minute I heard him stop, and later that afternoon, watering my back yard, I saw the pick just lying there, and it stayed there for months, and the hole never got dug, and I almost volunteered to do it for him but was ashamed and soon it was covered with mango leaves, the hole, the garden grave area, everything

Because he never cleaned his side our own backyard began to get invaded by five feet high California grass coming through the fence and some kind of white flower vine covered everything, even our plumeria tree like an umbrella ten feet high

Because he started to get rid of the cats on his own, it seemed, and soon only had three or four, then one with a collar and a bell

Because he would sit in his chair or be in his house and the phone would ring over forty times and he would just ignore it, driving us crazy

Because he started letting his thin white hair grow and it would stick up stiff like a Japanese Einstein

Because he started wearing the same brown pants and light brown plaid shirt everyday

Because each year we gave him New Year's mochi, which we always wondered if he ate or if it just stayed in his refrigerator, or what

Because he would have the Wong's nephew come over on his moped, park it right in front by the chair, and go inside, and we imagined it was his illegitimate son sleeping over for a visit but we still don't know what that was about

Because he started getting visits from his sister or brother more often, bringing him food or trying to clean out some of his junk, and his brother-in-law would just park the car in the driveway and lean against the neighbor's fence across the lane from the house and smoke until his wife came back out from that maze

Because I guess George didn't want that because sometimes he wouldn't open the door and his car was home and they'd ring his bell and knock on his door until finally they'd just go away, the mountain of black garbage bags they'd filled still sitting in front of his house, never thrown away

Because he started staying in the house with the front door closed all day sometimes, and we wondered if he was in the hospital again

Because the last thing he said to me was in his garage as we stood watching the Wong's new house being built, a backhoe digging for a new wall next to his fence, and he said to me over the noise *I wish they would stop*

Because I would be watering the ilima hedge and imagine him in his chair, smoking, watching me, smiling his quiet hello, then looking off through the drifting smoke—even though I knew he was in the hospital, probably dying

Because we talked to the brother that came and picked up the mail which we put for him in a baby blue plastic trash can on which he had written For Mail Only

Because he died in January we don't know exactly when, but he looked fine the last time we saw him and gave him New Year's mochi, and he was sitting on his same old chair eating the biggest bento we ever saw him eat, scarfing down the food with his chopsticks

Because we heard he's buried in Punchbowl with other 552nd Field Artillery Battalion World War II veterans

Because his name was really Toshiyuki which we always knew from his mail, some of his mail, not others

Because we were given one of several 25 pound bags of rice which were found somewhere in the house covered with gecko shit which we wiped off the bag and which we are now eating, the rice that is

Because a couple of weeks after he died someone else turned up and slowly started cleaning out the house, a pale, young guy with a limp, who would sit alone in the dim hallway for hours, sorting

Because this mysterious new owner got workmen to jackhammer the concrete, tear down the old gutters, rip out old furniture, smashing it apart to mash down in the back of a big truck which takes it to the dump, and we resent them for doing it

Because they're throwing out his old garden tools, his toilet, his 1936 McKinley High School annual, with the inscription in fine fountain pen flourishes saying that "Miracles can and did happen. . . ."

Because he has postcards from France of AJA soldiers during the War blowing around in the March windstorms we've been having, his water-logged high school annuals blowing their memories out the garage and down the lane

Because we were told he didn't graduate from high school, the annuals were his sisters, who he helped put through school

Because some of his magazines piled up in the driveway shocked us, and now we have a completely different perspective of him as a man

Because now that the drapes have been ripped off and thrown away we can see sunlight through his living room picture window for the very first time

Because I am holding on to his mango pole and his pole saw which I used to be able to just reach over from my side of the fence and grab, but now it's lying at the back of our house where the new tenants won't see it, but I know he wouldn't mind because he always told me just to keep it for cutting branches when, as he told me, you're in the mood

Because we're considering what kind of mail box to get, now that we won't be sharing George's with him anymore

Because I actually went over after the workmen left one day and took snapshots of all the cats' gravestones, before they threw them away

Because even after all the shit I scooped and grumbling I did I now wonder where is the cat with the bell? Where are all those hundreds and hundreds of doves beating the air and showering us with their downy gray feather rain when we come home?

After Hurricane Iniki, Kaua'i 1992

I rush by to claim my seat on the plane
past families who rigged blue tarps over houses
and line up for free meals at churches
and flush their toilets with buckets of green water
from a neighbor's stale swimming pool
who camp in garages with neighbors
and one day run home to their wives and yell
pack up a bag we're getting outta here
and they don't even know where
till they reach the airport

I pass the National Guardsmen
who have driven down highways of cracked branches
where galaxies of dead leaves swirl the black top
like some spreading disease
while dump sites erupt from canefields
like festering wounds
piles of corrugated iron roofs twisting
their rusty origami wings to the sky
bashed refrigerators, washers, water heaters
scraped together in mountainous gleaming scabs
and splintered wall sections, tongue from groove
beams snapped and jagged
like the ravaged tree trunks
lining the shores like monks in meditation
sea chants torn from them into the Pacific void
their surviving halves bent along beaches
for miles bowing still beneath the force that came over the ocean
to cripple and scar them

I rush past the children who will remember
hiding in black closets
held by grandma or uncle or mother
while the hurricane squeezed them closer together
their own screams binding them tighter
as a door slid open to rain on their faces—
the flash of the open ceiling sky—
then back in the darkness, the feeling of holding on
and blowing away

I rush past and somewhere the leaves
are sinking into the ocean
like the dark eyes of Kaua'i
staring toward the sky

I rush in the plane and take a space
among these survivors, construction workers,
psychiatric social workers of the Red Cross,
Salvation Army soldiers, insurance claims adjusters,
public health nurses, telephone linemen,
electricity restorers, visiting doctors,
forestry managers, architects, carpenters,
building suppliers, entrepreneurs,

glad to be leaving the island
of no electricity, of open ceilings,
lines for the bank down the block,
blue tarp neighborhoods, generators buzzing all night,
no telephones, people driving around lost all day,
no refrigeration for a cold drink after school,
no restaurants for dinner,
dark streets after sunset,
the island needing its rest

I take my seat behind the moaning woman in the first row
who cannot contain her cries for help
so the young steward leans toward her
drops his demonstration life vest
and suddenly feels his head in the grip of her hands
as she pulls it into her white blouse
begging please help me please
but he backs away trying to free himself
so she gives her whole body to his
says take it please take care of it
I'm only a woman!
and melts into him
smothers him down to the floor
behind the wall where the drinks are
moaning and sobbing for him to complete the act
as we stare, a captive audience strapped in
nobody moving to help

until the men with walkie talkies return,
pick up the woman by feet and shoulders,
carry her out with her luggage
so she's trapped on the island
source of the pain
which she couldn't hold in
or give away

Some clap and cheer All Right!
Let's get outta here we're late already
some of us sit with shock on our faces
others giggle nervously as
the captain apologizes for the delay
And the steward is so ashamed
the stewardess kneeling in his face saying
Stuff like this happens
there's nothing you can do about it, forget it,
it just happens
But he doesn't come out for the drinks down the aisle
he stays behind his wall and hides
when we leave the plane we try not to look in his eyes
we just lower our heads through the door one more time
and say Thank You Thank You

And I am thankful for the rental cars every 7 A.M.
muddy steering wheels unwashed for the rationing of water
I am thankful for the cups of coffee and Tylenol
and the high school health room bed with its crinkly paper sheet
where I lay as the carpenters ripped shingles off
over my head as I waited for my temperature

I am thankful for the Bed & Breakfast which offered me
a room with no ceiling, a shower from a plastic bag
hung like a transfusion
I am thankful for only an hour long wait
at the Hanamaulu Cafe for dinner
I am thankful for the last-minute room at the Tip Top Hotel,
water-damaged carpet ripped off, chocolate brown swirls
of Kaua'i mud decorating the floor,
the dead clock radio cord wound around its still numbers
all evening the roaches

And I am thankful for this airplane
so I can return again to Honolulu
and lie down in bed with my wife
and just let her hold me until
I don't need to be held anymore

Snacks

My husband say to me, "Eh, you so fat,
why you gotta eat so much?"

He only jealous
cause he was so poor wen he was small
he don't know how fo snack.

Yeah, ass what I said. Don't know how.

Get all da potato chip, Tostitos,
chocolate chip cookies la dat inside da kitchen closet,
he no even open da doah!

All my bags stay half open wit
da clothes pin on top,
he no even know da ting
stay waiting fo him fo come grind.

So, not my fault, eh?
I no like everyting come stale.
Poho.

I give chance,
but afta couple days
I look inside da closet.
If da bag still dere,
I grind em.

THE QUIETEST SINGING

PART TWO

Chinaman's Hat

Living on an island, I miss driving, setting out at dawn, and ending up five or six hundred miles away—Mexico—at nightfall. Instead, we spin around and around a perimeter like on a race track.

Satellite photos of the Hawaiian Islands show swirls, currents, winds, movement, movements of clouds and water. I have to have them pointed out to me and to look closely before I descry three or four of the islands, in a clearing, chips of rock, miniatures in the very shapes you find on maps. The islands, each one the tip of a volcano connected to the ocean floor, look like the crests of waves.

Logs and glass balls have creatures living on them too. Life gathers and clings to whatever bit of solidity—land. Whales and porpoises and sharks become land for colonies of smaller animals. And the junked cars, like sunken ships, turn into living reefs.

On drives along the windward side of O'ahu, I like looking out at the ocean and seeing the pointed island offshore, not much bigger than a couple of houses—Mokoli'i Island, but nobody calls it that. I had a shock when I heard it's called Chinaman's Hat. That's what it looks like, all right, a crown and brim on the water. I had never heard "Chinaman" before except in derision when walking past racists and had had to decide whether to pretend I hadn't heard or to fight.

When driving south, clockwise around O'ahu, there is an interesting optical illusion: at a certain point in the road, the sky is covered with Chinaman's Hat, which looms huge, near. The closer you drive toward what seems like a mountain ahead, the farther it moves away until there it is, quite far off, a small island in the midst of ocean, sky, clouds.

I did not call it Chinaman's Hat, and no one else calls it Mokoli'i Island, so for a long time, I didn't call it anything. "Chinaman's Hat," people say to visitors, "because it looks just like a Chinaman's hat. See?"

And the visitor knows right away what they mean. At first I watched expressions and tones of voice for a snide reference to me. But the locals were not yelling at me or spitting at me or trying to run me down with a bike saying, "Chinaman."

Although I don't swim very well, I ventured out to Chinaman's Hat three times. The first time, we waited until low tide to walk as far as we could. The other times, we left in the early morning. Snorkeling is like flying; the moment your face enters clear water, you become a flying creature.

Schools of fish—zebra fish, rainbow fish, red fish—curve with the currents, swim alongside and away. Balloon fish puff out their porcupine quills. How unlike a dead fish a live fish is. We swam through spangles of silver white fish. I hovered in perfect suspension over forests, flew over spring forests and winter forests. No sound but my own breathing. Sometimes we entered blind spots, darkness, where the sand churned up gray fog, the suit behind clouds. Then I had to lift my head out of the water to see and not be afraid.

Sometimes the sun made golden rooms, which we entered from dark hallways. Specks of sand shone like gold and fell like motes, like the light in California. Sea cucumbers rocked from side to side.

Approaching Chinaman's Hat, there is a group of tall black stones like an underwater Stonehenge, and we flew around and between those rocks.

Then we were walking among the palm trees and bushes that we had seen from Oʻahu. Under those bushes, large white birds nest on the ground. We hurried to the unseen side of the island, the other face of the moon.

Though tiny, Chinaman's Hat has its leeward and windward. The ocean side is less green but wonderful in its variety. We found a cave, a tiny pirate's cove with a lick of ocean going in and out of it; a strip of beach made of fine yellow sand; a blowhole; brown and lavender cowry shells, not broken; black live crabs and red dead crabs; a lava rock shelf with tide pools as warm as baths. Lying in a tide pool, I saw nothing but sky and black rock; the ocean spit cold now and again. The two friends with us stood in the blowhole, and said wedding vows while the ocean sprayed rainbows around their heads.

At day's end, tired from the long swim at high tide, we pulled ourselves up on the land, lay with arms open holding on to Oʻahu. We were grateful to return, relieved that we had made it back alive. Relieved to be out of the water before the sun went down.

After that first exploration, we heard from Hawaiians that the channel between Chinaman's Hat and Oʻahu is the spawning place for sharks. This information did not stop us from swimming out there twice more. We had the fatalism of city people who had lived on the San Andreas Fault. It will crack open at any moment, and California break off from North America, and sink like Atlantis. We continued to swim home with the fish we'd caught tied to our belts, and they did not attract sharks though pilot fish swam ahead of us.

The air of Hawaiʻi breathes warm on the skin; when it blows, I seem to turn into wind, too, and start to blow away. Maybe I can swim because the water is so comfortable, I melt into it and let it carry me like the fish and the frigate birds that make the currents visible. Back on Oʻahu, our friend who got married in the blowhole, often broke into hysterics, and she and her husband returned to the cool northern California woods.

There is a rending. The soul leaks out to mix with the air, the skin an osmotic membrane. But the eyes squint against the bright green foliage in the red light. These islands fool human beings into thinking that they are safe. On our second trip to Chinaman's Hat, a Hawaiian man and his son were camping under the ledge by the palm trees. They had a boat and meat hooks and liver for catching sharks.

On the third trip, Earll went spear fishing off the ocean side, where I did not go because of the depth and choppiness. I was climbing as far as I could up the crown, and finding seashells there. I watched him jump vertically out of the water. He had seen a giant thing and felt it swim under him, yards and yards of brown shadow under him.

Another time, we rowed a boat out there, our children sitting on the outrigger to weight it down on the water. A cleft in the hillside made a shelter for building a fire to get warm after swimming. At sunset, we cooked and ate the fish the men speared. We were climbing down to the boat, holding on to the face of the island in the dark, when a howling like wolves, like ghosts, came rising out of the island. "Birds," somebody said. "The wind," said someone else. But the air was still, and the high, clear sound wound like a ribbon around the island. It was, I know it, the island, the voice of the island singing, the sirens Odysseus heard.

The Navy uses Kahoʻolawe for bombing practice, not recognizing it as living, sacred earth. We had all heard it, the voice of our island singing.

A Sea Worry

This summer our son bodysurfs. He says it's his "job" and rises each morning at 5:30 to catch the bus to Sandy Beach. I hope that by September he will have had enough of the ocean. Tall waves throw surfers against the shallow bottom. Undertows have snatched them away. Sharks prowl Sandy's. Joseph told me that once he got out of the water because he saw an enormous shark. "Did you tell the life guard?" I asked. "No." "Why not?" "I didn't want to spoil the surfing." The ocean pulls at the boys, who turn into surfing addicts. At sunset you can see surfers waiting for the last golden wave.

"Why do you go surfing so often?" I ask my students.

"It feels so good," they say. "Inside the tube. I can't describe it. There are no words for it."

"You can describe it," I scold, and I am angry. "Everything can be described. Find the words for it, you lazy boy. Why don't you stay home and read?" I am afraid that the boys give themselves up to the ocean's mindlessness.

When the waves are up, surfers all over Hawai'i don't do their homework. They cut school. They know how the surf is breaking at any moment because every fifteen minutes the reports come over the radio; in fact, one of my former students is the surf reporter.

Some boys leave for mainland colleges, and write their parents heartrending letters. They beg to come home for Thanksgiving. "If I can just touch the ocean," they write from Missouri and Kansas, "I'll last for the rest of the semester." Some come home for Christmas and don't go back.

Even when the assignment is about something else, the students write about surfing. They try to describe what it is to be inside the wave as it curls over them, making a tube or "chamber" or "green room" or "pipeline" or "time warp." They write about the silence, the peace, "no hassles," the feeling of being reborn as they shoot out the end. They've written about the voice of God, the "commandments" they hear. In the margins, they draw the perfect wave. Their writing is full of cliches. "The endless summer," they say. "Unreal."

Surfing is like a religion. Among the martyrs are George Helm, Kimo Mitchell, and Eddie Aikau. Helm and Mitchell were lost at sea riding their surfboards from Kaho'olawe, where they had gone to protest the Navy's bombing of that island. Eddie Aikau was a champion surfer and lifeguard. A storm had capsized the Hokule'a, the ship that traces the route that the Polynesian ancestors sailed from Tahiti, and Eddie Aikau had set out on his board to get help.

Since the ocean captivates our son, we decided to go with him to see Sandy's.

We got up before dawn, picked up his friend, Marty, and drove out of Honolulu. Almost all the traffic was going in the opposite direction, the freeway coned to make more lanes into the city. We came to a place where raw mountains rose on our left and the sea fell on our right, smashing against the cliffs. The strip of cliff pulverized into sand is Sandy's. "Dangerous Current Exist," said the ungrammatical sign.

Earll and I sat on the shore with our blankets and thermos of coffee. Joseph and Marty put on their fins and stood at the edge of the sea for a moment, touching the water with their fingers and crossing their hearts before going in. There were fifteen boys out there, all about the same age, fourteen to twenty, all with the same kind of lean, v-shaped build, most of them with black hair that made their wet heads look like sea lions. It was hard to tell whether our kid was one of those who popped up after a big wave. A few had surfboards, which are against the rules at a bodysurfing beach, but the lifeguard wasn't on duty that early.

As they watched for the next wave, the boys turned toward the ocean. They gazed slightly upward; I thought of altar boys before a great god. When a good wave arrived, they turned, faced shore, and came shooting in, some taking the wave to the right and some to the left, their bodies fishlike, one arm out in front, the hand and fingers pointed before them, like a swordfish's beak. A few held credit card trays, and some slid in on trays from MacDonald's.

"That is no country for middle-aged women," I said. We had on bathing suits underneath our clothes in case we felt moved to participate. There were no older men either.

Even from the shore, we could see inside the tubes. Sometimes, when they came at an angle, we saw into them a long way. When the wave dug into the sand, it formed a brown tube or a gold one. The magic ones, though, were made out of just water, green and turquoise rooms, translucent walls and ceilings. I saw one that was powder-blue, perfect, thin; the sun filled it with sky blue and white light. The best thing, the kids say, is when you are in the middle of the tube, and there is water all around but you're dry.

The waves came in sets; the boys passed up the smaller ones. Inside a big one, you could see their bodies hanging upright, knees bent, duckfeet fins paddling, bodies dangling there in the wave.

Once in a while, we heard a boy yell, "Aa-whoo!" "Poon-tah!" "Aaroo!" And then we noticed how rare human voice was here; the surfers did not talk, but silently, silently rode the waves.

Since Joseph and Marty were considerate of us, they stopped after two hours, and we took them out for breakfast. We kept asking them how it felt, so that they would not lose language.

"Like a stairwell in an apartment building," said Joseph, which I liked immensely. He hasn't been in very many apartment buildings, so had to reach a bit to get the simile. "I saw somebody I knew coming toward me in the tube, and I shouted, 'Jeff. Hey, Jeff,' and my voice echoed like a stairwell in an apartment building. Jeff and I came straight at each other—mirror tube."

"Are there ever girls out there?" Earll asked.

"There's a few women who come at about eleven," said Marty.

"How old are they?"

"About twenty."

"Why do you cross your heart with water?"

"So the ocean doesn't kill us."

I described the powder-blue tube I had seen. "That part of Sandy's is called Chambers," they said.

I have gotten some surfing magazines, the ones kids steal from the school library, to see if the professionals try to describe the tube. Bradford Baker writes:

> . . . *Round and pregnant in Emptiness*
> *I slide,*
> *Laughing,*
> *into the sun,*
> *into the night.*

Frank Miller calls the surfer

> . . . *mother's fumbling*
> *curly-haired*
> *tubey-laired*
> *son.*

"Ooh, offshores—," writes Reno Abbellira, "where wind and wave most often form that terminal rendezvous of love—when the wave can reveal her deepest longings, her crest caressed, cannily covered to form those peeling concavities we know, perhaps a bit irreverently, as tubes. Here we strive to spend every second—enclosed, encased, sometimes fatefully entombed, and hopefully, gleefully, ejected—Whoosh!"

"An iridescent ride through the entrails of God," says Gary L. Crandall.

I am relieved that the surfers keep asking one another for descriptions. I also find some comfort in the stream of commuter traffic, cars filled with men over twenty, passing Sandy Beach on their way to work.

Letter from Jian Hui: 1

October

Dear Julia:

I think you finish your trip to USA
And I hope you send a back letter soon.
I miss you and I think of past good time
When we spoke English.
It was a good idea.
I am interesting in English.
It is important to me and I want to speak.
But nobody.

I stay at home but not any more at Uncle's house.
On National Day he tells me Go away, live somewhere.
So I cry to myself because I don't know where.
Then I go look.
I ask the grandmother I worked for when I came.
She tells me she is taking the train north
And I can help the grandfather till she comes back.
So I live there. Now I live somewhere else.

I go to my job every day at 8 o'clock but not on Sunday.
I ride bike to the office. I work by myself.
I answer the telephone. Sometimes my manager tells me
Shop or serve tea or go to Bank of China
Or Friendship Store or the Electric Teapot Factory.
He goes out.
Usually there is not much to do and I am boring.
At 5 is end. Also, not much money.
I do not like my job.

At this time I make a friend in my night class.
She is the same with me from Shan Dong.
Now she has a holiday and has gone away.
So nobody.
I miss my family in Shan Dong very much,
But I am more interesting to stay in Beijing
Because I live here now.
But I have no residence card, no work unit,
So it is change any time.

For weeks, I think, are clouds in the sky.
It is windy and the trees are yellow.
But the air is not golden as they say.
The air is smoke-color
And cold even inside the house.
So I wear slippers you gave to me.
They make the stone softer,
And they make the floor sound like grass.

I wish I can ever see you
But I cannot.
Not in my country.
Not in your country.

Goodbye, I love you,

Jian Hui

Letter from Jian Hui: 2

November

Dear Julia:

I am glad when your back letter comes. I read two times.

I work in the same office.
Not many people.
Mostly I stay inside.

I miss my family. I want to go home sometime
But I don't think so
Because I would have to give up the chance in Beijing.
Maybe January. Don't worry.
I will always tell you where I am.
I am very glad that I have a foreign friend.

I read English every morning but not speak
Because nobody.
This is prepare to go to your country USA someday.
This is my dream and my disappointment.
I really wish I meet you in USA
But it needs your help.
I only don't want you to help me. I mean it.
I am make a joke. Please don't mind. OK?

The grandmother came home from her sister.
I went to see.
The grandmother likes going to your country,
But the grandfather told me her permission was refused this time.

Maybe next time.
The grandmother doesn't like to go outing.
She like to watch TV and smoke
And always like to play card with friend
And late at night mah jong, a hard game. 4 AM.

The time passed very quickly when we spoke English
During when we stay together

When you were in China.
We had secrets like two girls.
I knew all you did not tell.
As if it is yesterday to me, that is how I miss you.
But you are happy now in your mother land. Not lonely,
With your daughter and her son Louis, Chinese Long Hua.
I think.

Goodbye, love,

Jian Hui

Letter from Jian Hui: 3

December

Dear Julia:

I didn't hear for a long time from you.
I look forward of your letter
But until today did not. Now today.
I am ever happy to receive.
Thanks for picture of your daughter
And Louis your grandson, Chinese Long Hua.
He is very lovely and clever and good,
And you take care of him harder than before.
Can he walk by himself now?
Can he speak English? Can he speak Chinese either?
When I help you he can speak.

I always work in the same company office.
I want to look for different job
But I have no good chance so I stay here.
Electric teapots have the success now
So I work too hard, but I don't want to give up.
I must go on. I must depend on myself.
Sometimes I have to work on Sunday.
But my manager gives me more money now.
He should.

I know I talked about I will move but didn't.
That house is far from my factory and my office.
That house is colder than this one
And the weather is colder now, especially at night.
The grass has turned orange,
And now I wish it would snow.
Snow makes me exciting.
But I think I can have a good time in this house by myself
I can cook. There is an ice-box, a bed, and pans etc.
I have a lock and the windows are not broken.
Nobody bothers me.
It is very cold and quiet alone.

I will be over my accounting class next week.
I have a machine of English writing I can use
And this letter was written by myself.
There are some mistakes.
It is true: "We live and ever learn."
Do you like reading my letter? I hope so,
But my English is very limit.

I hope we don't ever lose our bridge.

Love, goodbye,

Jian Hui

Letter from Jian Hui: 4

January

Dear Julia:

I am sorry to write you later.
A month ago when I got your letter I wrote to you.
At last I got myself your letter. It was returned.
I am so sad and I wanted to cry,
Because I am very afraid to lose our touch,
And I don't know how to say my heart.

Change has happened to me.
My company has moved to far from my house
And I have lots of works to do every day.
I get up at half past 6
And I wash my face and hands in a hurry and clean the room.
At 7 I ride my bike for 15 minutes.
Then I take the under road for 30 minutes.
At last I walk. So I am very tired on the way.

My office is half under room, half upper room.
The upper room in front is hotel and dining room.
I eat there every day and the food is good.
All of the people work in the hotel. They know me
So I am not lonely. I like it.
I stayed all day with my friend in the New Year.
We cooked ourselves. What a pleasure in a day!

Now the weather is colder and colder because the wind.
The water is frozen but no snow.
I wish it. I like the white world.
What is the weather in America?

I lost touch with Louise, your friend.
I called her once, then didn't.
I think she is too busy to bother.
She doesn't like you enjoy someone to visit.
Remember forever you.

We had good time together.
I hope our friendship is green forever.
I wish I could go into the lost life.

Love, Goodbye,

Jian Hui

Letter from Jian Hui: 5

March

Dear Julia:

I think you wrote letter I didn't get.
Also the long time I could not write.
I am sorry for long time.
I give this to your friend who goes to Hong Kong.
So I think, next it goes to you.

Something happened.
Someone told that I worked for a foreigner, I don't know who.
I work in my office and the electric teapot factory.
That is not foreign. Maybe joint venture. I don't know.
Then the police come to my manager and ask.
The trouble I do not have a residence card in Beijing.
So then they talk to me.
They want me to say something I don't know what.
That day they come I do not wear my coat,
Only sweater, and I am very cold,
In additional worried.
When I cook your lunch, is that work for foreigner?
I am afraid. Nobody to answer the question.
They talk to me. Then they think they have wrong girl.
After, they let me go. But not to Beijing. Shan Dong.
So I have to give up the chance after a short time. Sixteen months.

But I think I have succeeded myself.
I finish my accounting course and business experience work.
Also the English writing machine
And because you spoke English with me.
Also some new friends, Chinese and foreigners.
Anyhow the government said
We are allowed to go to foreigners' houses now.
I told the police that's what I did.
Not work. Open up the country.
But it is true when you came I helped you
When I take care of your lovely clever grandson.
I was afraid the police might think.
But they did not.

Now I am in Shan Dong.
So I will stay home for a while and see my family,
But then I will go back to Beijing even without a work unit card.
Like America. Free.
Don't mind. I am make a joke the way I did with you before.
I have good luck. I also think you.

I love you. Goodbye.

Jian Hui

Good Luck

May

Dear Julia,

Thank you for your letters.
Every time I am happy about it.
Now it is May and my job is another one.
I came back to Beijing from Shan Dong.
I work with my friend I met here. He is honest.
I like him and he like me.
We are easy to get along with.
Together we have a cloth shop in Wu Dao Kou.
Every day it is opening at 10 o'clock and stopping at 6 o'clock.
I am selling all kinds. For example, sheet, curtain, tablecloth.
If you need some, you tell me. I will send to you.
I hope we can make a big success. I think so.

I often meet some foreign in my shopping.
For example: Japanese, German, English, American.
One day a German came
And she spoke half-German, half-Chinese, so I spoke English to her.
She seems understand my what mean.
She told that she works in language department.
And I told that my friend did that also and I know about it.
She bought ten meters cloth in my shopping.
When I told about the place where you lived
I began to wish to visit your friends
But I can't ever speak English.
Not any. So I feel ashamed or crushed.
I still want to study more, but I am happy now.
I love you and I hope we will all ways stay in touch with forever.

Goodbye,

Jian Hui

Letter from Hai Bin

July

Dear Julia:

I am afraid my answer to your letter will not please you.
As you requested I have searched for Jian Hui
in the market at Wu Dao Kou.
No one knows who she is.
I asked at every cloth shop
and in addition all the neighboring stores.
The German teacher who remembered her also tried
but could not find the shop any more.
I'm sorry. I know how much you liked her
and tried to help.
But so many come to Beijing from the South
speaking a little English, live somehow
for a while, then disappear.
Maybe she went home. I hope that is what happened.
It's been a long time—seven months—more.

Maybe you do not know the many changes
since you went back two years ago
to your own country.
Think of it:
The old apartment's gone. The open market
where we bought peanuts next to the basket shop,
remember? That's gone too.
And the canvas covered stalls—they had to leave.
They moved I don't know where. I miss them.
And choosing my own fish from the tub out front
where they were swimming, taking it back to eat—
I liked that. We do that at home.
I liked the cook stalls—
the pork buns and fried bread with sauce—
and standing in the street with friends and eating.
We still do that in other parts of the city.
But it makes me sad that everything is new
in Wu Dao Kou.
I know that new stores bring in business.

Still, when I leave—I graduate this summer—
I want to remember things as they have been
these four years past, unchanged.

You asked about Snow White.
A teacher told her that her English name
was foolish, though it translated Chinese.
I liked her name. But she is now Elaine.
That teacher said that mine was foolish too,
but I have kept it. Fonda. It is my own.
But my life has changed.
I found the man
that I will marry in four years, a student,
advanced, whose work will take that long.
Both of us are certain. But he is from Korea.
Because of that I cannot get a job
though I am number eight in the senior class.
Of course I am willing to wait for him,
but I am ready to work, and I feel angry.
That will not surprise you.

I will keep in touch. It is easier for me
than for Jian Hui. I hope she writes to you.
Do not give up hope.
Perhaps she is safe after all.
You will stay in my memory,
a good teacher. My American friend.
Goodbye, and love,

Hai Bin

A Passage to Nowhere

. . . If I make my bed in hell, behold thou art there.

—Psalm 139: 8

It was an ordinary morning the day after New Year's in 1960. The weather was winter cold outside the apartment in Ocean Beach when Rockne Johnson drove his black Ford sedan from Bermuda Avenue to La Jolla, taking the shorter, inland Rose Canyon route rather than the longer way around the coast to Scripps Institution of Oceanography where he worked on projects which were then, in certain aspects, marked government-classified. It seemed as though he had just gone out the door but five minutes before I had taken the baby's laundry downstairs to put through the wash cycle when the phone rang upstairs.

"Hello. This is Navy Hospital in San Diego. Is this 4743 Bermuda?

"Yes, it is."

"Is this the Johnson residence?"

"Yes."

"Then you'd better get up here. He's been in an auto accident and is in critical condition."

Taken by surprise, I could say nothing. Strength seemed to ebb from my body. Then I thought, how would I do this? There was no other car. I didn't know where Navy Hospital was. I had a five-month old infant son and no baby sitter. Would the hospital allow this child into the ward? Not likely. If not, where would I put him? Maybe they had a nursery.

"Don't waste any time," the voice said. "He may not have anymore, himself. Goodbye."

What to do? I would take the baby with me in a taxi. I had no cash at home, just a checkbook. Would the taxi take a check? I called the dispatcher and explained the situation.

"We'll get you there, lady. No problem. Sure, a check for the amount is okay."

I bundled up the baby first then put on a baggy mu'umu'u that would be loose enough for me to hide him when he needed to be breast-fed. People might stare, maybe, so they would. Never mind what other people might think, I said, as I tossed extra cloth diapers, Kleenex tissue, diaper pins, plastic pants, and baby powder into a tote bag. The taxi arrived before I had even had a chance to brush my teeth or comb my hair. Never mind. Worry about that later. Get going.

"Would you hurry, please," I asked.

"Navy Hospital's a big place, ma'am. Know what building to go to?"

"No. I've never been there. I'm not from San Diego."

"Okay. We'll find the place. Ought to be somebody up there knows where."

Outside one of the buildings I saw a colleague from Scripps, Saxe Montgomery. I waved to him as I yanked 'Aukai out the door of the cab.

"He's in here," he said, "and they're working on him."

He was on a cart being moved from one room to another down the corridor. We could hear him moaning. I ran over to look at him, trying to get his attention, but his eyes shifted from side to side, unfocused, unseeing. He was unconscious.

"Wait in here," Montgomery said, motioning me to a chair in the reception room. "I'll stay with you until you know what's going on. Take your time. I can give you a ride home."

It was a long wait, and the baby got hungry again. I slipped him under the mu'umu'u, and he made a significant bulge underneath all the cloth. There was too much milk for him to handle, dripping down and soaking through my clothes. After he emptied one breast, I shifted him to the other one, not wanting him to cry or fuss and hoping he would go to sleep. Nobody stared. They paid no attention, or they were polite, keeping their eyes on newspapers and magazines they were reading. I moved Dane 'Aukai down until he was on my lap, pulled up the hem of the mu'umu'u so that I could take him out until he was outside lying over my front, peacefully asleep. The moaning had stopped. A nurse came down the hall, picking me out from the crowd.

"You may go in, now, ma'am," she said, "but not the baby and only for a few minutes. Keep it short."

"Yes," I said, handing the baby to Montgomery.

I found the right room on the ward. He was conscious but going through post-traumatic amnesia.

"Where am I?" he asked.

"In Navy Hospital."

"What for?"

"You were in a car accident."

For a minute he thought back, trying to remember.

"Must have been in Rose Canyon," he said, closing his eyes, as though expecting what would be coming next to test his will to live.

He would have little choice to influence the outcome. That he would undergo many changes, suffering through and surviving several crises, would not only empty his body of his own original blood, commencing to flow into plastic containers below the bed, but would undo, as well, the basis of any faith he may have had that man was of a stuff more than matter, that man was spiritual.

"How did he look?" asked Montgomery.

"Nothing shows on the outside. His head is bandaged, and there seems to be another over his chest, but I couldn't really tell."

"Well, nothing you can do now. Why don't I take you home so you can pack some things. My wife and I want you to come and stay at our house in La Jolla. Lots of room, and we have two cars. We'll see what we can arrange."

Seemed simple enough. Back at the apartment I had no sooner climbed the stairs to the door when the phone rang again.

"Hello, Ruby. How are you?"

It was Dr. Andrew Sheets' wife, Boots, who hardly ever called, so why did she pick such a time as this?

"I'm fine, Boots, but Rock isn't."

"What's the matter?"

"Automobile accident."

"Oh, no. Where is he?"

"In Navy Hospital."

"How bad?"

"He seems dazed from it all. I guess there are complications inside."

"Well, you shouldn't be without a car if you need to go up there everyday. Why don't you come down and stay here in Chula Vista? Andy will let you have the Thunderbird whenever you need it."

"No, thanks. I can handle things from here."

"Nonsense. We have two cars. Andy bought the T-Bird for me, but I don't drive."

"I don't know the way to or from Chula Vista. I only know the bus route to El Cajon and back. I'd get lost."

"After a few times you'll be okay. You need family; we're your family away from Hawai'i."

"I'll think it over."

In the afternoon Montgomery took me to Rose Canyon to find the site of the crash. Our car had left one hundred fifty-six feet of visible skid mark trying to avoid hitting the other car. The Ford was on the shoulder of the north-bound San Diego to Los Angeles freeway, where speeds over sixty and up to ninety miles an hour were commonplace. It was crumpled up to half its length, the right front door still open from the bang that had thrown him out on the road. Broken glass was glittering all over the highway. One of the cushions used to hold his head until the ambulance arrived was soaked with blood. The doctors' report showed that he had sustained seventeen rib fractures and a ruptured spleen. It would explain the steady bleeding that turned off about the third day, when his temperature then climbed, without any sign it would cool down.

On a Sunday they decided to operate. How long an operation? Anywhere from five to eight hours. Close friends of his insisted I should have a leisurely dinner with them and afterwards go see a movie, *Porgy and Bess*, a light musical operetta, just the thing to keep me preoccupied, but it didn't work. There was too much tragedy in the story of a crippled fellow, Sidney Poitier, falling for a beautiful drug-dependent girl, Dorothy Dandrige, who would skip town with her supplier, Sammy Davis Jr., all to the rhythm of George Gershwin's fascinating music. I was too anxious to get back to the hospital, where we met the team of surgeons coming out of the elevator with their patient under heavy sedation.

"How was it?" I asked the intern.

"Ghastly," he said. "A mess."

The head surgeon took me aside to explain that the ruptured spleen and stomach had pushed through a hole in the diaphragm, and the swelling of tissue had caused a halt to bloodflow into the spleen, so that while on the outside it had seemed he was getting better, on the inside he was ready to explode. They had removed the spleen, put the other organs back where they belonged, and sewn up the tear. Whatever that loss would cost him over the length of his life, its function would be taken over by the bone marrow. In the meantime no medication to ease pain could be given because of the head injury, and he should receive no food or water by mouth.

"He won't be feeling good when the sedative wears off. He should wake up sometime tonight, after visiting hours, but you can come in. Just ask at the nurses' station."

I drove back to the hospital that night and found him wide awake. He said nothing, pointing to his throat where the gauze over a piece of metal had worked off, revealing an opening into the trachea through which oxygen had been pumped into his lungs during the operation. Unless I covered it with my fingers, he could make no audible sound. I listened carefully to his words, just above a whisper:

"I . . . never . . . knew . . . such . . . agony . . . was . . . possible."

"Don't try to say anything more. I'll be back tomorrow."

The next night I found him burning up and desperate for water to drink. He pointed to a nurse, saying she was the kindest one on the ward, the only one who would wet a piece of gauze to put to his parched lips to cut the nagging thirst. He admired her because she had found a way around the nothing-by-mouth rule. She had, he told me, plenty aloha, asking if he could have another drink of water from the gauze. I soaked another strip of clean gauze and put it between his teeth. Satisfied, he drifted back into that state of suspension, neither conscious nor unconscious, of a mind afloat somewhere else in a vague dimension.

> *Thine eyes did see my substance, yet being unperfect; and in thy book all my members were written, which in continuance were fashioned, when as yet there was none of them.*
>
> —Psalm 139: 16

For a moment it seemed that I was looking down at the face of my baby brother, who was scarcely breathing, comatose. His head was fractured from the forehead to the plate above his left ear, one eye on the right closed, the injured left eye hardened into a flat red disk, somewhat the look of old, stiff jello. The eyelid wouldn't close.

He had been thrown from a motorcycle the Hawaii Hochi had given him for a daily paper deliver route in Nuʻuanu, except that he was not legally en route to deliver papers when the accident happened. He had taken the bike to a Shell Service station on Hotel Street to be fixed. Something was wrong with it.

The service station was next to ʻIolani Barracks, which then, in 1956, was across from ʻIolani Palace but outside the gate on the mauka side fronting Hotel Street. The problem with the bike having then been fixed, he waited for traffic to clear before pulling out of the station, gunning the engine. At the same time, a car came out of the ʻIolani Palace gate and smashed into the bike. The collision threw him headlong into the air, and he slammed into the pavement. The force opened a break in the bone above the left eye a half-inch wide, the fracture continuing backward over his ear. You could take his pulse by watching the soft space throbbing to clocked seconds per minute underneath. The doctor had taken the left eye, which had popped out, and simply put it back into the socket, there being nothing else to do. Warren's head injuries were of such a nature that it was too dangerous to do anything more than wait and see, the opinion of brain surgeons brought to his side in emergency medicine all agreeing, let him be.

They would just keep him comfortable. He would get better on his own with time. We waited and, after a while, the left eye closed. Maybe a month passed by. We waited through the next one. It went by. Three months later, he was still the same, no visible change except a gradual wasting away. He was moved to another room, causing me to suspect he would never wake up nor see out of those eyes again. I held these reservations to myself, not wishing to upset my mother whose mission of mercy was endless hope.

At this moment, as I stood at his bedside, I remembered a previous time when he was smaller, barely two years old, choking to death right in front of me. He was toddling around, not yet talking, and everything he found on the floor he popped into his mouth. Whatever it was he had swallowed I couldn't dislodge. I turned him upside down, trying to shake it out. It wouldn't budge. I tapped him on the back, as I had seen adults do when babies stopped breathing, but everything I did was useless. I was ten years old, and my ineptitude, fear and panic drove me out of the house, running to the garden where my grandmother was working. With hope in my breast then I felt that if there was anyone who could fix him, she would. The nearest hospital was three miles away, no car, no ambulance, no telephone.

"Grandma," I yelled, "Grandma!"

"What?"

"The baby, the baby."

"Who?"

"Warren Leihōkū!"

She looked up from the victory garden, as such vegetable gardens were then called in World War II. I didn't have to tell her what was wrong when she saw him, blue and purple. She threw down her tools and, with her unwashed dirty hands, put all of her short fingers down his throat, as though her whole hand could fit into it, digging compulsively away at whatever was down there, and once having found it, kept prodding until she brought it up—a small, blue plastic button shaped like a lily. I stared at it. It was my fault he had found it. I was folding clothes, and it had probably dropped down from a dress in the pile. He gasped and breathed, but she was furious and spanked him. At me she hurled words of disapproval, the sting of which was worse than a good whipping. I knew she was glad that he was alive but still mad that I had been careless. It was a wonder to me she knew what to do. I thought she even surprised herself. I took him back to the parlor, to the rocking chair, and sang him to sleep.

Now here he was, still sleeping, and all he had to do was wake up.

"Wake up, Warren," I said, "why don't you just wake up?"

"Ruby," he said, opening his eyes, "Sister Ruby."

"Warren, you can see?"

He could hear and see. He looked around, wondering where he was. The left eye moved together with the right, both at the same time, in the same direction. Nothing, then, was wrong with the muscle, but could he see out of the left eye, or was he using only his right? I held my hand over his right eye and asked him if he could still see me.

"Yeah, I see you."

"You sure?"

"Yeah."

Thou compassest my path and my lying down, and art acquainted
with all my ways.
For there is not a word in my tongue, but lo, O Lord, thou knowest
it altogether.
Thou hast beset me behind and before, and laid thine hand upon me.
Such knowledge is too wonderful for me; it is high, I cannot attain
unto it.

—Psalm 139: 3–6

Just then a nurse came into the room, telling me to step aside, that Navy Hospital visiting hours had been over a good while ago. She yanked the curtain around the tired hospital bed so that I would know she had work to do.

"I'm sorry. I didn't realize how late it was."

"Come back tomorrow," she said.

It was already tomorrow, and several more tomorrows, until the dreaded call from the desk would come that would be unwelcome news. Dr. Sheets got to the phone before I did, as I heard out the tail end of the message.

"We don't expect him to last the night unless we do another surgical procedure. We need a signature on the permission form, and right now he is not conscious. The doctors are anxious to operate. Get here right away."

When we arrived, the doctors and nurses were standing around the gurney, ready. They let me through for a minute, and I passed my hand under his nose to see if there was any movement of air. There was none.

"Here are the papers," said the nurse. She was the only one left at the desk.

"What do they think is wrong?" I asked, as the gurney went away with all hands pushing it.

"They think it's edema of the brain. With internal bleeding, too much pressure to the central nervous system causes it to shut down. If that's what they find they'll make an opening to drain off the excess fluid."

"I see. What are his chances?"

"They'll do everything they possibly can. Why don't you have a seat?"

There were leather chairs in the lobby and garden chairs out on the balcony. It looked like the balcony of Queen's Hospital in downtown Honolulu. Time to go home.

I moved out there where you could look over the city of San Diego sprawled out like Los Angeles, flickering with a million lights bursting from below and stars falling into the sea like a twinkling cascade. I went to the railing, bracing up against it so that I could say the words that mattered, just between myself and the Almighty Spirit way out there, somewhere.

"He belongs to you," I began, "so if you take him now I can't complain.

But, if you spare his life, I will do whatever it is he wants to do and go wherever he wants to go. I know he'd rather be out there sailing his ship over the horizon than spending his life in an office. It wasn't his idea to come back here if the *Soncy* could have made it down to Tahiti in November two years ago with a couple of friends, Jack Ward and Tom Keck. I should have told him when I was in Kona that time, that I was hapai, but he would have thought I was chicken. He had to turn the boat around in the doldrums. You know, I was morning sick all the time, eight days down to the doldrums, no food, no water would stay down. Four days to go back to Hawai'i, there was so much wind. Spoiled all his plans to go around the world that time, shucks. You know, he needs another chance, don't you think? You still my pal up there? Hope so. Whatever you do is okay. In Jesus' name, amen."

My half-Portuguese father believed you should think of Almighty God as your pal. Once Reverend William Castersen thought he wanted to go out on a Sunday afternoon with Kinney for a pleasure cruise down the coast. After church leave Koloa Landing on the south side of Kaua'i, go past Moyer's, Knudsen's, Po'ipū, and Brennecke's Beach eastward, around the lighthouse of Mahaʻulepū and Keoneloa. They took the minister's son, Ralph, with them. The once happy skies turned black with ugly squalls. Water began to fill the boat, so Castersen got up to pray for help. The weight shifted dangerously to one side.

"Sit down! You're rocking the boat! You want to get home, trust me. I'm the guy gets you back. Who you think you talking to? Just wave your hand like this and say, hello, how's it, pal?"

Another time he bought the *Taihei Maru*, an eighty-foot Japanese sampan and put a diesel caterpillar engine in it, hauled it out of dry-dock in Kewalo Basin. It was just his luck that the Japanese bombed Pearl Harbor the Sunday he was off Ni'ihau, fishing. Old man Otani, the fish captain, and his sons had gone out to show him their style of catching 'ahi, yellow-fin tuna, different from ika shibi. They came back to Port Allen at night, unaware of the blackout. Otani thought they had the wrong place.

"Kinney, dis not Port Allen. Mistake, I think."

"Naah, dis Port Allen. I no make mistake. I born 'Ele'ele, whassamatta."

"I think we make mistake. Port Allen get light. Ovah here, no more light."

"Yeah, but dis Port Allen. I know dis place, get light, no more light."

"Okay, you da boss, no blame me, broke da boat. No can see."

The Hawaii National Guard, thinking it was a Japanese sub, opened fire. Otani's boys started swearing. They were Japanese nationals and hardly spoke English. Bakatare. More shots, more cussing.

"Goddammit! What the hell!"

"Hold your fire, men. They're not shooting back. Maybe it's Kinney out there, coming back from Ni'ihau."

The harbormaster was pleading, but the guardsmen were not convinced.

"That's Japanese yelling out there."

"Sounds like Kinney to me. It's got to be the *Taihei*. Hold your fire."

"Whaddahell you guys think you doing? Gunfunnit. You putting holes in my boat, you stinkahs."

"E, sorry, eh. We thought was one Japanee submarine. No can tell was you guys."

"Sheezuz Chrissmas, where the hell the light? No can see Port Allen, sheezuz."

"No can put on da light, blackout, 'ass why. Japanese had bomb Pearl Harbor."

"Naah?"

"Yeah. Yesterday morning."

"Holy Smoke, no wonder. We was watching some planes, yeah, fly Honolulu."

"Mr. Kinney?"

"Yeah."

"Drotson, the harbormaster."

"Yeah?"

"Kinney, we have to impound your boat."

"Whhaat?"

"Kinney, the United States fleet in Pearl Harbor has been wiped out. We need your boat right now for reconnaissance purposes."

"Well, lucky for you, get new caterpillar engine. Works perfect."

"Can you have your crew off the boat tomorrow morning?"

"Sheezuz Chrissmass. An' where they gonna go with all their gear?"

"Well, I'm sorry to say they might have to go to concentration camp."

"What you mean? Sheezuz."

"E, ass' okay. We gotta go. Wartime."

> *If I say, Surely the darkness shall cover me; even the night*
> *shall be light around me.*
> *Yea, the darkness hideth not from thee; but the night shineth as*
> *the day; the darkness and the light are both alike to thee.*
>
> *If I take the wings of the morning, and dwell in the uttermost parts*
> *of the sea;*
> *Even there shall thy hand lead me; and thy right hand shall hold me.*
>
> —Psalm 139: 11–12, 9–10

Would he survive this night? What would I tell the folks? They would want to know if he would be celebrating his thirtieth birthday on January 20th. Back at the apartment in a file of family memorabilia was a letter from Knute Rockne dated February 3, 1930, Gulf Stream Apartments, Miami, Florida, to Mr. William E. Johnson, 716 and 1/2 Felix Street, St. Joseph, Missouri:

My dear Johnson:

May I congratulate you and Mrs. Johnson on the fine boy who has just come to you.
    I remember you quite well from the old days of Mozart and Marianna in Chicago, and I hope to be seein' you some of these days.
    Give my sincere congratulations to Mrs. Johnson and I hope the young man will be a whale.

I waited out on the balcony all night until the city lights disappeared with the dawn. At seven o'clock one of the doctors appeared, wearing a smile on his face.

"We're going to let you in to recovery. He pulled through. If you want to see him, follow me, come this way."

Tiny little rose tints had started to circle on his cheeks, or he was ashen gray and cold. Oxygen was barely reaching through tiny capillaries. He would revive, spend another week or two in physical therapy, come home and go back to work at the office, but he was hardly the same person as before. The difference was only slightly perceptible, vague, as though a significant aspect of personality at a deeper level of his being had been altered. Whatever it was that had once been there, I felt, had died in the wreck in Rose Canyon or been erased the night surgeons pulled him back from the threshold of eternity.

It wasn't long before he found out that his microbarograph design had been named, during his absence, for someone higher up the chain of command at the office. It was as though they hadn't expected him to recover and couldn't wait to get things done. He was still in transition, like the chambered nautilus, which, finding the shell he had occupied too small for him, needed to build a dome more vast.

"I'd like to quit my job," he announced.

"What are you going to do?"

"I'd like to go to sea."

"That's fine, when do you want to go?"

"Let's see. Dane will be a year old in July, so he will have a birthday in the Marquesas if we leave in June, what do you say?"

"Let's go."

We tidied up the finances and got the *Soncy*, a 38-foot Scandinavian double-ender Ingrid ketch ready for sail. On June first, 1960, we set out at three o'clock in the afternoon from Shelter Island, where *Soncy* had been moored for several months, leaving Point Loma behind. I would be leaving my younger brother Warren, who had come to San Diego wishing to be near me, and unbeknownst to me then, my father, who would be entering San Francisco Marine Hospital in a similar near-death condition while *Soncy* was en route through East Polynesia.

We sighted Guadalupe Island on the third of June, porpoises jumping off the bow and flying fish leaping over the cockpit. On June sixteenth we were in the equatorial countercurrent and on June twentieth crossed the equator. On the twenty-fifth we sighted Ua Huka at eight o'clock in the morning. The wind was brisk, carrying into our nostrils the smell of ripening breadfruit. Nuku Hiva was just ahead. As majestically as the cliffs rose out of the ocean to meet the sky, their ridges were covered with mossy green plunging to rocks at the base of the coastline, and the seas beat against them, like Wailau and Pelekunu on Moloka'i. The ocean rode right up to the waterfalls and forest. There were no fringing coral reefs, no gentle slopes, no *kula* plains. It was like Manoa Valley with the deep sea lapping at the base of Waiakeakua Falls, empty of the combined plain of Mō'ili'ili, Waikīkī, and Punahou. Sheer glory.

We espied the sentinel rocks of Taiohae toward evening and sailed into the bay at night flashing mast and stern lights, bringing the ship into line with a red beacon light on a hill we could not see but knew to be there. Cautiously the skipper tested the depth with a lead line until we kedged anchor with six fathoms of chain. What a magical moment of total quiet when the boat came to rest. No spume off the bow; no whining of the wind. In the distance, you could hear the rustling of water over pebbles onshore in the ebb and flow of the sea. In the air hung a strong scent of rich earth.

By morning light the land revealed itself in the southern sunrise as sounds of human life stirring *ki uta* reached our ears. On deck I made out a pavilion and by it gauged the distance to the beach as a five to ten-minute swim, but the government was already sending its launch to check our papers so we could go ashore. The posts of the pavilion were carved with tiki faces and the roof thatched with braided coconut leaves. When we spoke with Marquesan people who had gathered around, they seemed to understand our attempts to communicate with them in a kind of pidgin Polynesian we invented as we went along, some Hawaiian, Marquesan, French, Tahitian, and English words all mixed together. They loved it; their language capability was enormously flexible. They informed us that fourteen American yachts had already passed through on the way to the fête in Pape'ete on Bastille Day.

We responded that we were not going to the festivities in Tahiti. We would miss the fête. We were on our way to the Tuamotus, where we had promised the Bishop Museum we would again record stories collected by Dr. Kenneth Emory thirty years ago on the island of Vahitahi. The older ones were wire-recordings, and Emory had taped the samples to be used to refresh the old folks' memory of a generation ago in order to determine the amount of retention. For this purpose we had purchased a German-made Phonotrix mini-taperecorder.

From Taiohae we moved *Soncy* to Haka U'i, anchoring in Tai 'Oa. These names were related to Hawaiian ones, Hana- (or Hono-) uliuli, meaning 'dark-bay' and Kailoa, 'distant-sea'. Our decision to visit Ua Pou was foiled by unfavorable winds, forcing us to pull into Hana Menū, where we spent the first evening on Hiva 'Oa. Thereafter finding no safe anchorage in Vipihai Bay, we took shelter by nightfall in Taha'uku Bay, a narrow inlet at this time of the year so favorable to the open sea it was exposed to an incoming swell, causing the boat to pitch and toss at anchor.

The lack of a comfortable mooring for *Soncy* at Hiva 'Oa compelled us to depart for the island of Fatu Hiva to the southeast. At Atuona, however, we would leave behind a Hawaiian-Marquesan friend, Hapuku Kekela, veteran sailor himself of several yachts on the high seas, mostly American, on which he had admirably worked his way around the world. He had found his Kekela cousins in Hilo while on those cruises. He was descended from Hawaiian missionary James Kekela, to whom President Abraham Lincoln had given a gold watch for saving the life of American sailor, Jonathan Whalon, in the 1850s.

News of this passage from Ta'ahuku to Hana Vave, Fatu Hiva, did not reach friends and family until we had completed the route through the Tuamotus, when letters from *Soncy*'s skipper detailed the events of June through August from Pape'ete, dated September 6, 1960:

> ". . . We left our crew at Hiva Oa in the Marquesas which made everyone happy . . . After leaving them Ruby, Dane, and I sailed on to Fatu Hiva, an over-night sail, and spent eleven days there enjoying the peace and quiet. I got in quite a bit of upkeep on the boat, too, hardly going ashore. In fact, Hana Vave is the most spectacular anchorage I've been in being at the mouth of a deep gorge with the cliffs cut into huge grotesque statues. The gorge is a kind of bottleneck for a larger valley on inland which gives rise to violent gusts of wind blowing out through the bay. I put out 25 fathoms chain to the Danforth anchor and had no trouble holding . . .
>
> "This was the jumping off place for the Tuamotus so I took a solar

observation practically every afternoon to check my chronometer error and rate against the charted longitude for the anchorage. I have given up on radio time signals after reaching the Marquesas. I have enough trouble keeping up the batteries charged enough to start the engine next time without running them down with the radio and still not getting the time signal most of the time. It must be that the people who make charts are right, or at least close enough in their longitude as I've used this method from there on and have had no trouble making landfalls in the Tuamotus where you don't see land 'til you are right on top of it.

"Our first stop in the Tuamotus was Amanu atoll, 457 miles from Hana Vave. The wind was slightly forward of the beam which allowed the boat to be trimmed to steer itself.

"We had to run the gauntlet of four atolls on the way to Amanu. The first two, Pukapuka and Napuka are about 75 miles apart and not much sweat. We went through somewhere in the middle of the third evening and slept that night. The next two, Fakahina and Fangatau are something like 24 miles apart and consequently of more concern as my navigation was then impaired by heavy seas. (Which crest would you like to call the horizon and what shall we use for height of eye with the boat rising and falling 15 feet or so.) At least I could see the sun and on the evening of the fourth day sighted Fakahina six miles off the starboard bow. I bore off and sailed under the lee in the late twilight. It was all clear ahead so we slept the fourth night. My chronometer error determination was now reinforced.

"We had spent part of the second day nearly hove to because of the sea state. The sailing directions say that slack water of high tide at Amanu occurs about three hours after the meridional passage of the moon. I had chosen as our arrival date one where this condition obtained about one P.M. putting the sun behind us as we went through the pass. Amanu was sighted in the morning but it was apparent that we would be late. It was now a question as to whether the current would be too strong to stem when we did arrive. Sailing down the chain of islands we thought they would never stop.

"The farther we sailed the more of them came over the horizon. Finally we reached the northernmost of the two passes and I couldn't believe it was so narrow. It looked as though the *Soncy*'s sides would scrape on either reef let alone have maneuvering room. Turning was out of the question. The current was ebbing. The southern pass was purportedly wider and therefore recommended. As it was only a mile farther on and I felt the current wouldn't increase significantly in this much time we kept going. If the second pass is any wider it must be apparent only to the surveyor. *Soncy* has been through it four times and I'm still not convinced.

"There was plenty of water coming out and to say that we had misgivings is an understatement. But the only way to find out was to try so I gave the engine full power and bore in. There was no question as to where to drive but right up the middle of the road. It was a weird feeling to see the water flowing past the hull at full speed but the shoreline only creeping by. We had acquired an audience on the beach and, amidst real or imagined cheers, I'm not certain which, we steadily gained the lagoon. Here the channel makes a sharp turn to the right but now we were veterans.

"Inside the lagoon was at once a relief and a disappointment. The village is situated next to the pass and all the water in sight was too deep for the *Soncy* to anchor. You don't need a lead line to tell this in crystal clear Tuamotu water. Even if we did anchor the fresh breeze was building up an uncomfortable chop here at the downwind end of the lagoon. After four hard days at sea, we thought we deserved better than this.

"We were asking ourselves, 'What do we do now; go back out to sea?'" when a boatload of local boys came out and offered assistance. The leader had sailed to Hawaii in 1949 on an American yacht (the *Varua*) and could still remember some English. He came aboard and took the tiller saying he would show us where to anchor. He took the *Soncy* about a mile south of the pass and behind a lagoon where we found protected anchorage in six fathoms. This area is just off the edge of the Hydrographic Office Chart for Amanu pass."

We came ashore at Amanu atoll in the Tuamotus on Tuaira Kavera's boat. It had one of those English outboard motor engines with long stems. The view of colorful corals and reef fish beneath the boat was piercing clear through the water. On shore we passed through *naupaka* underbrush and chunky, dead coral, coming into a coconut grove so thick the sunshine filtered through only as sifted light. We noticed little houses strewn throughout the grove, but their sizes seemed to indicate you could only lie down in them. So, what were those? Graves, we were told. This was a graveyard and a copra plantation at the same time. One of the houses had louvered windows and lace curtains, indicating that the owners were well-to-do. We broke out of the grove into bright sunshine and found a paved coral pathway leading to a group of houses behind a fence of coral block.

Tuaira introduced us to his mother, Atera, who seemed to have the biggest house in the village, a community of about one hundred and seventy people. We were formally welcomed by the chief on the veranda. That evening, after a supper of boiled 'ulua fish, we sang out on the porch, exchanging Hawaiian and Tuamotuan songs. We brought out the 'ukulele, and they had a mandolin and several guitars. We taught them *Papalina Lahilahi* and learned *Ia Neki* and *Vahine Pa'umotu*. I asked if they would sing some of the old chants, but Tuaira said his generation could not sing the songs of his parents' generation. The older folks then began to offer the *paripari* and *teki*, and as they sang, a soprano voice rose above the others. It came from Hina Pe'a, originally from Rapa in the Austral Islands. It was her name that interested me, Pe'a. There were Pe'a families scattered throughout Puna district on Hawai'i, and they were related to us. Curiouser and curiouser.

Next day I sat down with the older women to transpose the recordings into Tuamotuan texts with some English translation by Tuaira:

> *Timanu te henua ra i te pae Kereteki*
> *Tapuni te pae Tokerau*
> *E niu te kopani.*

Timanu is the place, no coconut (on) the other side, Kereteki,
Tokerau wind goes all around,
The kopani coconut(s).

> *Ka matira koe*
> *Ka matira ra vau*
> *Koi tano a taua matira*
> *Kahiri kore pai, fati tau aku*
> *Kotahi a kai.*

You go fish, (with) pole and line
I go fishing, I go fish and you go, too,
We go fishing,
I have bamboo, you have bamboo,

We get fish,
If I broke my feet, I no get plenty,
Same as we get, two better than one,
If one get hurt, the other one catch fish.

> *Ko ia vau te ruku i vaho nei*
> *Te noho mai ra te tane i uta*
> *I Maehanavau.*
> *Maehanavau e teia ruki korari.*

I am the girl who goes outside to get pahua clams
While the husband stays upshore
Warm for one whole night;
I get warm if I go upshore tonight.

After a few days we decided to leave Dane 'Aukai with Atera Kavera and to sail on to Hao Island, then from there to Vahitahi with Tuaira, Etienne, and Petero Michele as crew. Four days later, as we came into the lee of Vahi-tahi, two boys on shore leaped into the sea, coming on deck to show us where to go along the coast, until Timothy Demos, a Tuamotuan sailor, presenting his captain's license in French, came out to sail *Soncy* in the lee while we visited ashore, there being no lagoon anchorage.

In the meantime, people who had gathered to greet us chanted a song, honoring Kenneth Emory as Keneti, whom they had not forgotten:

> *Keneti e, na mea topiko e ratinai ara kore*
> *I poro mai ia vaku e,*
> *Hararē poro mai ia vaku.*
>
> *Kavena e, na mea topiko e ratinari ara kore*
> *I poro mai ia vaku e,*
> *Hararē poro mai ia vaku.*
>
> *E Roki e, e ui ranga e ui atu vau ki au e*
> *No hea mai to taua tupu i hanga mai e*
> *E kimi ana vau e,*
> *Hararē kimi ana vau e.*

Say, Kenneth, heavy with sleep,
Sleep too much, don't call me to come in,
Sing again, don't call me to come in.

Say, Kawena, heavy with sleep,
Sleep too much, don't call me to come in,
Sing again, don't call me to come in.

Say, Rocky, ask, I ask him, you ask him,
Where do you come from?
I'm finding out.

It was a love song, *teki*, which they had adapted for welcoming purposes by attaching stanzas from other *teki*, one of which we had already heard on Amanu (Timanu) into which they interpolated the name of their island, Vahi-tahi (Titahi):

I Titahi te henua rai a te pae kereteki
Ua vatapuni i te pae tokerau,
E niu te kopani.

Titahi, land of barren reef on the south side,
Covered with coconuts on the north side,
Coconut grove like shut door (to weather).

Uppermost in our minds was the overnight exertion by the crew who were outside keeping vigil with *Soncy*. At the first stroke of morning light, the skipper resumed command of the yacht, having decided to take the yacht to Akiaki, an uninhabited island north of Vahitahi that was, in distance away, roughly equal to that of Nukutavake, where most of the local people had gone to make copra for the season. I later learned that Vahitahi and Nukutavake were one chiefdom under Tupuhoe, the population numbering about three hundred. Yet, at no time did I ever see more than five men, including the chief and people, supporting women and children left behind in Vahitahi households. Tupuhoe was very ill and had made no appearance thus far. He was the one to whom Emory had addressed the introduction on the taped samples with which I was to refresh his memory of thirty years ago. Time to move, but where, how?

The realization that I was by myself in the big wide world was sobering. I had expected to be left alone to some extent but not with the possibility of finality and in a foreign country. Yet here I was, exactly, in a totally isolated place, ringed all around by the ocean, huge waves bursting against the southern shore just three minutes away, surf boiling against the north shore, to east and to west, salt spume wafting through the air like fine mist, tons of imminent tidal surge force that could sweep over this island, no bigger than a large *motu* in Hao or Amanu, and coconut trees the only barrier to violent storms from the southern sea. Flimsy shacks of houses elevated on cement and coral platforms, so that they could be built up again, as these simple ditties sang of their only defense against imminent devastation from the sea, the coconut trees so thickly planted, *E niu te kopani*, so chary of the space above, below, side-by-side, to close like a door, *E niu te kopani*, the coconut grove as the only shield possible on a coral island the pace of a pygmy against the Goliath stride of the Pacific Ocean.

What kind of *niu* is *kopani?* Elaine Frisbie from Pukapuka in the Cook Islands was with Dr. Emory's petroglyph field survey team camped out in the summer of 1955 at Annabelle Ruddle's beach place in Pani'au where she entertained us with real-life stories of how her father, Robert Dean Frisbie, had saved his family during a hurricane by taking his children, one by one, as Polynesians on atolls did, and lashing them all in the crowns of coconut trees, one youngster per tree. I tried to imagine this: kids in coconut trees being whipped around in a frenzy of a hundred-mile per hour wind. Not a one of the Frisbie children perished. When the eye had passed over, he would climb down and go from tree to tree to check on them, giving them food and water, then lashing himself back into his own perch. Dr. Harold St. John, who taught Hawaiian Ethnobotany at Mānoa campus, would march his students around, calling out scientific names for all ornamental and economic plants such as the coconut tree, *Palmae Cocos nucifera*, forcefully recommending to us with obvious pride the life-saving flexibility of the coconut tree trunk as the primary means of Polynesian survival. It was the safest place to seek refuge as the land below became one with the sea. When the surge subsided, you would come back to earth somewhat shaken, but unharmed. As for the coconut itself, it held the purest form of drinking water in the world. *E niu te kopani.*

If I looked around I saw only the horizon broken by the coconut grove. Whose woods these were I did not know, but they were lovely, dark, and deep. I had many miles yet to go and promises to keep. Baby son more than a hundred miles away; husband gone, another hundred miles away; boat gone. What if the boat never came back? Boats do that sometimes. Not everytime. But I was carrying another child. I was morning-sick again, ready to heave on shore, cough my insides out, be a sea cucumber folding in and folding out. My God, have you forsaken me?

O Lord, thou hast searched me, and known me.
Thou knowest my downsitting and mine uprising, thou understandest my
    thought afar off.
Thou compassest my path and my lying down, and am acquainted with all
    my ways.
For there is not a word in my tongue, but lo, O Lord,
    thou knowest it altogether.

Such knowledge is too wonderful for me; it is high,
    I cannot attain unto it.
Whither shall I go from thy spirit? or whither shall I flee
    from they presence?
If I ascend up into heaven, thou art there: if I make my bed in hell, behold
    thou art there.
If I take the wings of the morning, and dwell in the uttermost
    parts of the sea;
Even there shall thy hand lead me, and thy right hand hold me . . .
                                                —Psalm 139: 1–4, 6–10

I walked back from the reef to the Demos' *fare*. The cooking fires were smoking above the roof. She waved to me to come in, to eat breakfast with her, and she set down in front of me a plate of cold rice with a piece of fish. Instantly, a swarm of black flies covered the whole plate. I knew I shouldn't eat any of it, but this being my hostess' house, I tackled the meal with accolades of gusto, asking Heimata, in between mouthfuls of buzzing food, if she could arrange for me a meeting with the chief, Tupuhoe.

Tupuhoe was not only the chief; he was Emory's peer and had to be approached with dignity and respect. If I arranged a meeting with someone else less in rank, it would violate rules of propriety in both Polynesian and French society. Then the door would close, I imagined, not only on me but also on the Bishop Museum, and, ultimately, the United States of America and the whole of institutionalized academia. It wouldn't be bad, for whoever would come here to find out?

Small diplomatic ponds have ripples, too, as do oceans of political gossip around the world, was it not said, so succinctly by Lunalilo, that voices on the wind travel afar, such that his insignficantly unrequited love for Victoria Kamāmalu was merely due to the rejection of their betrothal and marriage by her brothers, Alexander Liholiho and Lot Kamehameha, that no matter how trifling the matter of succession to the Kamehameha throne would have been as a minor principality among the monarchies of world powers in the mid-nineteenth century, it would eventually reach the courts of Great Britain as important news from the Pacific? I could not afford, even here, to blunder on this venture to a coral island on the fringe of copra schooner routes through French Polynesia.

Beautiful Heimata Demos, grey-haired, hardworking, patient, longsuffering, and kind to strangers, replied to my entreaties that she would go to Tupuhoe's family and ask them if it would be all right if the *vahine Vaihī* from *te 'iate Marite Soncy te ingoa* could bother him in the afternoon? She would go. *Haere atu au.* You stay. *Nofo koe.*

Tupuhoe would oblige in the afternoon, came the message. He would like to hear what Keneti had sent to him, and he would like to send a letter back, would the *vahine Hawaiienne* please *tauturu?* When I got there, he was lying down on a mat. I was told by the women present that he was very ill. Please play the machine. No sooner did he hear the crackly sounds of the old Vahi-tahi recordings, he motioned that I turn it off. *Taringa turi*, he said, meaning that he was made deaf; it hurt his ears.

What to do now? I immediately put on the chants from the day before recorded at Tapere's house with Tehio Tunui, Raka Ngapehu, Tehio Ruirui, Reitere Heteketanga, Tehio Kaurua, Terito Tehio, and Ngaheiariki Tehio, in three recording sessions, the oldest group aged forty-one to sixty-one, and another group aged twenty-nine to sixty-five years. He was enchanted by the playback of their voices. I recorded his voice and played it back for him. His eyes lit up. Play the machine again.

Tupuhoe called the attendants there, all the women of his household, to help him up from the mat. They feared for him, reminding me he had not long to live. He was suffering from bad kidneys. I could see he was in pain. Should we stop now? Should I come back another day? The yacht would be coming back. We would have no more time.

He waved us all aside, motioning to Petero Michele to interpret for the *Marite*. Petero had learned English from American soldiers on his tour of duty in Europe during World War II. No matter how fluent he was in Tuamotuan, however, his mother tongue was still Tahitian, and we stumbled along with Tuamotuan texts and broken English translations. Somehow, we made progress.

In Tupuhoe I saw the nobility of the real Polynesian chief. We may never see his like again. He waved away pillows brought for his back and sat upright, bending his body forward to ease his spine so as to be able to lift his feeble voice to chant the ancient *fangu* of Tahaki, the farewell *tangi* by Huauri to her son Tahaki upon his departure to the land of the Ponaturi to recover the eyes of his father, Hema. The women took the part of Huauri and he that of Tahaki, until all together they would join in the chorus of the refrain:

> *Purutia te tama riro i te tere he Rangai e*
> *E tangi ia e koro ai tu Ruhitange e*
> *E tangi te tama ki te metua purutia*
> *E koro ai to arā purutia,*
> *Ara te muri aroha kia mai Havaiki e*
> *Puhapuha ma Hinano te mea ka roha i Rangai*
> *Ua kore ranga ia e koro ai tu Ruhitange*
> *E tangi te tama ki te metua purutia*
> *E koro ai tu ara e henua*
> *Henua tangi ana i te hiti hanga o te rā e rangai e*
> *Ua kore rangi e matimati a Rua te kora tu i'i.*

The son has gone on fearless wings to a land of danger,
He has prepared himself, he goes on, like a bird he flies,
The son cries, he laments his father, bravely, he cries,
He wants to go on the path of danger, bravely, he goes,
On the path of the Muriaroha wind below Havaiki blowing,
Onward to Hinano, the son beloved (of his mother) goes on,

Unaware the father has already died, yet he flies on, like a bird,
The son cries for his father, who was brave before him,
Like a bird does the son fly onward to a high island, dangerous
The land of Rua's chiefs, land of ancestors in Vaerota,
Crying, he chants farewell, *tangi* at the rising of the sun,
Where Rua's chief perished in the rays of the dying sun.

I would return to record at Tupuhoe's house until seventy-one chants had been collected in the village. Tupuhoe readied the letter for Kenneth Emory, which I would deliver to him in person at the quay in Pape'ete in September, sending the taped materials on to the Bishop Museum by courier. Tupuhoe then took out a photograph taken thirty years ago identifying in the peer group himself, Tupuhoe Ateavai, who had been born on Vahitahi, and others who were part of the group whom Emory had known a generation ago, as those still living and present: Tehio Kauri, male, sixty-three years old; Ngaheiariki Tehio, female, sixty-five; Tuhiroro, female, seventy-nine. He pointed to a girl in the photo and said her name, after which, if I understood him correctly, was the princess.

"My daughter," he said, Petero interpreting. "She die, so much she love Keneti. When Keneti go, she go everywhere Keneti go on Vahitahi and stay there and cry. No eat, no come home. That's why they say, on Vahitahi, Keneti so handsome, everybody die."

I heard the children yelling, *"Te pahī, te pahī,"* "Boat, boat!" I looked and saw nothing.

"There, you see?"

I looked again, nothing. I was looking for the wrong thing. I should have remembered that all you see of an atoll in the distance are sticks of coconut trees above the horizon. I looked for a faint vertical line, and there was the mast, about a fourth of an inch high, leaning away from the wind, tipping through a stack of clouds, first one way and then the other, side to side.

"Te pahī," I yelled, *"Soncy!"*

The people walked me to the edge of the grove on the north side, inside the fringing reef, where they heaped shell lei upon shell lei around my neck until my shoulders sagged under the load.

Tuaira said, "Now you make speech in Pa'umotu, you make proud now, people like hear you say in Pa'umotu, better."

In Polynesian pidgin, mostly Tuamotuan, I said:

"Ko au e ferurira'a i teie fenua nei, ko Vahitahi te ingoa, e manako nei, he mea rahi to koutou aroha nui iā vaku, kia mātou, no Soncy mai, te 'iake Marite, kā mātou hanga e ferurira'a iā koutou, ki te korometua Tupuhoe, te 'ariki nui, nga famili, mea rahi te aroha, e horonga mai, e horonga atu a hoki mai."

"I will remember this land by name Vahitahi. I think how great your welcome to me, to us, from the American yacht *Soncy*, we will remember you all, and Tupuhoe, the wise elder, high chief, and all the families, from whom so much love is given, that such love shall be returned."

Then I sang with them the modern *teki* in farewell:

> *Vahine Pa'umotu taku, e-e*
> *Taku e manako nei,*
> *Tiaki te matangi Tokerau e-e*
> *Taku tere atu e,*
> *Mau aku ra taku taurā*
> *I te hakamau atu ra,*
> *'Avivi nga papa i ava i te kura Matavai,*
> *I te pihai ka momoe e*
> *I te pihai ka momoe e*
> *E taku hoa.*

Pa'umotu woman mine,
Mine to think about
When the Tokerau wind blows,
Mine to sail with,
I make taut the sheet,
To pass through the current of Matavai Bay,
Where I shall enjoy my rest
With you, my wife,
My companion.

Seventeen years later, on Thursday, October, 1987, *The Honolulu Advertiser* ran a story captioned "Ship Caught in Volcanic Eruption," with subheading, "Studying Seamount in the South Pacific":

"A rare underwater volcano in the South Pacific erupted just 130 feet beneath a research ship and enveloped the vessel in a swirl of murky water, gas bubbles and hot volcanic rocks, reports reaching the ship's San Diego home base said."

The eruption of the MacDonald Seamount 650 miles southeast of Tahiti sent gas-infused rocks clattering and clanging against the steel hull of the *Melville* and transformed the greenish ocean water into a churning, boiling dark brown, according to an account by the scientists aboard the ship as reported by the Los Angeles Times.

'Large gas and steam bubbles burst at the surface with chocolate-colored clangs and clamors but apparently undamaged.' Macdonald Seamount, 2,000 miles south-southeast of Honolulu, was discovered by University of Hawaii geophysicist Rockne Johnson in 1967. It is named after the late UH volcanologist Gordon MacDonald.

With it in the ranks of rare undersea volcanoes is Loihi, which rises to within about 3,000 feet of the surface 28 miles east of the hydrophones in the North Pacific.

In 1969, with his wife and four children, he sailed to the area on his 12-meter yawl Havaiki and found the seamount within 17 miles of the position he had predicted from the eruption echoes . . ." [italics mine].

Nine years after the 1960 cruise through French Polynesia, we had returned to a patch of the Pacific where the Austral and Tuamotu island groups share the space. Sounds less than music traced underwater had been coming from an active volcanic spot where none should ordinarily have been:

"On *29 May 1967* a 4 1/2-hour sequence of explosions was recorded on sofar hydrophones arrayed across the North Pacific. The source location was computed as 28.8 degrees S, 140.5. degrees W, on a southeastward extension of the Austral southeastward extension of the Austral Islands chain . . .

". . . To corroborate the long-range acoustic evidence of active volcanism, I searched the source region by echo sounder in *July, 1969.* The search was conducted from the yacht *Havaiki,* a 12-m fiber glass yawl, *with my wife and four children, aged five through ten years, serving as crew* [italics mine]. The echo sounder was a Furuno model F-812-H with a rated range of 2000 fathoms (3600 m). Electrical power for the echo sounder was provided by the main engine through alternator, batteries, and inverter.

". . . Engine failure 2 days before arrival in the volcano region severely limited the time available for echo sounding. Accordingly, the search was concentrated along the axis of major uncertainty of the sofar fix. This was estimated as the bisector of the azimuthal sector containing the hydrophone set. Although the echo sounder had previously been operating continously, soundings were taken only once each hour after engine failure.

". . . On *20 July 1969,* while on a south-southeasterly heading, *Havaiki* passed 7 km to the west of the predicted volcano location . . .

During local apparent noon (2128 G.M.T.) the vessel lay to while two 4-pound (1.8-kg) sofar bombs were detonated at a 4000-foot (1200-m) depth. At this time 53 solar-altitude measurements were taken during a 1-hour interval . . ."

". . . no signals from the sofar bombs detonated on 20 July were received at *any of the hydrophone stations although a pair of bombs detonated on 17 July, in a position northeast of Morotiri, were recorded 15 db. above background at Eniwetok and Wake islands."* [Rockne H. Johnson, Hawaii Institute of Geophysics, University of Hawaii, Honolulu 96822].

We had passed over the computed area at night. At first nothing showed up on the Furuno echo-sounder. We tacked back and forth until a profile of the bottom began to draw a sloping bottom on the screen. It looked as if we would run into it, so we sheered off.

"What do you think? I'm not sure we went over the top. There's a possibility that the reef is closer to the surface, in which case we could run aground."

"Well, if you don't try for the top, you will always wonder. Just go for broke."

"Ready about."

We went over it within twenty-five fathoms of the surface. Satisfied that we had done the best we could, we set a course for home.

In March 1998, thirty years later last year, the bronze medallion given to *Havaiki* by the French Societé des Etudes Oceaniennes at Pape'ete Museum was presented to the Bishop Museum. It had been struck in 1968 commemorating the Captain James Cook Bicentennial, 1768–1769, in French Polynesia and New Zealand. It was given to the *Havaiki* before we departed the quay for the Australs, as it was their impression that the yacht was heading for an undersea target on, virtually, a passage to nowhere.

We had to find the volcano first. It wasn't on the charts. Nor did I know that French geophysicists in Pape'ete may have been briefed that *Havaiki*'s progress would be tracked several thousand miles away on hydrophones, so when miniature sofar depth charges came out of the hold on July 17, 1969, to be detonated in order to calibrate the hydrophone network, my reaction was stupefied disbelief.

"What are those?"

"Depth charges.

"For what?"

"To set off."

"Now?"

"That's right."

"Oh, boy."

"Just hold this tape recorder on the side of the hull by the bunk."

"Sheezuz Chrissmas."

"Don't worry. They need thousands of pounds of pressure to go off."

"God Almighty."

"It's not going to blow up the boat."

"Oh, boy."

"Come on, kids, let's go topside."

Dane 'Aukai was at the helm, ten years old on July 12, 1969. At the age of fifteen years, he would sail his own boat, the twenty-five foot Japanese sloop, *Little Wings*, on a trans-Pacific solo voyage from San Diego to Honolulu, in April 1975. Six months later he would be injured in an automobile crash on Halekoa Drive. I had just gotten out of Queen's Hospital myself that morning and was on my way home when the news came that traffic on Kalani'ana-'ole Highway was stalled for a bad accident on Halekoa Drive. Three children had been injured, a man and his wife, who was also pregnant. They had all been taken to different hospitals. Mine were at Queen's. I asked my brother-in-law to take me back to the hospital.

Two other younger children were at school. At this moment none knew of the condition of the others since they had left the house at different times. I had asked my brother-in-law to go up to the house the night before and make sure he took away the keys to the station wagon. I didn't want my teen-aged son to be tempted to drive it. Only the older two, having stopped to meet their friend, had gotten into the car of a perfect stranger? A man who had no knowledge of the hill down which he was driving a rented car, accelerates it to speeds over sixty-five miles an hour with his wife almost ready to have her child, why did he do that? The children's father was thousands of miles away on an oceanographic research vessel, and he would know nothing of any of this until he got back, how would he react if this only son had died on my watch?

It wasn't as if I hadn't pulled him out of Ala Wai Yacht Harbor once before when he was two years old, when I was carrying his yet unborn sister. We had both nearly drowned then, thirteen years ago. He was jumping from *Soncy* to the dock but his timing was off. As he took a broad toddler's leap, the stern rope pulled away from the pier. He fell into the canal, came up briefly, then sank out of sight. I was right behind him. Usually I was somewhere else working on the deck, but fortunately I happened to be by the cockpit. In the dark water I was frantically feeling around on all sides hoping to catch hold of him, letting the air out of my lungs so I could go down faster.

It was a good thing we had let his hair grow. I felt those loose strands in the water and tightened my grip around his locks, pulling hard on his hair so I could get his head out of water. I knew it hurt but I didn't have much time to get him out before his lungs would fill up. Each time I pushed his head out above me, the weight displacement dragged my head under. He was choking. If he broke free from my grasp, he'd go back down, and I might never find him again. This was my only chance to save his life. I aimed for the slack in the line when the yacht moved toward the dock. Lunging for the lowest part. I got hold of it. My right arm seemed as though it would pull out of socket, but I wouldn't let go of the rope or the baby in the left arm. Someone, hearing my call for help, came by. I gave him the baby, hauling myself out on my own. The man was spooked speechless by it and left without a word.

When I got to Queen's Hospital, I found Dane hovering between life and death and his sister, Moani, unconscious. He could not have the necessary operation to drain a blood clot on his brain until the afternoon, all surgery rooms fully occupied that morning. Even after surgery, he stayed in a coma for weeks. I looked down once more at that familiar injury, the left eye, the left side of the skull, and the forehead, fractured into pieces.

When he awoke one evening and saw me standing there, he said, "Mommy, don't go home. Stay here and don't go."

"I can't. There are hospital rules."

"No. Don't go home. I don't want you to go."

"Okay. I'll stay."

I found a place on the floor, put something on it for my head and until midnight we managed to fool the nurses. When the R. N. came in, I got a full dressing-down for breaking the rules. I dusted it all off, as I had been through that too many times. I was the daughter of a practical nurse and daughter-in-law of a registered nurse. (What could be worse)? Nothing was new.

As I left, I said to my son, whose sight in one eye was hidden under a big bandage around his head, "Save yourself, my son, that's what the Bible says, only you can save yourself."

Outside the hospital, in my fervent prayers to overcome my fears for his life, I could not rest until I gave him back to God. Acceptance.

> *For thou hast possessed my reins; thou hast covered me*
> *in my mother's womb.*
> *I will praise thee; for I am fearfully and wonderfully made . . .*
>
> *Thine eyes did see my substance, yet being unperfect; and in thy book*
> *all my members were written, which in continuance*
> *were fashioned when as yet there was none of them.*
>
> *How precious also are thy thoughts unto me, O God! how great is the sum*
> *of them!*
> *If I should count them, they are more in number than the sand; when I*
> *awake, I am still with thee.*
>
> —Psalm 139: 13–14, 16–18

In the end we bear our own burden, by ourselves. We face our own limit; our own death is totally alone. Against what force are we vulnerable each day? Life is taken a breath at a time; death is only a lack of breath away, constantly. This I discovered when I went to swim at Kuhiō Beach in Waikīkī with a group of undergraduate varsity swimmers at Mānoa campus. I would swim with them as they trained under coach Soichi Sakamoto, but I never joined the team. I didn't want an Olympic medal, just an ordinary diploma. They were attracted by the news that a big surf had built up offshore. The weather was ugly. The uglier the better for body surfing. I went along.

At Kuhiō Beach is a pier running out on the reef. I casually swam out beyond it, and in no time at all it looked no bigger than a thin, black line about a quarter of an inch long, using a squint-of-eye ruler from where I was, bobbing in white caps. How had I gotten into the shipping lanes? There was a fast undercurrent, a riptide. The distance to shore was a football field or more inland. How to get back? It was late in the day.

The waves were not of the rolling-face type. They rose into a bursting curl, which, if you were spun into it would coil you under, slam your body to the reef below and drag it over the bottom. That is to be expected, except that these were not the usual Waikīkī waves. They were long-period waves from a storm surge to south and packed with power. The back of each one was a long swoosh outward against which swimmers find it necessary to swim around, farther down the beach, to escape the undercurrent. Although this was common knowledge to beachboys, I was a rookie.

Even if you come up through one of those long-back waves, the next one is already holding you down, forcing you to duck it by going back out under the curl. Even then you need extraordinary staying power in the sweep. Take a deep breath and hold it. After the long-period waves came short-period combers, one after another, between which I had too little time to dive down to escape the thundering burst overhead or to breathe any sufficient air to withstand another duck. Soon I found I was sucking water into my lungs, losing strength even to take in a little bit of air. Pretty soon one hour had gone by, then another. I knew I was drowning.

There came the moment when I was so tired I could no longer move arms or legs and gave up trying. I let the ocean make decisions for me. The last great wave came rising out of the sky. This is it, I thought. Instead of diving under, I stayed where I was, floating on the sweep. Lord, I said, I'm going to die out here today. No one will know. The ocean crested, curled, broke, and swept down, yanking me to the bottom. It rushed over the reef, out of control, with me in the boil. I was drinking tiny little rocks with seaweed and salt water. I tried to stay awake. Somehow I was still floating, up to the next wave, and the next, until the pier was only a few fathoms to dry sand. I crawled out on my hands and knees, moving only so far on the wet sand to put my face down and let the water out. I was still alive.

> *Whither shall I go from thy spirit?*
> *   or whither shall I flee from thy presence?*
> *If I ascend up into heaven, thou art there;*
> *   if I make my bed in hell, behold thou art there.*
> *If I take the wings of the morning, and dwell in the uttermost parts*
> *   of the sea;*
> *Even there shall thy hand lead me, and thy right hand shall hold me.*
>
> *I will praise thee; for I am fearfully and wonderfully made;*
> *   marvellous are thy works; and that my soul knoweth right well.*
>   —Psalm, 139: 7–10; 14

Encountering Sorrow

1. The Chinese Magician

My fahdah, he so funny. He tink he related to everybody. Sometimes when my friends come ovah our house, my fahdah ask dem all kine questions about who your fahdah, what's his name, where he went school, la dat. Pretty soon, he can figgah out dat he know da guy or my friend's uncle stay related to somebody he know. All from asking, "What school your fahdah went?"

"You da Hu boy? Your fahdah used to go St. Louis? He used to play basketball? You related to da Hus from Kaneohe?"

My older bruddah Russo gotta get in da ack and tell my friend, Herbert Hu, "So, Hu you?" Russo donno dat Herbert catch gas from everybody cause dey call him "Sucka" cause Hu sound like da President Herbert Hoover, which sound like Hoover vacuum cleaner so dey call him "Da Sucka."

But dey get me too. Sometimes in school, somebody tell me, "Eh, you da guy, eh?"

And I tell, "What guy?"

And den dey tell, "You, das you, Daniel Wat. Wat guy. Heh, heh, wop yo jaws."

Shet. Everytime I fall fo dat.

When Mr. Sakamoto, da P. E. teacha make basketball teams, he like to call out our names, "Hu on da shirts, Wat on da skins." And dat start everybody saying, "Who? What?" And Andrew go tell, "What about When and Where, Mistah Sakamoto?" We all laugh and Sakamoto he trying fo be serious but he stay cracking up too.

Or when Sakamoto trying to be funny, he make up teams like Chu, Fu, Goo, Loo, and Kahanu against Chang, Dang, Pang, Yang and Macadangdang. And if your name no rhyme, he make um rhyme. He call you Doo-doo and assign you to da *oo*s or Walla-walla-bing-bang and tell you play fo da *ang*s. Sometimes he make all da K's go against da LMNOP's cause get plenny K's. Or Sing gotta go wit Song. Of course den, somebody gotta tell, "Well den, Ding gotta go wit Dong!" Or when Sakamoto like play wit us, his favorite team is Dicky Wee (we call him Pee Wee when he go *shishi*), Calvin Hee,

Stanley Yuu and Norman Shishido so he can tell, "Yuu, me, Hee, Wee and Shi going be da shirts."

Of course, Andrew gotta tell, "What about Dem and Us!" Crack me up!

Even my fahdah started calling me "Wat guy" cause one time he went pick me up from school and some guys was razzing me, "Eh, Wat Guy" and Daddy tawt dey was talking Chinese, and he ask me, "How come dey call you one chicken, *wat gai?* Das pot roast chicken, you know? Your mother make good *wat gai.*"

"I not one chicken, Daddy. Let's go."

"Who's dat kid? His fahdah went Roosevelt?"

"Ho, Daddy," I tell him, "you tink you know everybody, eh? You must be *somebody*, eh?" I was trying fo be sarcastic but he nevah catch.

"Nah, not errybody. But good to know who's who, eh. Maybe dey can fix you up wit one discount or someting eh?"

Ho, das when I come all shame cause j'like he ask all dose questions about my friends fo get someting cheap. My fahdah, he always trying fo get someting cheap. He so cheap, he go late to da Islanders game aftah da fit inning, cause you can jes walk inside da stadium and dey no say nutting, no even ask you fo your ticket. My fahdah jes make like he get one ticket, but he booshet, you know. And we gotta share *one* bag peanut and he no buy me soda so I gotta go da batroom and drink from da water faucet if I get tursty. I used to peek chru da cracks in da seats and try figger out where da batroom stay. Kinda good fun go batroom undah da grandstand cause you can look up and try find your seat. I try look fo my fahdah's skinny chicken legs and his plaid Bermudas, but no can tell who is who, all da old futs look da same. And every-time I go, I check if somebody went drop money but probably not my fahdah.

He stay rubbing off da peanut skins in his hand when he went ask me, "So you going to da seventh grade dance? You know how to dance or what?"

"Yeah."

He laugh little bit, "Huh. And what's dis about you going be a magician at da dance?"

"For da Talent Show part. Mrs. Sherwin said everybody on da committee gotta do someting. John's band going play couple songs. Shirley going do Japanee dance, Gerald going play accordian. I going do couple tricks: I going borrow Russo's magic vase, do da magic cones one, and I donno what else. I need one more. You can buy me one new one?"

"Naw, no need. Go ask your Uncle Reuben show you some tricks; maybe he lend you his costume."

No ways. I ain't wearing dat stupid suit: red silk jacket, black beanie hat, loose black pants, and kung fu shoes; look like one China Jack. And he put on da goofy buck teet and talk funny kine, Charlie Chan talk, look stupid. Sound stupid, "I Doc-tah Ting-a-ling Ah-Fut-Fut, da Chinee Houdini and dentist. Dey say my show so bad, jes like pulling teet!"

Uncle like to do tricks wit fire and smoke and he can make da coins disappear den pick um out of your ear. And guarantee, he do da trick wit da balloon and da long needle. You know da one you blow up one balloon and poke da long needle chru and da ting no bus except Uncle, everytime he do um, da balloon bus so he yell, "Hap-pee New Yee-ah!" and den he tell, "Poor man firecracker." He bow and smile and he start blowing up one nudda balloon. He always bowing and smiling, always smiling. He ack stupid cause his tricks no work all da time. My bruddah Russo said was on purpose dat. Was part of da show fo chrow people off. I not too sure.

*   *   *   *   *

It's Ten-Ten, October Tenth, overthrow of the Imperial dynasty, and I'm thinking about my grandfather. Ah Goong was one of several revolutionaries in Hawaii who raised money for Dr. Sun Yat-sen in the 1920s.

Uncle Reuben used to tease me, call me professor after my goggle-eyed, awkward looks. Said I looked like one Professor. Was smart like one professor. Maybe he was trying to make a connection to Ah Goong, who was a professor of some kind in China. Perhaps like my father, he was hoping that I'd become whatever I was called.

The Chinese have a thing about names. My Chinese name is Ling Chun, Perfect Justice, my father told me. My grandfather named us all. I didn't even know what Justice meant when he first told me. And whenever I screwed up, my excuse always was, "Nobody perfeck," even if my name meant I was supposed to be. Perfect Justice, no such ting. What a stupid name, I had a whole string of stupid names: Daniel Ling Chun Wat. Once my mother put my name in big letters on my sack lunch: D. Ling Wat. I don't know why she did that but once everyone saw it, I become "Dealing Wat" for a week.

It was always important to my father whenever we visited my grandmother that we call out her name. Not her real name, which I never really knew, but Russo and me, we'd always run through the front door, shout, "Hi, Ah Po!" and run out the back to play, our filial obligations done. Years later Russo would always refer to our cousins who had died by using complex descriptions or circular references, never using their names: *the cousin who was a welder and used to work at Pearl Harbor, the cousin who had cancer and used to teach at the University, the one who died of pneumonia after mowing the lawn in the rain.* I'd say their names like a mantra in my head: Michael, Donald, Henry. Michael, Donald, Henry. It was bad luck, according to our mother, to say their names out loud and I guess he believed her. Once I checked the gravestone of her mother, my Ah Po Lee, before a trip to the National Archives to try to look up her immigration records and discovered it read, Lee Number Three Girl. I guess I'll never know her name either. Despite my Chinese name and being called Professor all my life by my uncle, there was no magic in my name. I couldn't fool anyone. I wasn't Perfect Justice. Wat Guy was just a bad magician.

Had Ah Goong been like my father, always mocking, always scolding? *S'mattah wit dat boy? No can talk Chinese, no can catch, no can squeeze the grass clippers, no can drive standard shift? Gonfunnit!* Was Daddy just repeating what his father had told him? Playing out Ah Goong's disappointments: that he would never understand what it meant to be a revolutionary, would never truly know Chinese well enough to say anything important, never be able to make speeches, to write words that would make someone give up a couple of days' pay. He sold appliances, for Christ's sake. Refrigerators, ranges, washing machines. He swept his hair into a wispy pompadour held up by Dixie Peach pomade, wore bow ties and two-toned shoes.

Ah Goong sold a revolution. How did you ask poor people for money? How could you point toward the homeland and say that this money was part of being filial? Did the people turn away, slam doors as he asked again and again for money. For the cause. Years later he would build a writing gazebo, have the audacity to name it Pavilion of Filial Devotions, and his friends would come and point west, talk about the homeland, knowing they were already home. Who would go back there now? To poverty, famine, and war. How filial was that? How much smoke and magic did they put up?

* * * * *

"Stoopid trick," I hear somebody say. Da string around my cape is choking me. I finally settled on wearing black pants, white shirt wit red bow tie, black cape, and one homemade black top hat. I wanted one coat wit tails like Harry Houdini but couldn't cause my muddah no can sew. Maybe the Chinese outfit would've been better. I went practice so many times in front da mirror: pull up da sleeves, show da hands, palms, backs, sprinkle da dust, wave da wand. I wanted to be perfect. But da tin foil is unraveling and I am sweating it's so hot. The black crepe paper on my top hat stay all wet wit sweat and everytime I wipe my head, my sleeve come more black. I'm dying, bleeding black. And now all my moves feel funny. Wave figure eights with the wand over the plastic vase. More foil peels away from the two chopsticks masking taped together. A few impatient notes and a noisy chord from the band behind me getting ready. Everybody call um John's band cause he da leader but sometimes we call dem da Motos, cause had Dennis Yamamoto, George

Miyamoto, John Akimoto, and Roland Pagan, tree guitars and drums playing surf music. Andrew call dem "Tree Motos and a Boto." I turn around. John gives me a small wave with his guitar pick. I wave my wand and lift the cover of the vase, remember to grip the false shell of the ball along with the lid. Show with an open palm that the vase is empty. I turn, my cape whips the plastic vase over, I lunge for it, drop the concealed ball. It rolls off the table toward the audience which has inched up closer trying to figure out the trick, to catch my mistake, and I want to do Uncle's Doc-tah Ting-a-ling Ah-fut-fut routine instead of chasing the ball across the floor. Someone throws the ball back at me; I miss the catch, have to scramble on the cafeteria floor after it. Shet. Shet. Everyone laughs.

Move on to the last trick: the two cones taped together which will magi-cally roll uphill on two angled wooden rods. Wave the wand which now looks like a small foil flag on a stick. Wipe my sweat. Sprinkle magic dust, which is now glitter smeared across my forehead. Try to tear off the cape which is still choking me, no can. The knot is stuck and now the cape is hanging in front like I'm at the barber. It's tangled with the Reddy Kilowatt bow tie from Hawaiian Electric which I borrowed from my father. The one that lights up, batteries in my pocket. I know I look really stupid, the flashing, the bow tie is giving me a headache. I hold up the cones, spin them as if they have some magical power. It's all in the set up. You just need to make it look hard. Make like it's not going to work. Pick them up, knock on them, pass them around: *no mechanical parts, no hidden motors.* Set them on the rods a couple of times, make hand motions: *come-to-me, come-to-me, come-to-me.* Like you going hyp-notize um. Pick them up before they roll, so when you finally lay them on the two angled sticks da ting going come to you cause dey just roll that way. Cones always going roll uphill if you put the sticks the right way. But now I'm starting to rush and I know people no can hear cause da guys in da crowd getting bored and stay fooling around and now da drums in the band getting impatient, *da dum dunt. Doom, doom.* I feel like I'm talking Chinese. Nobody understands what's supposed to happen. I should have been Ah Foo Ling Yu, the Chinese coolie magician. Borrow my fahdah's straw coolie hat. He get one fo working in da yard. Would've been better to be funny and stupid, like Uncle Reuben. Now I know why uncle does it. It's so easy to act stupid, to be the Charlie Chan Chinese wimp. Comes natural, talk wit buck teet, Chi-nee, half sentences, chrow in some "*ah so*s," bow and smile a lot. But Andrew would've turned it into Ass-o, da Chinese Magician, in no time, I know. And the whole damn seventh grade would have made buck-teet "Ah So" to me for the rest of the year. I rush through the rest of the trick. The cones roll. Small kine applause. I'm pau. I grab all the stuff, take a short bow, put the top hat back on my head still dripping black crepe paper sweat. Mrs. Sherwin tries to lead a second round of applause as I rush past her. I only hear her clapping. Make ass. Make total ass. The band starts up the first song, "Wipeout" by the Surfaris. John steps up to the microphone and laughs in that high falsetto, "He, he, he, he . . . wipeout!" *Da da da, duh-duh, duh-duh, duh-duh . . .*

* * * * *

The Young Locals for Peace. In college I wore my hair long, wore the Young Locals black armband every day, slung my bookbag over my shoulder and smoked my first cigarette of the day on the way to school, lighting up before I was even out of the driveway. Never smoked at home. My mother and I pretended that the smell of cigarette smoke wasn't on my clothes, or the matches and the disposable lighter she took from my pockets and lay on the nightstand when she did the laundry weren't really there. My father never said anything about my long hair or the cigarettes or the late night hours except to look at me and shake his head: poho, waste time. I knew he dreamed of having an engineer in the family like Aunty Etto's boys (it was years before I figured out that aunty's name had an H in it) or a doctor like Ernie Ho's boy. He must've wished he had called me a doctor, lawyer, or engineer. Never once called me an artist, writer, or revolutionary. Once he sat me down and pointed out that a dentist, like Uncle Reuben, ". . . not bad you know, dey no call you up any kine hours, you keep regular hours."

Later, I figured out that nobody died on you if you were a dentist. You did-n't have to go to all those funerals that my father went to with alarming reg-ularity nowadays because he was president of the Chinese name society. It seemed like everyone with our name was dying. Every Sunday, he wore his black funeral suit and when he came home, set a couple of sheets of old news-paper on fire and stepped twice over it: warding off bad luck, the evil spirits. More hocus pocus.

The Chinese society was mostly Wats. Some with one T, some with two. Aunty Etto said that the one-T Wats were more pa-ke cause dey saved on a T. Russo used to say that James Watt, the inventor of the steam engine was pa-ke. There were some Chus or Choos or Jous or Joos. But not da Koreans, my father would warn us. All the same character, he told us.

"So how come no mo any Wat-anabe's in da Wat Society?" I asked him. He nevah say nutting. I knew he was hurt by my rejection of his Chinese-ness. The Wat name society. Why should we feel any connection to unre-lated others with the same surname. What did it mean? Daddy said that all the Chus were from the same village, that the patron saint of the village was a poet, who searched for love through all of China, never finding it. He trav-eled all the way to Heaven, sought true love there and didn't find it. Heart-broken, he threw himself into the river on the fifth day of the fifth month.

Better to die in the search than live without true love. So now on the fifth day of the fifth month, the Dragon Boat festival is held and people still search for the poet and toss rice wrapped in bamboo leaves into the river to keep the fish from eating him. Stupid story, I thought. Another stupid Chinese poet. Maybe *that* was perfect justice.

The Young Locals for Peace was the farthest I could get from being Chinese. It was about radical, anti-war politics. I liked the idea of working for peace, demonstrating, sign holding and leafleting the snack bar; holding teach-ins until the night they organized a march and called on us to torch the ROTC building. I veered off toward the parking lot and headed home. This wasn't any kind of justice. Turned out I *was* a Chinese chicken, *wat gai.* Maybe a wimp like my father. Hardly a revolutionary. *Wat gai,* pot roasted chicken. I had to smile, that was me: *pot* roasted.

Truth is, I had been a Young Local to be with Pearl. It was the only time she wasn't with her tall haole glassblower boyfriend—at Young Locals meetings. We had gone to the same intermediate and high schools but never really got together except to be in the same homeroom, Woo and Wat. Lost touch with her until I saw her at Young Locals. She called me to help her move out of her mother's house. I don't know what happened to her father, never met him. *Find out what school he went,* my father would say. But I knew her mother if only by her abrupt replies on the phone: *Pearl no stay home. Who dis?* Tell her Daniel called. *Pearl no stay home. I donno when she come home.* I know, tell her Daniel from school called. *You call back bumbye. Okay?* Okay. Sometimes she used her Chinese name, *Ling Siu, no stay home.* Perfect Love. *Sometime she no come home.* I know.

When I dropped by to pick up her stuff, her boyfriend's MG was already loaded and he was sitting in the car looking like he wanted to be somewhere else. I heard Pearl's voice and her mother talking Chinese, fast, short, unmistakably angry. I tapped on the screen door. She managed a smile and we loaded what we could into my car. I'd have to come back.

"I gotta go," her boyfriend told her, "see you there." I secretly hoped that this would be the cause of their breakup. I couldn't see her mother beyond the screen door but she poked her head out to look me over after he left. She knew that *Ling Siu* was going out with that *bahk gwai,* the big haole. I imagined them in bed, she astride him and I felt like the Chinese wimp again. Maybe I was too much like my father. I could almost hear her mother's challenge to me: *How come you no go out wit Pearl? Wassamattah you? You let da* bahk gwai *take her? How come? Why you let her go with him?* As if it were my fault. Sorry. I'm no magician. I was just the Chinese coolie, haul stuff, put up shelves in a rooming house near campus, a place where she never really lived because she stayed most times with him in a messy artist's studio, beaded curtain, mattress on the floor covered with cheap India Imports covers, ashtrays full and a couple of yawning cats wandering around.

Wassamattah wit you, pa-ke *boy?* I could see it in her eyes. "You Chinese?" she asked. She tried something out in Cantonese. I could only shake my head, "No, no sa-be." I shrugged I-no-understand. *No talk Chinee, eh?* No. *Your fah-dah talk Chinese?* Yeah. *Your mother talk Chinese?* Yeah. *Why you no talk Chinese?*

Pearl laughed at our pantomime. It was good to hear her laugh. We didn't say much on the drive over. Talked about the Young Locals. I had stopped going. She didn't have time. I sweated her boxes up to her second floor room. Put up the bookshelves. Remembered the magic show and the first dance. Drove her a couple blocks to her boyfriend's house. She invited me to stay for spaghetti. He looked at her and said, "Yeah, stay." Almost a challenge. I chickened out and left. Wat Guy.

It happened again in the cafeteria at work, the woman who cleans up the condiment counter and refills the sugar packets looks closely at me. *You Chinese?* Yeah, I say.

"What's your name? Wat. *You know how to write?* I struggle to remember the character and write it on a napkin in baby strokes, the only thing I remember from one summer in the first grade Chinese school. *Ah,* she says. *I'm Chu. Wat, Chu, same same character, you know. You talk Chinese?* No, no can talk. *Ah ABC, eh? American Born Chinese.* Yeah. ABC. *What gen-ration you?* Ah, my father born in China, my mother ovah here. *No talk Chinese, eh?*

I start to edge away. Smile, nod, bow. I'm nervous, chicken. Start to sweat. *Wat and Chu, same character, you know.*

I know, I know. But not the same, there was no magic here. Her character was much stronger, much sturdier than mine.

* * * * *

Two weeks before the seventh grade dance, Mr. Sakamoto, the P. E. teacher arranges for us to practice dancing with the girls' P. E. class on the basketball court. We're dressed in our P. E. clothes and the dance lessons look more like basketball drills than dancing. We line up by height and I'm partnered with Wanda Chu. Dicky wants me to answer the question once and for all: fake or real? He keeps a tally of everyone's opinion but there is no evidence either way. He sees his investigation as preparation for a future in gynecology.

"C'mon Dan-yo. You jes gotta hold her tight and you can figure um out. Or try bump her chest accidentally when you dancing."

"Why you no do um?"

"I'm too tall fo her. You, on da uddah hand, are just da right height."

"How can? Mrs. Sherwin over dere telling us six inches between boy and girl. And no dancing surfa style."

"C'mon, Wat Guy, you chicken? You like know too."

Mrs. Sherwin didn't have to worry. Wanda tries to dance without touching me, like I have some disease. She already knows how to dance and spends her time looking at everyone else. Some of the girls are getting timed for the 600-yard run-walk on the field, so she cheers them on. I pretend to watch my feet and wonder how she could ever run the 600 without her tits getting in the way. Chu. I wonder if we're related. Aunty Etto is always telling us watch out who you like, might be related. No good marry your relative, your kids going come out all retarded. I decide she must be Korean. Nobody in our family looks like Wanda.

Halfway through the song, Wanda tells me, "S'cuse me, I gotta go batroom." She waves to Mrs. Sherwin, "Teacha, I gotta go batroom." I'm left without a partner so I watch Pearldean Woo running her P. E. test. She's flushed and panting but happy that she's made a pretty good time. She has circles of sweat under her arms and flaps her T-shirt to cool off. The teacher tells her to be my partner. Wanda never comes back.

The cafeteria is hot in the late afternoon. It gets even hotter when we close all the louvers and make um dark cause da committee like um be like one real dance but we know it's just after school and we stay sweating like crazy and da whole place beginning to smell like da P. E. locker room and Hungarian goulash all mixed up. Da boys stay hiding from Mrs. Sherwin so dat dey can comb their hair into one stiff black helmet, all shiny wit sweat and too much pomade, except da grease is beginning to melt in da heat and everybody's North shore wave coming flat no matter how much you comb um. And if you nevah pack on da pomade, your hair stay on da south shore: no waves, watch-da-small-kids-splash kine, absolutely flat. The Talent Show is over and everyone's waited out the first few songs. Mr. Sakamoto is the MC, acting like a clown, but no one has actually gotten up to dance yet. Finally after so many I-going-if-you-going deals among the boys, it's as if the light turned green and a mass of boys head across the room.

I'm caught up by the wave and Dicky points out that Wanda Chu is there, "Eh, Dan-yo, Wanda like you. She stay waiting fo you, Dan-yo. You ever wanda about Wanda?" He laughs at his own joke. "Falsies or real? She went ditch you in P. E. eh? Now's your chance."

I no care if she went ditch me, she is definitely North shore. She looks up and sees me headed her way. She shuffles behind Pearldean Woo and I'm face to face wit da south shore. Flat, maybe one to two feet, good day fo diving.

Shet, I no can surf, anyway. Can barely swim. I jerk my head toward the dance floor and tell, "Like dance?" She has on regular school clothes: plain white blouse with a small handkerchief pinned above the pocket, plain white slip, plain white bra, additional chest protection provided by her sweater tethered by an alligator clip strap across her neck, and her math book and portfolio clutched across her front. I imagine her mother reminding her, "No fo'get your sweater, now. Bumbye catch cold," but really meaning, *don't show the boys your breasts.* Pearldean no say nutting, puts down her books and we head toward the center of the floor.

The record scritches off the player and Mr. Sakamoto laughs crazily into the mike, "Everybody do da bird!" He puts on the "pa-pa-pa-pa-pa oo mau-mau, pa-pa oo mau-mau" song and everybody's acting crazy, doing the bird, flapping our wings and even Mrs. Sherwin, who's got a "fine pair" as Dicky puts it, is bouncing around wit Mr. Sakamoto. And Pearldean is holding the ends of her sweater flapping and I still have my cape on and I flap and we're the best flapping pa-pa-oo-mau-mau birds on the floor. *Bird, bird, bird. The bird is the word. Do the bird, bird; bird, the bird is the word.* The song finally ends and Pearldean says thank you and rushes to the sidelines. She looks like she did in P. E., flushed with stray bangs stuck to her forehead. I start across the floor a couple more times but chicken out halfway. Pearldean's not looking at me so I can't tell if she going to say yes again. Maybe she knows she was second choice.

Dicky tells me, "Your hair looks like shet."

Mrs. Sherwin advises, "Maybe you ought to try to wash that black stuff off your forehead."

Forget it. Wat Guy sits down.

"Last dance," Mrs. Sherwin announces, patrolling the sidelines. "Pick somebody and get on the floor. Everybody up." I half expect Sakamoto to blow his whistle. Dicky is still trying to get me to dance a slow one with Wanda so that he can get another opinion, but Timmy has beaten me to her and I'm in front of Pearldean again.

"Uh, you like dance again?"

"Sure," she says. We hear the first strains of "pa-pa-pa-pa . . ." We're almost relieved that it's not a slow song.

"Nah, jes joking," Mr. Sakamoto's voice booms on the P. A. He changes to "Surfer Girl." I look over to Wanda Chu who is hanging on to Timmy Yuen, her chest pressed to his. He has a smile on his face. One more vote for real.

Pearldean and I stretch toward each other like we're in P. E. class. We hold each other lightly. I have an itch.

"Try check out Timmy and Wanda. Dey dancing surfa style," Dicky says and winks at me as he sweeps by with Louise who's desperately trying to keep up with his big steps as he cruises the floor spreading the gossip. We both turn to look, our glasses clink like we're making a toast. We mumble sorry to each other and laugh. I stumble toward her nearly tripping, I wonder if I've stepped on her foot. Shet. She leans into me, I think so that she can get her feet farther away. And we stumble some more. I'm sweating profusely now and wondering how I'm gonna push up my glasses without just dropping our hands. I think I could grab her close and hold our hands up high and nod casually into our clenched hands and then push my glasses back up my nose, but I know it's a stupid idea. Pearldean says something.

I say, "Wat? Wat Guy, dat's me," automatically. How stupid. She must think I'm like Dicky or Andrew. I lean closer.

"Hot yeah!" she yells in my ear.

"Yeah, my glasses falling down," I say. She pushes them back up for me and wipes some glitter off my forehead with her palm.

"Magic dust," she says and pretends to sprinkle.

"No tease, eh. Only make A at dat stupid Talent Show," I tell her.

"No, you were good," she says and the song is over.

We're still holding hands when Mr. Sakamoto blows into the mike and says, "That was the second-to-the-last song because the committee said it wasn't dark enough. Now is the real last song." And now all the lights go out, even the mirror ball and the light organ, and Mrs. Sherwin looks nervously at Timmy and Wanda.

Pearldean leans into me and puts her cheek on my shoulder. It feels heavy. My pants is poked out, shet. What if she can tell? I don't know where I'm step-ping, it's so dark, I can't see. The sweat is pouring down my face and I smell awfully stink. She breaks loose and unpins her handkerchief and wipes my face with it. I protest, "No do dat, going come all had it."

"That's okay. I never used any of them before. My mother actually thinks I'm gonna use these, like to blow my nose in an emergency." She dabs at some of the crepe paper smear on my forehead, "Whoa, look how black."

"See, I told you. Your muddah going tink you get black hanabuttah." I can't believe I said that.

Afterwards, I sit with her outside while she waits for her mother. We don't say much. I'm about to ask her for her phone number, for the math assign-ment, for tips on running the 600 yard, anything but her mother comes.

She says, "Thanks for dancing with me. See you next week." And like magic, she's gone.

*　*　*　*　*

I came across my name in a book of Chinese poems. Ling Chun, Perfect Justice. The poem is titled "Li Sao," Encountering Sorrow. I wonder more about Ah Goong these days. I wonder if I was meant to find Perfect Justice, to even try. The poet sought perfect love. Fool. My wife and I bicker over the smallest of irritations. The children won't wash the dish that they've just eaten from. I no longer know what is right or fair, holding what was certain in the past up to scrutiny. What was chicken before has become courage. What was insight has become babble. I tire my wife and children, I'm afraid, with stories told too many times, too many different ways. And I suspect they look upon me with derision, a fool still trying to do magic. And what is left after all the tricks are done? Just a deep and satisfying sorrow. Perfect Justice.

2. Fish Uncle, Sleight of Hand

We all stay in da living room, me, Russo, and Mr. Ho while Daddy practice his speech for the Wat-Chu Society dinner. Mama stay in da kitchen cooking, so she no need be da audience. Mr. Ho helping Daddy pronounce da hard Chinese words. Russo call um da Donno Wat-Chu Doing Society. Daddy tell us one mo time, "Your granfahdah went start dis society, you know. Fo help all da people from da same village stick togedda." *We know. We know.* He tink we going learn Chinese if we listen to him practice because every now and den he stop and explain someting to us. We no like know.

Russo go tell, "So what Daddy, dese guys in da club all our cousins? We stay related to dem or what? Aunty Etto going tell me I no can marry anybody ovah dere?" Auntie Etto always telling Russo, "You bettah ask me first if da girl related to us or not, Russo, cause if you cousins, no good you marry each uddah." Russo get nervous when Auntie and Ah Po start talking about who would be good fo him to marry. Which of their friends get eligible daughters. Who might be suitable Chinese mates: who got carsick, had mental illness in the family, or bad teeth. Russo not even pau wit college and he no mo girlfriend so Auntie says she gonna help him out. She always trying to get him to go Hong Kong wit her so she can introduce him to some nice Chinee girls.

"No ways," he tell me.

Daddy's hand stay shaking and he keep moving his head up and down following the words Mr. Ho went write fo him. Finally he fold up the paper along the creases, and worries it into the back pocket of his shorts, "I no can talk dis kine fancy stuff, Gunner, I not smart enough fo say dis kine."

"Can, Cowboy. You can. All da old folks expect you to say dis kine fancy speech. You da president, president gotta talk la dat. No matter *what* you say, jes *how* you say um all fancy. Like one politician."

"Yeah," Daddy says to him, "dat's what I tell da boys all da time . . ." Russo and me look at each uddah, we move our mouths to Daddy's words, "No mattah *what* you know, jes *who* you know." One of Daddy's favorite sayings. Russo always acking wise, he tell, "So we should've been named Hu instead of Wat, yeah, Daddy?"

At da dinner, Daddy stay up at da main table in da front of the restaurant wit all da big shots. We stay at one table in da back next to da kitchen wit all da uncles la dat cause my uncles not big shots. My fahdah told me dat da president gotta buy one table, one hundred twenty bucks.

"Get twenty five tables. Wow, you gotta talk to two hundred fifty people," I said.

"Shet, I know. I know."

"I tawt being president was good," I told him.

"Yeah, for dem. For me, I'm out one hundred twenty bucks and I gotta do all da work!"

So he went invite da uncles and aunties to one free dinner and told us boys we bettah learn Chinese cause, "Ah Goong, your grandfahdah, was one of da founders of dis society." *Yeah, yeah. We know.* So I told Russo, "Ay . . . you going have to be president of da Old Fut Society when you get old and buy one hundred twenty dollah table and learn one old fut Chinese speech."

*   *   *   *   *

I was president of our YMCA club fo little while in da seventh grade, da Epics or da E-pricks as da Imperials used to call us. We used to razz dem back dat at least we wasn't named aftah da margarine. *Ta, dah, dah, daah! Imperial Magarine makes you feel like a king!* I nevah like be but everybody said should be me cause I da only one who knew da Robert's Rules of Order la dat. Was between me and Andrew, but Dicky told me to be da prez cause I was jes one figgahead anyway cause everybody only going listen to Benjamen because whatevah he said was what we all wanted to do anyways, so we might as well shut up and let him tell us what fo do. Besides nobody wanted to beef Benjamen or have him razz you cause den everybody join his side and you get razzed by everybody. So if he said you was going be prez, you was da prez. I found out afterwards why Benjamen nevah like be one officer.

Being president meant you had to be everybody's stooge cause whatever had to be done, dey said, "Das your job, you da prez." You had to call up da girls' club fo invite dem to one social. But first you had to fill out da forms fo get approval and if you tell, "Das da sekatary's job," Benjamen tell, "Yeah but your job is to make sure da sekatary do um."

Anyways, dey only wanted to get one social wit da Les Shondelles, da club dat had Wanda and Cookie and Big Head Shirley, she make her hair all big wit hair spray and *plus* she get big head. One time Andrew went blow one paper dart in her hair from da back row and she nevah know until da next period. I donno if she knew was Andrew dat did um but da Les Shondelles nevah like have one social wit da Epics. Not dis month, not next month, not evah, dey was so stuck up. And when I couldn't get da social wit da Les Shondelles, Benjamen made like was my fault and said, "Maybe da prez gotta be somebody who can get dem."

And everybody went tell, "Yeah."

And Benjamen went tell, "Wat Guy, you outa here."

And dey went impeach me and elect Andrew aftah he went make one stupid speech about how he was going get plenny socials cause his cousin was friends wit da Les Shondelles adviser. Of course Andrew always get one cousin who had better stuff den you or know somebody who could get someting cheaper den what you went pay. Sheesh, sound like my fahdah. One time, we went figgah dat if Andrew really had dat many cousins, he would be related to everybody. He said he was going get car washes too wit da Les Shondelles cause he like see dem in wet T-shirt. Everybody went laugh and started talking about who dey tawt was da cutest Shondelle. I like see him get one social wit dem. Sucking Andrew. I tawt he was my friend. Used to be he nevah even know how to say Les Shondelles, he kept calling dem "Less Shondelles." I told him was "les" like "lay," like you like lay one Shondelle. But now, piss me off, he nevah even tell me he had one cousin or dat Benjamen was planning to impeach me. So little while mo I jes stopped going to da meetings. My fahdah was glad, he nevah have to drop me off and pick me up aftahwards. He nevah even ask why I wasn't going meetings anymore. I nevah tell um.

* * * * *

The Wat-Chu banquet was at Golden Duck Chop Suey, the same restaurant Ah Goong used to take da whole family to dinner when I was small. Our family wit all da uncles and aunties and cousins take up two tables plus one kids' table fo da small kids who no can wait fo da real food to come, so Ah Goong gotta order noodles and chicken fo dem. Russo hate it when he gotta sit at da small kids' table and watch us. Das when he taught us stuff like how to eat shoyu by sticking your finger inside da shoyu plate and how fo play fight sword wit chopsticks while we wait fo da food to start coming.

Fish Uncle usually came late with a fish wrapped in pink butcher paper, which he took to the kitchen right away. All the kids loved Fish Uncle cause he always had a pocketful of quarters which he traded for little favors from each of the kids: pour him a cup of tea, get him a toothpick, put money in the meter, help him carry his packages to the car.

Once we went out to Kuapa Pond, where he raised mullet. He gave us each one small bag of *ebi*, dried shrimp, and a piece of string he cut from a dwindling cone he kept in his truck and sent us to catch black crabs along the rocks. He sold them to the Filipino fishermen to use as bait. Russo would always be the first to tattle on me, "Uncle, Daniel went eat all da bait!

"Huh! If he no catch nutting, bumbye I gotta sell him to da Filipinos." He would test my arm between his thumb and forefinger and say, "Aiya! Too skinny. Das okay, let him eat da bait. Bumbye when he come mo fat, den we can sell him." He wink at Russo. "Here boy, eat. Eat." And he would pour another handful of *ebi* into my sack.

* * * * *

The program has started and the MC is introducing Daddy. Fish Uncle comes in late and slips into the seat next to me. He still smells of the fish market, even though his aloha shirt is fresh from a day on a hanger swinging from the nail holding up the calendar from Kowloon Mercantile, the stack of days thin and ragged now that it's September. He takes the seat next to mine and slips his feet out of his worn, brown, cross-strap leather slippers. His feet look like two pale fish, white and shriveled from standing in water all day, and smell faintly of black rubber boots. He's absorbed the scent of the market, the sharp, harsh exchanges in Cantonese, the waft of a cold cigar sitting in the ashtray, and the shouts and laughter that cross the aisle between the stalls. Fish Uncle is teasing the Korean lady that her *bak choy* is too high. He calls out to Take's Meats and Poultry, "How many chicken feet for one akuhead?"

Take shouts back, "Only have couple pounds. You want some ass for your head?"

"Okay, okay, hap dozen turkey tail," Uncle says.

He takes off his aloha shirt and hangs it on the back of his chair. His undershirt is damp on his back and along the sides and his trousers wet from the knees down. All the parts that his rubber apron doesn't cover. His fingers, shriveled from pawing ice chips over the fish all day, seem to thaw out as he holds his teacup out and I pour cup after cup for him, if only because the teapot sits in front of me. I set the lid ajar to tell the waitress that we need more. The leaves have sunk to the bottom into a morass but somehow when she adds hot boiling water, the tea tastes fresh and fragrant.

We can barely hear Daddy say his speech at our table. The noise from the kitchen drowns him out each time the doors swing open. Daddy gets a funny Texas twang when he tries to talk haole, only ting he talking Chinese. Russo and me look at each other. We can tell he's nervous, pausing a lot, the paper shivering. The uncles don't notice or don't care and continue to eat. Nobody is listening except Fish Uncle, who listens like he's asleep, eyes closed, head tilted back. He's the only one listening because he laughs at the right places and leads the applause at the end. We all follow, glad that it's over.

When Daddy comes to our table, he's gotten back his big-shot swagger.

Fish Uncle pours him a jigger of whiskey and everyone toasts his speech but we can see Daddy's hand is still shaking when he sips.

Fish Uncle tells him, "Eh Cowboy, too good eh, you. You sound like one Chinese Texan. So das why dey call you 'Cowboy' . . ." My fahdah, he no catch, but me and Russo, we catch and we stay laughing and poking each uddah until my muddah give us stink eye and we stop. Daddy is still sweating when Uncle asks him, "You know what you was talking about or what?"

"*Tsien tsang, pahng yau, gok wai* . . ." Daddy starts to recite again, explaining to us, "dat means, 'Friends' . . ."

"Romans, countrymen, lend me your ears," Russo mutters into my ear. I pretend to pluck off my ears and hand them over. We bus out laughing and now everybody stay looking at us acking up and my fahdah stay wiping his forehead wit his napkin, "Wassamattah, you guys no understand Chinese anyway," he scolds us.

My fahdah is popping one vein and sucking down Johnny Walkers now and coming mo loud, standing up every time he pour one jigger, offering the bottle around da table before pouring his own. Finally he says, "Whachumean I sound like one Texan?"

"You sound like one Texan talking Chinese. No can undahstand what da hell you saying cause you sound like Bonanza talking Chinese." Fish Uncle does John Wayne, "Waal, tsien tsiaaanggg, pahng yall, gawk wai. Yeeehaw! Who went write your speech, Big Bert and Ernie?"

"Ernie Ho. My friend Gunner went help me," my fahdah says.

Aunty Etto who most times stay on another channel says, "Not Big Bert, Daddy, Big *Bird*. Big *Bird*."

"Bird, bird, bird. Do da bird, bird, bird," Russo sings in my ear. I bust out laughing again. We go into our routine, "Pa-pa-pa-pa-pa oo mau-mau, pa-pa oo mau-mau. Everybody do da bird, da bird, bird, bird." And we flap our arms like chicken wings. "Bird, bird, bird. The bird is the word. Bird, bird, bird." Mama gives us a look.

"Yeah," Uncle tells Auntie, "Das what I said, Bert. Big Bert went write da speech, eh?"

Mo worse me and Russo no can stop laughing and flapping our papa-oo-mau-mau-everybody's-doing-da-bird wings. And by now all the high maka maka pa-kes stay looking at our table and pointing. A couple are flapping too. Wing Duck Chu, the funeral parlor guy, get one bolohead he stay trying to hide by combing all his hair straight down in front and greased into a point. He look like da Count. You don't forget hair like that. He somehow reminds me of *larp ahp*, the greasy Chinese salted duck: a pale, white bird salted and flattened and half-dried, the meat tough like leather. There's something spooky about *larp ahp*, the color I imagine of all those dead bodies he handles.

I start to giggle because I'm reminded of Daffy Duck and Looney Tunes cartoons, I don't know why. I think of Mr. Chu closing up each coffin saying, "Ah-bee-ya. Ah-bee-ya, ah-bee-ya . . . duh, duh, duh, dat's all folks!" in a Porky Pig voice. Mr. Chu is looking at me now because I'm trying so hard not to laugh, my stomach hurts and Russo is getting the look from my muddah and he's hitting me in the side to shut up.

Russo used to tell me that all those dried things in the Chinese grocery were the dried up toads you saw on the road. They would clean um up and they'd end up as *larp ahp* or *hahm gnee* or *pei dahn*, duck or salted fish or thousand year old eggs. Everytime we went to a store in Chinatown, I'd look around and try to see if any of the dried things were toads. I couldn't tell. They were all dried and salty, like Daddy, like Ah Goong, like all the fancy pa-kes. All too salty for Uncle's taste. Too salty for me.

Daddy no say nutting to Fish Uncle. I no can tell if he's drunk or pissed. His words stay stuck. I know he's scared to say anything, scared of sounding like one Texan. He finishes his whiskey and goes back to the big-shot table. All salty.

Uncle holds out his teacup. I am careful not to spill hot tea over his hand as he motions me to fill it.

The fish course comes out of the kitchen, a mullet steaming on a platter, peanut oil still crackling; the scent of scalded Chinese parsley and green onions mixed with the shoyu rises with everyone's quick intake of breath.

Aunty Etto sticks a chopstick into the swirl of peanut oil and shoyu and sucks on the end, "Da shoyu not low salt."

Everyone laughs and chatters, "Das awright Aunty, fo today, can use da salty one."

"Ah, steam fish," somebody says, and Uncle is already dividing fish into flaky portions. The head and the tail remain until Uncle pushes the platter around the table, "Errybody had nuff to eat?" He lifts it as if to clear the lazy Susan then tilts the rest into his plate. We only hear sucking sounds from him for a while and the splutter as he spits out the scales and bones into his rice bowl. I wait for the eyeballs to clatter into his bowl and I imagine them rolling around the bottom of his rice bowl. He sees me watching him and swirls the pearls around his bowl a couple of times and tells me, "Good fish. Now he's a blind mullet . . . hee, hee, hee."

By the end of the meal, Uncle is leaning back in his chair sucking air through his teeth and vigorously digging the remaining bits of scale and fish head from his teeth. He rinses his mouth with tea, swallows, then sends me to the cashier to get him another toothpick. Daddy is glaring at me from the big-shot table because some other old Chinese guy is talking. I shrug and point to Fish Uncle. When I bring back Uncle's toothpick, I find a quarter next to my teacup. He sucks his teeth and laughs, looking me over, "Still too skinny to sell to da Filipinos. Eat, boy. Eat." He stands, turns to the podium and puts his aloha shirt back on. Amazingly the speeches end at the same time and while everyone else is applauding, he announces to Aunty, "Time to go home, Mommy." Aunty gathers her sweater from her seatback and hustles after Uncle. He sticks his head into the double swinging door to the kitchen, "*Hau, hau. Gum do.* Delicious and plenty. Next time, I bring you fish and you make sweet sour style," he says.

"No, no," the cook protests, "the fish you bring is too precious to spoil with sweet sour sauce."

"How can I tell if you're any good," Uncle teases, "unless you cook me a fish with some sauce? Anybody can steam a fish." The waitresses laugh.

"See if I can cook. Huh!" the cook puffs. "I will cook you a crab sauce next time. Crab and sweet scallops."

"Okay, okay. Next time you cook dat for me," Uncle says and winks at me.

"Bring your wallet," the cook says, "I don't know if you can afford my cooking." The waitresses are hanging around to see if Uncle can get in the last word.

"I donno," he says. "Maybe I have to bring two fish, in case you spoil da first one." Everyone laughs but the thought of fish with crab sauce lingers. We remember the time at one of Ah Goong's dinners when Uncle brought three small kumu and a mullet, and they came back to our tables caught in a net carved from a turnip and the mullet fried into a leaping arch held up by a wooden chopstick garnished with carrot crabs in a sea of shredded cabbage and steamed kumu. Auntie made everyone wait until she took a picture.

Uncle's the big shot now and I look up at the head table way at the front of the room. Daddy looks small and far away.

3. Measuring the Speed of Light, a Trick with Mirrors

The quantum connection, persists between any two particles that have once interacted by ordinary means . . . in effect, after two particles interact in a conventional way, they move apart outside the range of interaction, the particles continue to influence each other instantaneously via a real connection, which joins them together with undiminished strength no matter how far apart they may roam. . . . A quantum particle seems to 'leave a part of itself' in everything it touches, a part to which it always retains instant access.

— NICK HERBERT, *Faster Than Light,* 1988

By now Daddy look small and sad. He giving Russo orders to ask for take-out boxes to take home the leftovers and no use too many boxes cause cost quartah extra but no jes jam anykine food togedda. Only certain tings can go with certain stuff, den let errybody take home one box if dey like. And whatevah leftover take um to our car, no foget da bottle likker coming home wit us. I kinda feel sad fo him especially when Russo gimme da Neopolitan signal. He put his hand inside his shirt and make like Napoleon whenever Daddy start acting like one short, swell-head dictator. Except when he first told me dis, I nevah know what dat was. I tawt he said "Neopolitan," j'like da ice cream, cause Russo always eat all da chocolate part, da ding-a-ling. Anyways he giving me da Neopolitan signal but not funny to me anymore.

It's not a good way to remember your father. A lifetime of shrinking, as if he's been getting farther and farther away. By the time I sit down to ask him to tell me his story, I am already 35 and he is 71 and we are light years apart. I've studied a little physics: the state of entropy, randomness; things at rest tend to stay at rest, things in motion tend to stay in motion; *que sera sera*. I never quite figured out relativity: time, the absolute, turns out to be relative. If you travel at the speed of light, could you come back before you started? If you went out your front door and walked in a straight-line, would you eventually end up at your back door? Time dilation and length contraction. Moving clocks run slow so by the time I had returned from college, Daddy seemed a lot older.

And if moving yardsticks got shorter traveling at the speed of light, I suppose from his vantage point, returning from a mainland college after only a year away made me smaller.

The weekend before I went off to college, my father sat me down in the kitchen. He told me, don't be afraid to speak up, talk good English, and don't come home with a haole wife. I don't remember exactly how he did it but I got the message just fine.

"Bumbye you get tied down with one wife and kids and you all jam up." *Yeah, yeah. No worry. I know, Daddy. I know.*

I attended Case Institute of Technology in Cleveland where, after making you buy the class tie, an ugly-striped number in brown and orange, they tell you that two Case physicists, Michelson and Morley, measured the speed of light in 1887 in a lab along the train tracks. Michelson and Morley had really hoped to find something else, an ether that slowed or speeded up the speed of light according to the direction of the earth's rotation. Existence of the ether would confirm the principles of Newtonian physics. When they failed to find evidence of the ether, the need for an alternate explanation, Einstein's, arose. This was the paradigm shift, that quantum leap of knowledge (or was it mostly faith) that transformed how we viewed the world. It must've been a trick with mirrors. I saw pictures of the two men looking dapper in three-piece suits and hats, thick mustaches, cocky and confident, the way my father looked in his wedding picture, the way I was in 1968 when I showed up in Cleveland. Local boy takes on the Midwest. I couldn't imagine such an experiment, the air wasn't clear enough. It was thick, like an ether. All the time I was there, I felt disoriented. Sometimes I'd wake up and think the long plane ride had been a trick: this place was really somewhere around Kaimuki except colder. I had just gotten on the wrong bus and had ended up in Cleveland. I rode the train often. Maybe I was hoping to find the one that would take me back home. Sometimes I'd ride backwards in the last car and watch the lights and stations rush away from me, just a particle in the measurement of space and time.

Daddy was talking and I wasn't listening. He was nervous, began to talk Texan. I snickered at the idea of coming home with a girlfriend or wife, is that all he's worried about? So it's okay to talk like one haole, just don't marry one?

We were all measuring ourselves against the light. Michelson, apparently unconvinced, spent the rest of his life repeating the experiment, not once getting a different result.

Seventeen years later, on the pretense of doing an oral history for a graduate course, I sit down with a tape recorder and ask my father to tell me about the "olden days." We arrange ourselves awkwardly around the desk in Russo's old bedroom so that we don't have to look directly at each other. When I look up, I see the family photos on the vanity. Others are reflected in the mirror from the top of the dresser across the room: Mama and Daddy in their wedding photo, Daddy looks young and slick, the photo is sepia toned and hand painted, he's wearing Oxfords, a loud tie with a crane flapping in the front; the dramatic sweep of hair, a cocky smile. He has the confidence and patter to sell hundreds of refrigerators and ranges in a year and still keep the shine on his shoes. Mama looks demure, slender in a heavy brocade jacket and more serious, a curly bob and a half hat pinned in her hair. There's another with our entire family: Russo and Daddy flanking Mama who holds me, my forefinger poking my fat, two-year-old cheek. The background looks fake, a seamless mottled grey but my hair is slicked into the same wave as my father. Russo at 8 or 9 years old wears a ragged crew cut and a contrasty Hawaiian print aloha shirt probably in red or dark blue because it photographs nearly black in the picture. Daddy is wearing a silky Japanese print aloha shirt and Mama looks practical in a shirtwaist dress. We look nearly all-American, like

Homer Price's family. Through the mirror, a picture of my Ah Goong, my father's father, in a coat and tie with a feather boutonnière, his shock of thick white hair mowed close at the sides, metal-rimmed glasses with tortoise shell at the top. He is tall, thin, and stately. And there's the one with Ah Po Lee, my mother's mother, flanked by her eight children, no sign of my grandfather. Mama stands by her side, the youngest at four or five, distinguished by a huge bow in her hair nearly the size of her head.

The interview is going badly. My father has a poor memory of his immigration and early childhood but can remember nearly every job and supervisor he's had in his entire life. He remembered every injustice, every slight, every unfair act that each boss has done to him. Instead I ask about Ah Goong. My grandfather, it appears, was involved in countless moneymaking schemes throughout his life, most which failed miserably. But Daddy says Ah Goong's enterprising nature taught him to take chances, "When you see an opportunity, you gotta grab it." I wonder if you have to be this optimistic to sell appliances.

Apparently my grandfather grabbed at any opportunity to make money, joined any number of huis, invested in stores, real estate, and business deals. When Ah Goong and his friends saw how much money the Princess Theater was taking in, they started a theater of their own. But even my father ended up at the competition when he played hooky from Chinese school on Saturdays because they had the Westerns with silent stars Tom Mix or William Hart. Ah Goong was the principal but never noticed him missing from Chinese school? Or the kids calling him "Cowboy"? Didn't he see the new swagger in Daddy's step like Bronco Billy's? My father loved the Wild West so much he later invested his money in Montana ranches, Las Vegas land, and Alaskan oil wells. None struck.

He has prepared a list of names and dates for me which ends in a cryptic list: *Obstacles I had to overcome—shyness, lack of confidence, lack of communication between father and mother, participations in school, confusions and don't know who to turn to.*

The list goes on. *Major Breakthru: YMCA formation of boys club, affiliation with Beretania Church with religion, health, participations, competition and challenges in sports and life closely related. Objectives and philosophies; accept and copy (if can) how others do it and succeed.*

Somewhere midway through the list, he speaks directly into the tape recorder and says, "I try to teach my sons the things I learned from my experience but my biggest regret is that they never learned how to speak Chinese." It's been only fifteen minutes and already I'm embarrassed and ashamed. He's going down his list of aphorisms like the old master on "Kung

Fu," *Ah, Little Grasshopper, always take business courses so you have someting to fall back on.*

> *You gotta have connections to get ahead in the world.*
> *Speak up. Talk good English.*
> *How you gonna learn if you don't ask?*
> *You gotta be aggressive if you wanna get ahead.*

I'm not much better with my mother. Auntie Esta says that Ma could sing, that she sang in the McKinley Glee Club. I've never heard my mother sing. Not the Andrews Sisters, not Rosemary Clooney, not How-Much-Is-That-Doggie-in-the-Window Doris Day. Ma just clears her throat when I ask her about it, no song emerges. She just says that choir was easier than taking band. She didn't want to lug around an instrument, she'd have to take the streetcar home and she hated riding it, made her carsick. I still couldn't imagine her singing. I imagine my father with the rest of the St. Louis boys sitting at the back of the auditorium at a school concert picking her out of the back row of the choir, laughing and poking each other and deciding right then and there that he was going to marry her. He wouldn't tell her this of course, but I'm sure he had a plan to win her. He saw everything that way: a game, a strategy, and a large measure of good luck. Being in the right place at the right time . . . being under the basket when the pass came . . . being there when they called the winning lucky number. It became a credo he'd repeat to us all his life: *timing is everything, you gotta be at the right place at the right time.*

And all I can think of is the fine print, *Must be present to win,* on the back of his winning raffle ticket after he has given up and gone home before the last number is called. He is at the right place at the right time when he collapses at the YMCA while Emergency Medical Technicians are training in the gym upstairs. They take him to Queens Hospital in minutes. Then he lies in Emergency waiting to see a doctor for two hours as his speech leaves him. I try to get him water, but the nurse says, "No"; try to remove the neck brace, but the nurse says, "No"; try to get the doctor, but the nurse says, "Soon."

I call his own doctor and am told he will call me back. I watch him utter his last request in the Emergency Room for water, so thirsty, water. And I can't even give him that.

How many times have I replayed the scene: I throw a tantrum, I charm the nurse, I call his doctor back and curse. The emergency room doctors behind each curtain seem to be unhurried, attending to patients who can speak: a broken arm, a strain, a stitch. I think to wheel him out of there because, "Dammit, this is my dad and if you can't help him now, I'm taking him where he can get some help!" Years later I will read stories about complete recoveries from strokes if you get medication that reduces the swelling in the brain within the first hour. I will be reminded that I blew his hour.

I hold his hand, talk to him, watch his eyes alert and scared, his mouth slack on one side, trying, I know, to make his tongue and lips form words that I can understand. He's been doing that all his life. Never realizing that it's me who's never learned the language. He will raise one arm again and again to signal something to me but his goddamn, good-fo-nutting son no can even help him. He wants to smack me. How many scenes of dying has he seen in those Tom Mix movies? Like William Hart, John Ford, or Bronco Billy Anderson, dying brave, silent, like a real cowboy.

Perhaps he hears mama singing.

THE QUIETEST SINGING

PART THREE

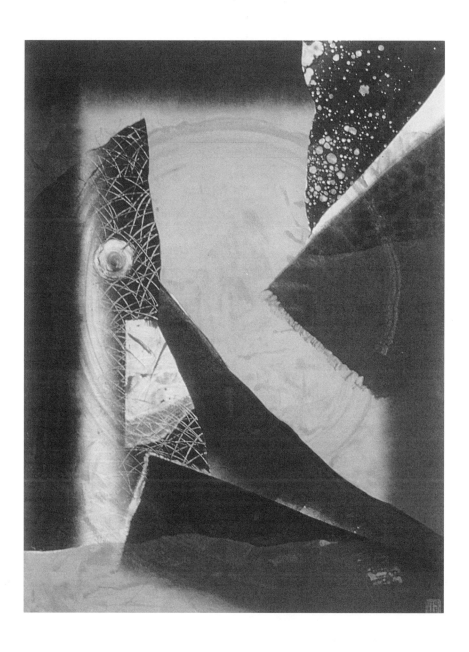

from *The Folding Cliffs*

The Folding Cliffs tells the story of a Hawaiian couple, Pi'ilani and Ko'olau, and their young son Kaleimanu, just over a hundred years ago. Ko'olau, a cowboy, locally famous as a crack shot, is found to have leprosy, and he and his wife know that their child is likewise afflicted. Ordered to prepare to be sent to the leprosy settlement at Kalaupapa on the island of Moloka'i, Ko'olau and his family go instead to join a band of fugitives from that verdict, in the deep, remote, and all but inaccessible valley of Kalalau, on the north coast of Kaua'i. There, in the cliffs, Ko'olau holds off the officials who go to the valley to force the fugitives to surrender and be taken away. Finally only Ko'olau, Pi'ilani and their child are left in the valley, and they live on there alone. The child dies, and then Ko'olau, and Pi'ilani buries them and lives there all by herself for some time before returning to her own family on the west coast of the island. The story begins with her return to the graves, upon hearing, not for the first time, a rumor that Ko'olau's has been discovered.

— W. S. MERWIN

I.vii

A light rain reached down to her face the fringe of a mist
    there was no color yet in the ghost dawn but around her
through the full consonance of the stream came here and there
    clear voices opening as she passed close to them
trills telling of water questions not continued
    some of the voices were lights flying beside her
the amakihi a yellow brilliance the olokele
    a flicker of scarlet but the light was the complete gray
before daybreak with the black bands of the trees floating
    through it then before a condensation of green seeped
into the tall reaches of the valley opening ahead of her
    the house appeared Halemanu at the end of a long rise
with the lifted shell of high trees raised above it
    the mountain palm towering behind and as her feet

brushed the wet grass she saw the four pale long uprights
of the verandah the new wide steps leading up to it
and the dark arms of the house reaching forward toward her
someone was there the smell of woodsmoke floated in the mist
and as she stepped forward a small light passed at a window
she stopped and watched and a woman came out with no light
and stood at the top of the steps a tall figure in a long gown
the hair built high on her head the same color as the hour

I.xiv

She looked into the fire until Anne was wondering whether
she had forgotten where she was but then at last she said
—They are telling me again three times now someone has said to me
that he has been found that the grave has been discovered
and they have dug him up and have taken his bones and his gun—
Who told you that—Anne asked—Kekaha people—Pi'ilani said
—One of them whispered to my mother but said not to tell me—
Where did they hear it—Anne asked—One said he heard it
in town from somebody he had not seen there for
a long time—What kind of person—He told me it was
nobody from here but they know all about how to
sell things like that and who will give money for them—
Did he tell you any names—Anne asked—No names—Pi'ilani said
—Nobody's names ever but they talked about his gun
how his gun had been found somebody had dug it up
and his bones—Did you talk about this with anyone else—
No—Pi'ilani said—I never said anything
only that nobody knows the place where I left them—

I.xvi

How utterly still she sat as she was saying it all
Anne thought and then Pi'ilani went on—There was
so much talk and talk when I came out of the valley
back to Kekaha the first time they had been talking
ever since we had left and they believed themselves
each of them telling something else that was nothing
playing cards with their own stories that they said were us
so the bets got big and they asked me one thing or another

and I would not know what they had inside their heads
      that had been growing there while they knew nothing about us
when we were in Kalalau talking to nobody
      except each other those years while day by day there were
more things that we did not have to say or that we
      did not want to say again and what we said lasted—
Did you see no one at all—Anne asked—After they were all taken
      out of the valley—Pi'ilani said—sometimes we heard voices
sometimes maybe voices of people we had known sometimes
      calling our names sometimes talking about us but
never seeing us they always sounded like echoes
      even when they were close to us and I have learned since
that friends came looking for us at the beginning
      bringing food for us and clothes but they did not find us
it was only our own voices that made no echoes—

                              I.xxiv

—You walked all night—Anne said—There is till a long way to go—
      Pi'ilani answered—I want to be down there
in the valley before it gets dark—She took off
      the borrowed shawl folded it on the bench and lifted
her old black steaming wrap from in front of the fire
      and slung it around her shoulders Maka'e came in
and embraced her again and then Pi'ilani
      turned to Anne—Good-bye—she said and they kissed near
      the cheeks
with the distance in place between them like a pane of glass
      that had always been there and Pi'ilani stepped out
into the sunlight that changed her into the color
      of a shadow and she went down the nine steps like a shadow
and up the trail among the old trees and was gone and there were
      only the trees as Anne stood looking and she could almost
see what she had known there and would not see again
      faces and garments in the sunlight of the early days
husband children friends certain that it was all theirs
      the certainty swelling their voices as they sang
their hymns under those trees on the mountain repeating
      their claim to the wilderness she kept holding off
memories of Valdemar who knew so much Vally
      so much older than she was showing her the skulls

he had dug up at Manaulepu many years
　　before he had known her it had all been for science
she recited a psalm Blessed is the man she said
　　stiffening slightly as she stood there becoming the severe
bony old woman her grandchildren would not like
　　she heard a step on the boards and nobody was there
and she remembered the time soon after they were married
　　when he was away from home at the legislature
and she heard footsteps that the servants told her
　　were the sound of a spirit but she had gone out
with a lantern and seen the night heron fly off over
　　the garden and she smiled because she took no stock in such
　　things

I.xxxix

She was sure now as she lifted the tangle of branches
　　guava and then oʻhiʻa and kopiko remembering
Kawaluna looking at her steadily each time
　　and then shaking her head and saying—You know that nobody
has found him—and yet Piʻilani had come each time
　　to see what she knew the litter of moss and brittle twigs
undisturbed the russet fur along the fern fronds
　　untouched the sunlight floating on patches beyond
reach she say it all in her mind as she came up
　　between the rocks and there was no path there were no
footprints or broken shoots and then the hollow in the crag
　　and the corner into it and she saw the place before her
almost as she had seen it in her mind only
　　a little changed in itself a little estranged
giving off no sign that it knew she was standing there
　　the shadows whispering among themselves the cliffs
with their backs to her the new growth on all sides not
　　knowing her it was what she had known and been sure of
she stood watching the ragged light scattered across the leaves
　　tears were running down her face and under her breath
from the center of her body she chanted to the place
　　Kalua i Koʻolau nobody knows where you are
nobody has found you nobody has found you

IV.xxiii

—But that was long ago at the beginning—the Judge said
    —back when you were at the Pastor's school and at that time
none of us knew what went on there and the constables
    kept rounding up lepers and shipping them over
dropping them off at Waikolu along the coast
    to find their way to the grass roofs at Kalaupapa
some of them scarcely able to stand and they say that in less
    than a year two hundred of them had been thrown out like that
and the inhabitants could not feed them or shelter them
    but were crowded out of their own fields and houses
with lepers everywhere lying sitting hobbling begging
    until those who had lived there left the peninsula
where they had been born and they shipped out or climbed the cliffs
    into the rest of the world when it seemed that the world
was gone and the lepers moved into their empty houses
    and ate up whatever had been left there and they brewed
alcohol from the sweet potatoes and lay around
    naked so that the place became known on the island
as the crazy pen but the Board of Health kept sending
    more of them from Kalihi in Honolulu
putting up shelters and buildings sending a doctor
    and rations of meat and taro root so much a head
and not much of either and as for anything else
    they wore their rags while those lasted and were lucky
to have one scrap of blanket on that rainy coast
    and I hear the crippled were given nothing to eat
unless they did their share of the daily grave-digging
    and when it came to coffins those who had no money
were buried without them and this priest Damien says that
    he has seen a body dug up by the pigs and eaten
some died alone and unnoticed for days some forgot
    who they were and wandered into complete mindlessness
but now they tell me that with the mission it is better
    with more food and a hospital but just the same nobody
would go there willingly and now there are hundreds of them
    dragged away by the constables as your sister was—

Hon W D Smith Pres Bd of Health Honolulu
    Sir in accordance with your request herewith a complete list
of the residents of the valley of Kalalau there are
    twenty three households four of which consist of only
one old man each In nine households no leprosy
    is visable sic to a casual observer
in three households all the inmates are afflicted with leprosy
    while in eleven underlined households the inmates
are part lepers and part non-lepers the population
    numbers one hundred and two with seventy four apparently
non-lepers twenty eight lepers eighteen of them male
    eighteen adults ten minors only six rifles
could be heard of and only three of these are available
    one of them belongs to a non-leper the lepers do not wish
to be taken away as they believe the new Japanese
    doctor at Kilauea may be able to cure some of them
J Kauai and Paoa are the two lepers most likely
    to give trouble it is my belief that if these two
and perhaps one or two others were removed most underlined
    of the others would go voluntarily I also believe
that these leaders could be taken with a small force
    two or three men like Sam Ku with what material
we have here would do Two weeks later after Stolz's own visit
    he wrote again to Hon W D Smith now
Attorney General Dear Sir in accordance with your
    instructions I went to Kalalau and interviewed
most of the lepers six of the reported cases
    I would not undertake to move some of them I am sure
being non-lepers As for their going peacefully
    my trip was only a partial success the majority
among whom is J Kauai desire to go and will
    make no trouble but about four or five of the young
strong fellows say they will not go while as many more
    were non-committal the amount and kind of intimacy
existing between lepers and non-lepers at Kalalau
    is simply abominable I believe there will be fifty cases
of leprosy in consequence of lepers having been
    allowed to remain in Kalalau Then three weeks later

he wrote again that eighteen of the lepers had decamped
    for parts unknown including J Kauai they had vanished
into the tangle of ravines up at the foot of the cliffs

VI.xxxx

Without Kaleimanu to take care of any more
    and keep warm and carry with them it was easier to move
around the valley and to her it seemed too easy
    as though she had been cut adrift and was floating away
but Ko'olau's feet were much worse after the day
    when he climbed the cliff and after they buried Kaleimanu
the torn sores were deeper and they never stopped bleeding
    and rotten water came out of them and she saw him
walking on the open sores of his feet as his feet shrank back
    and when he walked he left prints of blood and fluid and rags
of flesh trailed behind his footsteps then she took pieces
    of clothes that were falling apart and she washed them in the
    stream
and wrapped them around his feet and he cut a stick to walk with
    —We do not have to travel very far or move very fast
the way we live—she said and it was a summer of plenty
    they watched friends of theirs come and rebuild their houses
and take care of the fruit trees beside their taro ponds
    and there were fruit trees wild or untended up through the valley
fern shoots and shellfish from the streams and he still carried
    the rifle from one sleeping place to the next and it lay
within reach at night but she saw the way he held it now
    distantly absently as though he had forgotten it
the kamani stick that he used for walking was nearer
    to his mind and grasp than the rifle seemed to be
and they had hidden the other guns months before that
    she saw that his hands were curling tighter the fingers
shrivelling until it was awkward for him to eat
    and he picked up more things with the heels of his hands
but he seemed almost well that summer although he was weaker
    than she had ever believed he could be and in
the evenings they would sit in the dark as the coals
    closed themselves in the ashes and they would say nothing

for a long time and then find that they had been thinking
of the same thing and they would talk of what they remembered
without sadness or it seemed to be without sadness
and then would be silent again and she would start to chant
under her breath patting a shell or her knee bringing the chant
out of the darkness around them and offering it
to the darkness ahead of them and she thought of his face
as it was crumbling into itself that summer and autumn
and winter and when they slept to the sound of the rain
some nights she dreamed of white sand and voices along the shore

VII.11

She remembered Kaleimanu saying that he was falling
asleep before he died and his face was in front of her
all during the days when she could see Koʻolau
sinking from beside her those months when he was going
the same way the child had gone it was more than seven months
like that and at the beginning of that time he could
still talk to her as they had always talked and they stayed
close in their words but later when he tried to talk to her
it sounded as though he were calling from a long way off
in a hoarse voice though there was a day in one of those long
spells
of green sunlight and fragrance and stillness that arrive sometimes
in the winter with the drops shining at the end of the leaves
when he spoke to her again from no distance and told her
that after he was gone he wanted her to bury
his rifle with him because he said she had never been
the one who had used it and it would stay in the ground with him
afterward and that then she should leave the valley
and go back to Kekaha and their house and families
and when she was questioned she should tell them the truth
that she had stayed with him and their child as she had always
said she would do and as she had promised to do
when they were married and that she had killed no one
but had come with him and stayed with him until the end
and when she had buried him in that ground where she way lying
and had left him there in the sleep of the seasons

and gone down the stream through the trees and close to the
     houses
of people she knew who had come back and had passed by there
     down into the sea and out through the turning of the waves
and had lain there again looking up at the clouds and the stars
     that appeared and vanished between them she stepped out
onto the rocks and went around by the side of the valley
     to leave no trail and went to a spot near a side stream
where there was a thicket of lantana next to the water
     near a path that led along by the taro ponds
a place where she could be hidden from everyone
     but look out and see them and hear what they were saying
and she crawled into the deep thicket and made a bed there
     and slept alone for the first time in the valley
wanting to be near some of the people she knew
     but not wanting to show herself to them not yet not yet

VII.xv

Half waking again knowing that she was in the valley
     but under a roof once more she lay still in the darkness
it seemed to her that she felt nothing and knew no names
     no stories and that she was flying without moving
in a night without stars without end without morning
     or memory and then she thought This is the grave
that is not a grave this is the wind that is not air
     this is where they will never find us and even as
she thought it she knew that she was Pi'ilani
     in the house of their friends Kelau and Keapoulu
her hand was touching the black grass of the wall and she knew
     why she was there with Kuala sleeping outside
and then she slept and woke knowing that it was near day
     and she got up and went out to watch the clouds trailing
their long arms across the sky showing a fragment
     with its stars in their places fading as she looked
and then closing over them again and the dark valley
     under them seemed to her like the sleep of a child
closed in itself then she heard the grass rustle in the door
     and Keapoulu whisper behind her—Sister—

and they stood together at the edge of the rock platform
    with their arms around each other and then sat down
and Keapoulu began to tell her who they should visit
    and Pi'ilani spoke of friends she had seen in the valley
when she was alone and living in the lantana thicket
    listening to them and Keapoulu told her
which taro ponds they were working now and which families
    had rebuilt their houses and had babies and who was fishing
down in the caves and out in the bay and she said
    they were dancing again up on the temple platforms
three of the teachers were back and the children went up there
    almost every day and danced the way they used to
and Kelau came out and joined them and told Pi'ilani
    who was planting new fruit trees beside the ponds there would be
more oranges than before and papayas on the banks
    and mangos in the lower places and tamarinds near the shore
—It is beginning over again—he said as the first
    daylight revealed the valley below them under the trees
and she thought of all of them waking there and of going
    down there herself and them seeing her as she was now

Secrets

He got out of the van and waved at Janie. She blew him a kiss. He didn't notice the spiral of dust as she drove off. He seemed detached—already on his way toward the ridge.

The dirt road was much as he remembered except that grass and a stunted growth of lantana encroached on the wheel tracks. He loved the grass the way it was now, tall and pink in its seed-time. In the past he had watched its many moods—how the wind traveled across and darkened it in streaks, how the color changed from season to season. There were more guava shrubs now. The fruit was ripe and falling, the smashed yellow and pink rinds along the way—birds and rats had had a feast. The smell of fermented guava hung in the still air. It would be hot later without the wind.

On the edge of the forest, the first sweep of emotion struck him. In the chest and belly—a strong and airy presence. There was throbbing. A mixture of anticipation and fear, he thought. And a small trace of hope. He couldn't for a moment remember just why he was walking there. That is, what his real reason was. He knew only that he wanted to come, that he had been impelled by some secret force. Janie had seemed to understand. Perhaps she understood more, but she hadn't said.

In the trees, the old road dwindled away. He had to trust his remembrance and sense of direction. He walked on for 20 or 30 minutes, quite certain he was going the right way, although nothing seemed at all familiar, except the kinds of trees and plants—the eucalyptus, the small ohia, a few large old koa and a scattering of kukui. It had always been a curiously mixed forest.

Sweat began to drip into his eyes. He pulled out the red bandana Janie had given him and tied it around his forehead. For a few minutes he rested on a fragment of an old Hawaiian wall—walls ran all through this country. The silence and heat were oppressive. He remembered that a heavy stillness often dominated the forest. The land in this particular place dipped into a hollow; it held the air like water in a stagnant pool. Just the other side of the hollow and up the slope was the abandoned road. Years ago, farmers and Hawaiians had used it as a short cut to avoid the road which followed the precipitous profile of the coast.

He took a sip from his canteen and started out again, climbing the slope. The earth, which was never quite dry in this area, steamed. Sometimes he slipped, falling almost to his knees. He realized he was winded—he was pushing too hard. He would be glad to reach the ridge and the sea air. About half way up, the going became rougher because of pieces of *aa*, clinkery and crumbling. There were a few hard water-smoothed rocks. He tried to hop from stone to stone to avoid the mud underneath. He steadied himself on the thick branches of guava. By the time he reached the ridge, the sun was lower in the sky than he had realized. The walk had taken longer, soon the one night he had allotted would be upon him.

At the top of the slope he moved toward the sea, some five or six miles distant. That was the way he remembered it—the old road and the village straggling along the ridge. After a ten minute walk he saw a cluster of large mango trees ahead. His heart commenced a heavy painful beat, and tears came to his eyes. Strange that the emotion should be this strong after so much time. In the clump of mangoes there used to be an old house stained green. Inside the house were the splintered frames of a wooden sofa, a broken rocker and a table with one leg missing. He had tried to get his father to help him carry the table home. But father had said with unusual roughness that the things did not belong to the family.

He planned to go straight to the house and set up his little camp there. It had been his favorite of the half-dozen deserted buildings in the area. He used to sit on the dusty floor and imagine old men and women minding babies, children climbing mango trees to eat the green fruit, a young woman washing clothes, someone pounding poi. The only trace of these people was their empty houses with broken sticks of furniture.

The clump of mangoes was thicker and darker than before. Underneath the trees, the earth was bare except for a few shriveled brown fruit. Flowers, which used to be kept neatly in beds, had grown wild throughout the lawn. He looked for the house. He couldn't see it. Was his memory playing tricks? —surely this was the place for the house. He moved closer. The lava rock steps were there; the foundation was there. Beyond the steps lay a sagging heap of lumber through which weeds and grasses grew. He wanted to cry. But he sat on the steps and put his head in his hands. Why hadn't he thought of this—of the erosion of time? He knew that the other houses too must have collapsed. The lives, which he had once imagined there, could no longer exist. When walls fell in on each other and only stone steps remained, the people had truly gone. They could walk up the stairs—but only to a jagged heap of lumber. They had no space. In the distance the sea hummed faintly. The dusk came heavily through the trees.

He removed his backpack and took out the thermos of coffee. He drank the sweet bitter coffee slowly. Janie had made it just right. He then put his backpack by the side of the steps. He wanted to explore the village before it was too dark.

Where some of the houses had been, little was left; splintered termite-eaten boards, piles of stone. No walls remained standing. The banana and mango trees were lush. And the old soursop tree still stood in the yard of the red house. Years ago he had taken soursop fruits home, and his mother had made delicious chiffon pies. He had watched her cut through the snowy white pulp, he had smelled it cooking. There had been fruits then he seldom saw now, the surinam cherries, the starfruit. A vague inner feeling arose in him: he began to wish that he hadn't come. Such places as the village are better off in memory; only there do they remain the same. He walked heavily back to the green house, hardly aware of what he was doing. The dusk thickened.

He moved his backpack onto an open grassy spot. Gladiolas and periwinkle gone wild sprouted all about. He took out the blanket and spread it on the grass. Then he opened the plastic container Janie had prepared. He munched on fried chicken and rice balls. When he finished, he cleaned up the trash and put it at some distance away under a rock. He scratched a bit of earth around and over it.

Returning to the blanket, he stretched out. The fragrance of the mountains was all about him—that special green-pungent smell. Only Hawaiian mountains had that smell. In California and certain parts of the south of France the pine dominated the air—sharp, sweet and resinous. In Greece the bare mountains smelled of hot, dry rock and wild herbs. He had never known the smell of snowy mountains. This green-acrid Hawaiian smell was in his memory and in his blood. In the Hawaiian mountains, waterfalls slid over moss and had deep still pools at the bottom. The sound of birds was always there, yet one seldom saw the flutter of a wing. Ferns so deep a man couldn't walk through. . . . Ancient lava flows. Lichen, all kinds of lichen. Stone walls wandering everywhere.

He was afraid to allow too much to come back. It made him feel guilty all over again. And angry. Mother was always in the doorway peeking anxiously—her hands always stained with fruit and earth. His father riding down the mountain slope on his horse, stinking of horse and saddle; his father like a giant, threatening at times and distant at others. . . .

A voice startled him. "Eh, Kimo! Long time you no come!"

He jumped up to peer through the darkness. The old man stood exactly as he had thirty years before. His white hair ruffled, his blue jeans stretched tight over the muscles of his strong thighs, his palaka shirt faded. "Mr. Kahalewai! I didn't know you were still here."

"I stay. Where you been?"

Kimo didn't know quite what to say. "Pretty much everywhere, I guess. But I wanted to come back."

"I hear you marry that Rapozo girl, then get divorced."

"Yeah, I did."

"Then I hear no more nothing about you."

"I go the mainland to university. Then work. I marry one other *wahine*, Janie."

"You get any *keiki?*"

"Only one, she died, she *ma-ke*."

"Oh, I sorry."

"But look at you! Just the same."

"Sure, us old folk, we no change. Hey, you come my house tonight. Humbug sleep out here. Plenty mosquitoes. We get one extra bed. Come on, pick up your stuff."

Kimo stuffed his things in the backpack. Mr. Kahalewai started down the road. He flashed his light along the way. The path was rocky and sticky weeds grew at the side. Kimo recognized very little.

They went to a house Kimo could not remember, small and brown. Inside, kerosene lanterns cast a dim orange light on the table and chairs. One had a red glass shade over it. Old calendars hung on the wall, some with dried leis draped over them. On a small round table with a crocheted cover were the pictures of the family. Mr. Kahalewai pointed to them—"All *ma-ke* now. Only Roselani and me left."

Mrs. Kahalewai brought a plate of hot beef stew and a bowl of poi. He ate to please her, although he had already had Janie's chicken. Mr. Kahalewai wanted to talk.

"You know that house where I find you? Well, old Antone Freitas live there long time ago. He your father's uncle. You know?"

He didn't know. Father never talked much. Kimo had always been wary of the secretiveness. "When I was a kid, I used to go in that house. They left some furniture behind."

"After Antone *ma-ke*, his daughter Marie and her little girl live there. They call the little girl Violet. Then one day the two of them go away. They just leave the house like that."

"When I was a kid, no one lived in any of the houses in the village."

"Yeah, everybody move away. This place too far from everything. Nobody want stay."

"I remember meeting you once on the road. You look just like you are now. You no change."

"I been old a long time. A long long time. Some of us just hang on."

"You know my father?"

"Yeah, I know him. From kid time."

"I was in Europe when he died."

"Yeah, you no come home for funeral." He paused. Then went on, "That Violet, now, she became a singer. She sing in the nightclubs in Honolulu. Make plenty of money. Big name. She call herself Nohelani. She get fat now, but she can sing."

"Mr. Kahalewai, they no tell me my father was dying. The funeral was over when I heard. That's why I no come."

"He smoke too much, he get cancer."

"I wonder why they no tell me."

"Your father no want, I think." The old man talked about Kimo's father, and Kimo saw him again, stern and rigid, remote. On his horse he was another kind of person—a part of the animal and of the mountains, the wind. "Your father number one paniolo. No one could ride a horse like him. . . . Only thing, sometimes he was mean. He get mad and shout. No can blame him. He get tough time in his kid time."

Kimo wanted to ask more, but Mr. Kahalewai said abruptly, "Time for us old folk to go to bed. You can sleep in the extra bedroom. Everything clean. Mother keeps everything too clean."

Mrs. Kahalewai kissed Kimo and turned down the white cover of the bed. The couple went into their bedroom, and he was alone. He heard the surf from the distant sea. Insects crackled against the screen. He lay down and stared into the intense darkness of a countryside with no light in a house or on the road. The sheets smelled of mold.

Antone Freitas. He spoke the two words. His father's name had been Anthony. Marie and Violet. Once father had mentioned Violet, with disapproval. But never Antone and Marie. He never talked of family. Yet he had taken Kimo to the Freitas house. He said he wanted Kimo to see an old place and that he wasn't to forget it. The tone his father used was like a whip cracking.

Kimo didn't forget the house. It became his secret place for years. He tried to remember the details of the first visit. They rode up on horseback. Father claimed that the only way to know a place was to ride to it and through it on horseback. He said you could feel earth and the air of it. At the green house they dismounted. "You go look in the house. I'll be back." He walked off down the road, his boots clumping heavily in the dirt.

The house was a spooky place for a kid. I thought it must be haunted. I tiptoed up the walk and steps. The door was open. I stared through. A gecko dropped on my arm. I had to choke a shout in my throat. "You little shit," I said, glad to have something to talk to. I stepped through the doorway and saw the old three-legged table and the broken chairs. There were calendar pictures pasted on the wall, mostly pretty Coca-Cola girls. I chanted to myself, "You little shit, you little shit." It made me feel braver to hear my voice while I walked through the rooms, and on through the kitchen to the back porch and steps. I sat on the steps and stared into the trees. The leaves moved and made small sounds. A bird trilled and another answered. I liked the smell of rotting mangoes. A strange excitement stirred in me—I wanted to capture this whole experience, to hold it as simply as one can hold a stone or a piece of wood. There was some kind of magic. It put me in touch with the trees, the earth, the house. And with the mysterious lives lived there.

When father came back, I asked who had lived in the place. "No one you know," he said.

"Why did you bring me here?"

"I brought you here. Now we'll go home."

After that visit, I returned to the house every time I could steal away from the family. It was where I started my "book," A scrapbook in which I put down things I saw and felt; where I made small drawings of plants, trees, birds, and the old houses. I needed to put things into words and drawings. Only then did I begin to understand meanings.

A sudden squall beat the walls of the Kahalewai house. Kimo sat up. He had not slept. Leaves scraped like small animals on the roof, loose shingles rattled. The moldy smell was overpowering, and more so with the squall. It was curious, he thought, that the smells and sounds were there, undeniable there—but the house itself seemed unreal. He could see nothing. Only blackness—not even the slightest thickening of this blackness for a chair or dresser shape. He would rather sleep in the open, even with the rain. He crept out of bed and pulled on his clothes. The floor creaked under his feet. He didn't want to wake his hosts. As he went down the stone steps, a thin branch of something brushed across his arm. His body shook. He was glad to reach the road through the village. At the Freitas house, he spread his sleeping bag on the wet grass and finally went to sleep.

The sun was beating on him when he woke; close to noon, he guessed. The mango trees had shaded him from the bright light until the sun came over head. He wanted to wash and wandered about the remains of the house to look for a container which might have rainwater in it. Near an old back gate was a galvanized tin tub with an inch of brown, leafy water. He cupped his hands and poured water over his face. The cold washed his sleepiness away. . . . The Kahalewais—he must go and apologize for leaving them so discourteously during the night.

He walked down the road. He was sure the path to the Kahalewai house started just a little beyond the village. The dusk had been thick; he hadn't seen a great deal. There were some sticky plants. He seemed to remember a series of old fence posts and a sake tub with rusted wire holding the ribs together. The Kahalewai house was in a place where the trees were thick and overarching. He couldn't see any trees which looked like that. The trees he saw thinned considerably at the edge of the village. He walked on for half a mile or so until he came to the edge of pineapple fields. Strange that he couldn't get his bearings.

He returned to the Freitas house determined to walk very slowly and hoping that some small clue, even the feel of the ground under his feet would help him. He had begun to sweat, not from exertion but from anxiety. The experience of last night was real—he had no doubt of that. Why couldn't he find the Kahalewai house?

Suddenly he saw an overgrown trail which he must have missed the first time. The grass was stunted and coarse. No foot had recently walked there, he thought. But he followed this vague green path into the woods. On a stump he saw an old tin cup and further along a coil of rusted chain under a lantana bush.

Finally he came to a house. The roof sagged dangerously. The walls tilted —it would not be long before it too became a pile of splintered lumber. He went up the stone steps and peered through the doorway. He could see nothing but the deep gray luminosity of air and the weeds which had grown up through the floor. In a far corner bits of red glass glinted. The house had been stained brown.

He thought of last night. It had been very real. He could not doubt that he had paid a visit to the Kahalewais. The old couple themselves with their brown skin and white hair, the beef stew, the moldy sheets, the photograph of a small girl which had been isolated from the other photos on the round table —set apart for a special memory, perhaps a special love. He remembered that once his father had spoken of the Kahalewais. "They are a strange people. They stay apart. Some say that they have chiefly blood, the kind that must be hidden." When Kimo asked for more, his father said, "Everyone has secrets. We have no business to pry."

No business to pry. Secrets—any and everybody's. Here in this village were all those lives—lived and forgotten. The Kahalewais, in that little house with kerosene lanterns and stew and poi to eat, went on day in and day out knowing something. What? And father had never talked of Antone Freitas. Or of his own brothers and sisters. He had a picture of his mother, a photograph brown with age of a woman one could hardly see. She had on a full white skirt and her hair was in a bun.

Father, in a community where family was the center of life, seemed without family. He kept himself apart. He appeared from a mountain slope like someone from an old legend. An Oedipus, perhaps. He remained aloof.

Kimo hated his father for his cold secrecy. Once in a burst of adolescent nastiness he shouted: "You're not a real father. You don't give a damn about any of us." Mother had slapped his face. He remembered with shame that he had laughed at her. His father had his revenge. All through the years he moved farther and farther away. He didn't even allow them to tell him of the cancer. The distance between them remained intact, solid as a rock.

Back at the Freitas house he wrote in his book for a while. All about the crumbled village, Antone Freitas (there was little to say—he was father's uncle), the visit to the Kahalewais. He wrote about how he could still taste the sweet-sour flavor of the stew; the lamp with a red glass shade and the little pieces of broken glass in the old brown house; the stifling smell of mold and the feel of coarse muslin sheets on his naked body. Senses had their own memory. Senses don't lie. He had always believed this.

He packed his gear and hoisted it on his back. Janie would be waiting by now. He walked along the ridge and started down the slope. The heat slapped him in the face and wrapped around his body. The *aa* lava rolled under his feet. The wet earth had a fishy smell which he couldn't recognize. Finally he came out of the hollow. In the distance he saw the van.

Janie came running down the road shouting his name. She was in a panic.

"Kimo, Kimo!" she cried and flung her arms around him. "Where have you been? I thought you were dead!"

"Darling, I was where I said I would be."

She began to pound him on the chest. "You shouldn't do this to me! You shouldn't frighten me."

"Janie, what's the matter?"

She pushed back from him. "Kimo, you've been gone three whole days!"

"That can't be. I was gone overnight."

"Three whole days! I've been camping in the van, waiting. Last night I was about to get the police when an old Hawaiian came alone. He said he'd seen you. Talked with you. That you'd be coming."

"Mr. Kahalewai! Strange, I was with him in his house last night."

"Maybe you were with him in his house last night—but he was here too."

"That can't be. Janie, you're confused. I was gone just the one night."

She pounded his chest again. He could feel the force of her anger and love. "Don't tell me such stories. I know how many days have gone by. I had to do the waiting. What did you do up there?"

He took hold of her flailing arms. He didn't know what to say. "I didn't do much." He paused. "I just explored here and there. Ate your good chicken. That's all."

She laid her hand on his mouth. "Kimo, don't do this to me. You know how I hate your secrets."

In Praise of Oʻahu:
Kaopulupulu, the Prophet,
and Kahahana, Chief

KAOPULUPULU, PROPHET

Feet thundering to seal your doom,
to shut your mouth, to silence your call
to the gods that the ravishing of men
in battle or peace come to an end—for this,
your son is staked to a tree and you, staked
like a thin, foreign dog placed in his sight:
he must die, commanded your chief.
O Prophet, O Priest,
who seek from Kahahana, the Dog of Oʻahu
like a foreign chief with no respect for the mana
of the gods—for him,
you, too, must die. You dared warn him.
No more killing the people!
No more wanton sacrifices!
O Kaopulupulu, Prophet!
"The gods see; gods hear," you say, your tongue not tied:
"Do not betray the gods! The blood of your kin—
your warriors—is stained deep on your hands
quick with the shark-toothed bladed dagger!
O Chief," you cry, "spare these your warrior sons.
Your mad dog spittle runs. Spare! Spare!"

Kaopulupulu, you give the lie to the teeth of a man
who belies due honour to common toilers of land.
Your tongue, carved out to the figure of your heart,
your hand on the knife that you ask your son

to wield on himself that he die—shows you know
you too must die. Laocoön, his sons—
again prey to the fate of the hour, unrepentant,
fierce as prophets must be, without end.

Sons choose.
Without question, this son of the land,
turned the blade in his side.
And you, not weeping, but seeing him, held
the mana of his blood on your head—your wife
trembling in your sight—sealing his/your fate.
Oʻahu stands
silently weeping forever the long Prophet's voice.
From the peak of Puʻu Kahea
to the deep of the bay, blood runs
where today toddlers bathe, children swim,
purifying the air again in innocence.
Clear minded was the vision: a man is a man.

O Kaopulupulu! Dragged to Puʻu Loa,
tied like a choice hog for sacrifice
to Kahahana for crossing his will—
you are no innocent, but warrior priest.

Kahahana honoured your last wish,
for the presence of the gods of the ocean
and fish to see. Puʻu Loa is your altar.
How often did you sacrifice men?
You carved them in pieces
and set out their bones in the sun,
like those of common animals who had run.
But here at your altar you stood.
And gave up your god for a truth
wedged between—your chief and the people.
Afterward, fleshed out in small pieces, quartered—
the bones of your hand,
the substance of feet,
to the gods, which are the people of the land.

Even
in peace, you speak, long after, to us
abiding even as you did when you fell,
for the worth
of a warrior to be as he is, even in war,

Kaopulupulu: Prophet, Priest!
A man.

KAHAHANA, CHIEF

Disputing Kamakau's View of the Young Oʻahu Chief As Cruel

The young ʻIwa, Kahahana,
fledgling of Maui's Lightning/Hawk
Nosed Chief Kahekili—
was fortune sorceried into war:
a favourite for the embattled gods grown thin
at the batten,
spare spoilage for all the running blood unspared.
Was it ever enough?
You were raised never to count the costs.
All was praise and blessing
like your great, wide-eyed innocence of heart.

To Oʻahu, then, the Hawk/Lightning Flash returned you—
having taught you to fly and never wield if faint
heartedly a flesh-cutting sword drew warm blood
from a man; set you under Kaopulupulu,
your father's own priest, that shrewd rat-eyed
priest, his wizardry.
Hawk/Testing, he asked that you give up all lands
with the word Wai—all villages of the living,
all game, all life force that any boy-chief,
any man of the soil should need for his people to plant
their life's heart, deep, filling up the taro fields to the sky,
down to the sea. Happily, you agreed, then discovered
the Hawk's cunning eyrie's view, a vision:
Oʻahu shall bow down to Hawk, be stolen, for sacrifice.

All water sources are given to the gods,
shall stand sacred to Kane and Lono: all gods
but one, Hawk-Lightning his Name,
Striker of fear in the heart!

You offered instead: "anything else,"
As the Priest Kaopulupulu advised,
without trembling. All the wai lands, he said, never,
screwing you to the wall like an insect by a stone.
The wizard's rat eyes shrank to notice your leap
of heart, your faith, your hope. And would have
all or nothing: with you or without.
Any boy-chief would recoil and seek a sweet
maiden love instead. Pinned between
Hawk/Lightning
and Stone Priest
your own chiefs' answers
came by the sword.

Did you not read
the signs in the sky?
You did not.
You saw, instead,
a beautiful woman.
and freely loved her.
And lost your way:
lost Hawk/Lightning,
lost Stone Priest,
gulled by both
when you sought only life
in the love of your youth.

Lightning spear thrust in the ground
is death: which Warrior-Chief chooses
a woman over land,
over produce, over people to govern?
None do. But you neither Hawk, nor Lightning,
walked with your Love,
with more power for the gods,
more marked than marching soldiers
(their spear-tips poisoned)

for the Hawk, his Lightning strikes.
Should thunderous Maui rule Oʻahu's shores?
In your sight, a Boy-King's, Love rules.

Your warriors, conscripted by the Hawk
who had tutored you
to follow orders as a Prince, a King,
followed Hawk/Lightning
or Stone Prophet. And tore you
from Love. War is for men, they said.

With each high-staked demand, the Hawk
tested you for chiefliness—read as war,
killing, on command. unflinching, loyal,
until you, growing mad, between well laid
suspicion placed between you and the Rat,
you killed the Rat, Oʻahu's own . . .
Only Hawk/Lightning, now, stood to lay claim.

He ordered your soldiery
to seek you out, to hunt you down in ʻEwa
And he came, burning villages from mountain
to sea, in the peace that is Night. Sought fleet-
footed spies to ferret out from cool volcanic caves
the might that is fear. It was a chiefly prerogative:
to kill and kill and kill.
He hunted you down in your own ancestral lands,
by the hands of your own men.

Oʻahu's beautiful chiefess, she whom you took to wife,
against the Hawk's and Rat's advice—for sheer love
and little else—sought out her brother, bargained
with him that you might sneak out at night, given
time to escape, for the knowing where you were.
Brother to your Light, your Life-of-Heart agreed.
and told him: He hides in ʻEwa, in a cave. He hides by day.
By night, he roams for food.

Set up between Hawk and Rat, spear and club,
you bit both hands trained for feeding you in youth.
And wasted fair Oʻahu in slaughter, in sacrifice.

Nor were you spared. A cave in 'Ewa for burial bed
as you were eating grub—your wife/lover,
would-be rescuer leading a traitorous brother
to the den. They speared you startled rising up
simply to defend. . . . Once your owl hooted
and flew away, the day was closed. Blood everywhere.

Which was your fate, my young warrior chief!
To those who knew you
you loved better than you fought
and risked your royal life for mortal beauty of a love.
The goddess La'ila'i knew you. She took you for her own.
And brought the wrath of men upon you.
for defying the god-chief Hawk who was Lightning.
Lover, alone, now a spirit, elepaio, of sky, of tree,
not land.

The 'Iwa is scavenger-god of cliffs, feeds,
heeding the common fish of sea-worthy life.
It falls from its own feeding, self defeat
on its own terms, for triumphs in innocence without disgrace.
Maligned you were, my Chief! I who am from Maui born!

We set our sights on 'Iwa once again
and haunting sites. We sing to your sweet innocence
of choice: no small, no simple gain.
The anguish of your broken heart, the treacheries of Hawk,
doubts of Rat. We sound your name and fondly
call your spirit back,
O young and faithful, honoured Chief who lies dismembered
in some common grave, nameless and shamed
after torture, rack. Where was Father? Where was Mother?
Brother died to brother.
It rains. We weep for you, Kahahana, and the wife
who loved you well. When the sun rises, we will rise
and bathe in the ocean. We will remember
O'ahu's 'Iwa, O Kahahana, O'ahu's own!

Hoʻoulu Lāhui

At dawn, the chanting called Kahikina out of sleep. She sat up and parted the bedroom curtains from her upstairs window. No, she wasn't dreaming, he was still there. Only the wooden gate separated him from the stone path which led up to her door, but she knew he would never come across unless she chanted back to him with her own kāhea, welcoming him in the formal and polite way of their ancestors. Unless she did so, the flimsy wooden gate might just as well have been a forty-foot moat swimming with sharks and water snakes. She could see him clearly, his white hair, his tall figure against the morning, his vibrant breath rising in his chest and falling out through his voice in rich, dark tones.

Anger pricked at the back of her neck. What the hell does he expect? Three days and he's still out there thinking I might welcome him in. Why should I? I don't even know him. I don't even want to know him. Let him wait. Let him wait forever or go back to where he came from. It's all too ludicrous.

Kahikina sat at the edge of the bed and stared at the floor. She stood up, grabbed her robe from the chair and walked downstairs to the kitchen. While she waited for the water to boil, she brushed out her long dark hair with its streaks of white. She could take the pill, the gene therapy pill that would keep her hair its natural color forever. She'd already surrendered to the same kind of treatment for aging skin, but Kahikina wanted the gray in her hair. She liked having a sign that announced the kind of maturity she felt she'd earned after 67 years of living. She braided up her tresses, twirled them around and secured them with a wooden hair pick, carved in the shape of a lizard, at the back of her neck.

The man at the gate began chanting about Papa and Wākea. Papa, the earth mother, and Wākea, the sky father, progenitors of the Hawaiian race. Kahikina listened and for a minute mused over his version. I guess he never heard the *old* story, the way it was told before the Ministry of Hawaiian Culture reshaped oral history. "Kānaka nouveau," Grandma used to call the proud new bureaucrats. But I remember hearing a different story, from Grandma's lips, alone, in secret.

That was Kahikina's first year in school, the year 2035 when Ke Aupuni Hawaiʻi Hou, the New Hawaiian Nation was only ten years old. She used to think her grandmother made up that story. It was certainly different from the one she learned in school, but now it all made sense. Yes, there *was* a great darkness. And in that darkness there *were* great shadows, and in the shadows dirty hands sealed secret deals—without the knowledge or consent of those whose lives their plans would splinter.

His chant was closing and Kahikina could almost feel the calling in of his life breath like the smoke of a genie spiraling back into a bottle. Yes, he has a voice. Kahikina knew she must have met him at some time in her life. He was about her age and looked full blooded, kānaka maoli piha. All the families met every year at the counsel when she was growing up. They were only a handful by then. At the time the new nation was formed, pure Hawaiians had dwindled to 500 men, women and children. The first sovereign parliament set aside the best land for them, subsidized their housing, provided educational benefits, job counseling, training, and complete medical care. The medical programs were the most intensive. On a compulsory basis, pure Hawaiian children received extensive bi-yearly physical examinations. In addition, every month their weight, diet, and exercise regime was monitored. At the age of 18 the program became voluntary, but almost all of the other benefits required "voluntary" participation in the medical programs, so the routine continued. The doctors must have watched her for a long time.

It didn't seem so strange then. She'd grown up being treated like one of an endangered species. All of them were subjected to the poking and prodding, but in return, they were always given the best, always an honored place at ceremonies, always invited to every national event and to an endless series of public occasions. Kahikina remembered how she hated going out in public when she was a child. Visitors to Hawai'i had somehow come to believe that it brought good luck to touch a pure Hawaiian. She hated strangers always grabbing at her, trying to touch her hair, her clothes and even her feet. She hated it. She looked out at the man again through the kitchen curtains. He must remember those things. He must know how she valued privacy.

Maybe he was the Kapuahi boy, the one from Ni'ihau. The family was tall and slender that way. Why won't he just go home?

Alika arrived when Kahikina finished her first cup of tea. She heard his bicycle on the back gravel path. When Kahikina's husband died a few years ago, she closed off the driveways with pass gates, strung up laser fences around her thirty acres to prevent trespassing and rarely left home. She couldn't figure out how the man got through without a passcard. Alika didn't have one. He was programmed on voice security. Kahikina thought about calling the police and having the man removed, but what if it really was him? How could she be sure? She couldn't bear more publicity, more exposure, more invasion. She asked Alika to speak to him again.

"He said he doesn't want to talk, Auntie. He said he's waiting for you to greet him."

"He trespasses on my property, uninvited and expects me to welcome him?"

"It's not *his* fault, Auntie." Kahikina knew that Alika thought it *was* the man, the one she'd read about. And was it her imagination or did Alika say the word "Auntie" with a hint of mockery? Kahikina looked at him in confusion.

Alika walked out to survey the loʻi. Across the taro ponds the heart-shaped leaves of the plants fluttered in waves. He stopped and examined the two new varieties, the Uahi-a-Pele and Pāʻu-o-Hiʻiaka. They were named for the volcano goddesses Pele and Hiʻiaka because of their smoky-colored foliage. He checked them carefully, and then he went into the house, taking the laser key card from its place in the kitchen drawer. At the water data board, he keyed in and ran a house water treatment and recycling process. All waste water would be converted for garden use. Water and land conservation had become the first priorities of the New Hawaiian Nation, and Hawaiʻi was now a model for other island communities. Alika walked back out to the loʻi and put his hand in the water near an in-flow valve to check the temperature of the circulating water. A fish glided by. Alika had recently introduced them in the ponds, starting with the traditional awa, āholehole and oʻopu. The water felt cool and soothing on his hand.

A nitro-evulsion process extracted liquid nitrogen from the air, making an affordable cooling agent that kept the water below 25 centigrade, the perfect temperature for a thriving loʻi. Taro cultivation previously depended on naturally circulating water to maintain the low temperature. Now, despite a dramatic increase in production, streams and rivulets flowed freely and ground water was necessary only to make up for evaporation. As in the ancient days, taro once more filled the valleys and terraced hillsides.

Kahikina sat in her rocker on the lanai and watched him tend the plants. Taro was said to be one of nature's most perfect foods. Hāloanaka, a taro, was the first born of the gods. Hāloa, a man, was born second. Born of the same parents, the taro is the elder brother, man being younger. Alika looked back toward the house.

The sun climbed through the sky, and at noon time, awakea, the world was bright. Kahikina made sandwiches and set them out on the lanai for Alika. The pitcher of water on the table dripped its transparent beads. From the kitchen, she could hear Alika come up the back stairs and leave again. Through the window, she saw as he went around to the old man sitting under the tree. The man rested peacefully, leaning on the tree, protected from the brilliant light. Alika offered him a sandwich wrapped in a napkin, and gave him water from a cup. The tree's umbrella shade shaped them into sculptures, a dark tableau of shadows against a world of light—the old man looking up at Alika, Alika's hand held out with the cup of water, his head tilted to one side the way it did when he was intensely interested.

Kahikina turned away from the window and sat at the small table in the kitchen. Hearing Alika come back, she rose, picked up her plate of salad and moved out to the lanai. She always ate lunch with him. She listened to his reports about the plants and the grounds, and sometimes he told her things about his life outside her world, what he did, his friends, different things. He made beautiful bowls at home in the evenings, beautiful wooden bowls that he turned and polished. Kahikina imagined that the small house he lived in was illuminated by the warm colors of wood. She saw bowls like dark amber hanging from the ceilings, set up on shelves and window sills, filling up his world with the essence of trees, with the hearts of trees, making him strong. Alika has the heart of a tree, she thought, growing sturdy and full of life. On this day, they ate in silence until Kahikina finished. She looked at him and felt a pang of quick, sharp hurt.

"Why did you feed him?" As soon as the words left her mouth, she knew they were wrong, wrong words gone out, not to be taken back.

Alika stopped. He put down the cool glass he was about to drink from. He took a second to look at her making sure their eyes met. His head tilted slowly to the right and his voice was soft and silken.

"I'd do the same for you, Auntie," he said quietly.

Kahikina stood up, her face hot and flushed. She grabbed her bowl and vanished into the house slamming the screen door. She couldn't tell what he meant. Was he rubbing it in, she asked herself, or am I just oversensitive and vulnerable, seeing it everywhere? Why shouldn't I see it everywhere? God damn it, it *is* everywhere. At the sink, while rinsing out the bowl, she let the cold water run on her hands—water, running water to calm her down.

After a few minutes, she moved into the cavernous living room where her quilt was stretched across the frame strewn with its pattern of breadfruit leaves. She sat, breathed deeply and took up the needle, moving it in and out, in and out, quilting a pattern of lines that emanated from the applique, "like waves around our islands," Grandma used to say. The rhythm of the stitches began to soothe her, like chanting, like the swaying ocean, like her breath coming in and going out.

She had just turned twenty-one, and Ho'oulu Lāhui, Increase the Race, was the slogan of the project. It was an ancient slogan from another century, but the health clinic had revived it, and now it stood out, emblazoned on a holographic wall poster. In the image, the words Ho'oulu Lāhui stretched out through a rainbow that arched over Waipi'o Valley. Light rain fell in the valley over fields of fertile taro gently moving in a slight breeze. Under a black umbrella, two Hawaiian children meandered on the web of paths that separated the taro ponds. Raindrops swelled on the translucent leaves and rolled off. A dragonfly flew by. The sound of flowing water drifted from the poster image. It mesmerized Kahikina, making her feel peaceful and good about the project.

Dr. Haulani Haehae entered the room. She had been Kahikina's kahuola, her personal health care giver, since Kahikina was about eight years old. Her dynamic and comforting presence gave Kahikina an immediate and almost child-like sense of security. Dr. Haehae had cared for Kahikina during all her childhood illnesses. She had seen her through a difficult adolescent depression when Kahikina's mother had died, when anger and fear nearly swallowed her.

"Participating in this project would be a true act of aloha to those who can't have children." Dr. Haehae's voice began with sincere compassion.

"It's like the old idea of hanai, isn't it?" Kahikina mused. "Like giving your child to be lovingly raised by others."

"Exactly," smiled the doctor.

"But this project *is* confined to people of Hawaiian ancestry.?"

"Of course, one of the partners has to be. I'm sure that's mentioned in the written information I gave you." The doctor's voice became subtly authoritarian.

"I guess I missed that point." Kahikina hated appearing less than smart with the doctor. "Well, most of it I've read before, about how stress, pollutants and chemicals have affected infertility. But I didn't realize that fifty per cent of our couples can't conceive."

"Sad, isn't it? Carrying a child is not the problem, it's conception. Low sperm counts and defective ovum."

"I just didn't know it was that bad."

"It's a very serious problem," said Dr. Haehae with a hint of emotion, it especially when you think about the long term survival of Hawaiians as a group." The doctor let a few moments of silence pass. "But the hopeful news is that in-vitro fertilization is now well advanced, and through this program we can offer Hawaiian couples the chance to raise a child of our own race."

"And you think this selective screening process that you're doing might improve fertility in the next generation?" Kahikina did remember reading that and hoped the question would please the doctor.

"I'm quite sure, Kahikina." The doctor smiled and watched her.

"It sounds like it would really make a difference."

"Absolutely. And I've asked you because I know your records, and I know you could make an excellent contribution. Most of the donors, as you can probably guess, are only part Hawaiian. Being a full-blooded Hawaiian, your participation would be a great gift to the future."

"How will you . . . ? I mean how does it . . . ?" Kahikina didn't quite know the exact words for her question.

"How will it work?" Again, Dr. Haehae smiled her reassuring smile. "The procedure takes about twenty minutes for women. We extract ovum from you at the right time of the month just before release from the ovary, which in your case will be in about four days. We take the specimen, make sure it is an absolutely healthy one, and then we begin the cloning and storage processes. We expect about 300 specimens from men and women. Specimens will be matched through a random selection process that assures usage of every healthy specimen on a rotation basis so that they are all used equally."

"And you're only giving children to people who really, really want them?" Kahikina asked.

"Oh, of course dear, a child is precious, especially one which carries our blood. Any couple requesting our help will be thoroughly evaluated."

"And no one will ever know who—"

"Absolutely not," the doctor was emphatic. "Nothing about this project will ever appear as part of public information. Our government has guaranteed the tightest security. We want to protect *everyone's* privacy."

Kahikina knew the New Hawaiian Nation carefully monitored the media, in order, as they always said, "to avoid the self-serving and divisive confusion perpetrated on our people by the irresponsibilities of mass communication in the late 20th century." She felt confident that everything was simple and straightforward, and so she agreed to help. She was one of only fifty pure Hawaiian women of childbearing age left in the world. She had half the potential for precious human life, for full-blooded Hawaiian human life. At the time, she felt a kind of obligation to participate. Dr. Haehae knew everything about her and probably counted on her to have those feelings, but this woman she thought of as her guardian and friend had lied. Had all her nurturing kindness been just to take them both together to this one day? If so, it all worked very well and Kahikina had certainly done her part to increase the race. Four days after her conversation with the doctor, she had submitted to the simple procedure that sealed her commitment.

She looked up from her quilting and out at the healthy taro leaves sparkling and ripe in the sun. Rapid advances in genetic engineering had revitalized everything, beautiful crops, beautiful animals, and beautiful children too, beautiful healthy children.

How could she *have* ever noticed? Two years after she had participated, she married a man in her own field of work, agricultural economics. Modeled on old-fashioned home economics, they were trained to help people establish the maximum self-sufficiency in home environments. Aquaculture, productive home gardens, small-scale agriculture, were all part of the home systems they designed and helped maintain. Almost too easily, she reflected, they were offered really good government jobs in this quiet rural setting. Because of her pure ethnicity, Kahikina's eligibility for a land grant became automatic upon request after age twenty-one. She and her husband, were nevertheless astounded at the stroke of luck which awarded them through commission lottery the exquisite thirty-acre parcel complete with restored historic plantation manager's house. In such an idyllic setting and with such an engaging daily routine, she never had an inkling of what was going on. Of course it must have been part of the plan, the jobs, the house, the raises, and the special new projects. They were far too clever for her. They were far too clever for everyone. Their dispersal had been so meticulously planned, everyone and everything so carefully monitored for all these years, that no one ever suspected a thing.

Two weeks ago, everything changed. Dr. Haehae had recently died at the ripe age of eighty-seven. Her last years were spent in her comfortable home where she passed the days reading mystery stories and propagating orchids. She died without much fanfare or public notice, bequeathing all of her worldly goods to a niece who had also become a doctor. While sorting through her Aunt's personal belongings, the young woman came upon a little leather bound book with pages of handwritten text. On the first page were inscribed these words: Hoʻoulu Lāhui. Charmed at discovering her Aunt kept a journal, she sat down and began to read. In one afternoon, she read the diary, which documented the project and Dr. Haehae's passionate feelings about her work. This niece had always suspected her own mother and father were not her biological parents, and she pursued the clues in the book wanting to discover her true genealogy. She was also determined that history would not forget her Aunt's heroic work.

The Minister of Health had come himself to tell Kahikina before the story became public. "I've ordered national security to delete your name and address from any and all public files. I've changed your communication numbers and covered any other possible traces, which could lead strangers to you. The government is willing to provide permanent security for you for the rest of your life, but now, after what's happened we can't guarantee complete anonymity."

"Can't or won't? You don't seem to have any trouble controlling other information." Kahikina wouldn't look at him.

"It just happened too fast. She gave out the information as if it had been approved. It's just too late." The Minister paused and cleared his throat. "At any rate, the Sovereign Parliament, in a special session, asked me to tell you that Ke Aupuni Hawaiʻi Hou would like to honor you. We would, if you agree, in a religious ceremony of the most elaborate and ancient formality, invest in you all the power of the highest, I mean the highest, aliʻi. We could even establish certain kapu for you to make your life more private. We would create a special name for you and the nation would hold you always in the greatest esteem."

Kahikina continued to stare out the window.

"You see," the Minister was doing his best to sound concerned and sincere, "the nation needs figures of substantial proportion, figures which in some way echo the grandeur of a great past."

"Like a queen bee."

He ignored her remark. "I know you need some time to think this all over. It must be quite a shock to find that your family is so, so big. I think I understand how you might feel."

Kahikina turned to him with a stare so cold he couldn't disengage from it. "Oh, I don't think so," her voice was steel. "I don't think you will ever know how I feel."

The Minister left hurriedly saying he would contact her soon.

And then two days later this man, she shook her head at the thought, this man at the gate.

Kahikina stopped to rethread her needle.

Instead of selection on a rotation basis, they had simply chosen two donations of the very best, one male and one female, both of them from pure Hawaiians. First they were cloned for grooming purposes, and then altered to withstand inbreeding. Lab technicians combed through the strands of DNA, searching for and removing all defects. They engineered, strengthened, and activated enough genetic traits from each ancestral pool to produce an infinite variety of looks. Next, they cloned these perfect specimens again. Not once, but hundreds, maybe thousands of times. In hundreds of sterile dishes they were joined. She, Kahikina, had been joined to a man that she did not even know, a man made as perfect as herself, and thousands of pure Hawaiian children came into the world. They didn't come all at once, but were properly spaced and placed to avoid arousing suspicion. The race didn't die. It began to flourish—Hoʻoulu Lāhui.

How ironic, thought Kahikina, that my husband could not have children and didn't want to use the available alternatives. How ironic that my one disappointment in life was that I never had any of my own. She sighed and lost herself in a sea of stitches. Kahikina didn't know if minutes or hours had passed before she saw Alika standing in the door with the afternoon sun behind him. In a touching gesture, he removed his hat and nervously fingered it.

"Don't stand there looking at me like that. Come inside and sit." She said it kindly.

Alika sat in his favorite chair right next to the one her husband always used to sit in.

"Well," Kahikina kept her eyes on her quilting, "You want me to welcome him, don't you?"

"It's not like *he* did anything to you."

"I never said he did," she paused. "But do the words *violated, deceived, used*—do those words mean anything to you, Alika?" She hadn't intended to be close to tears.

"I'm sorry, Auntie. It's none of my business. I didn't mean to intrude on your privacy." He rose to leave, but turned at the doorway. "He's just a simple man, Auntie, mahi'ai, dirt farmer, like me. He says he doesn't know what to do, where to go. I'm sorry. I just feel—I'm sorry." Alika left the house quietly.

"This is our secret," whispered Grandma. "Now don't tell Mommy. Wākea was the sky father and his wife Papa was the earth. They were man and wife and together they had a beautiful daughter, Ho'ohokulani. In time, Wākea developed a great desire for his daughter, but he was afraid of Papa's anger. Wākea went to his kahuna and asked him for help. The kahuna created the kapu, all the laws, which include nights, nights when it was forbidden for man and wife to sleep together. He told Wākea to go and tell Papa about these laws and to say they were declared by the gods. So on the forbidden nights, Wākea crept away to sleep with Ho'ohokulani. She had children with her father. First she bore Hāloanaka who became a taro. Next she bore a man who was named Hāloa and from this man came the Hawaiian race. Papa found out about the deception and spat in Wākea's face. People today don't like this story. They don't like that it tells of how our people came from a lie, a lie to use and deceive women, but this is the story our ancestors told, my pua."

Kahikina continued quilting until the old clock chimed four. She started out through the screen door, and saw Alika in the lo'i cleaning something out of the water. He looked far away and golden in the sunshine. As a boy he was shy and eager to please. Now, he was old enough to have a family of his own. The thought that he might have been one of them was too painful to be anything but a brief stab in her consciousness. Suddenly the big house seemed very quiet and empty, just a big wooden frame yawning and creaking and growing old. Would it have been different if children had run through it? She thought of a house full of children laughing and playing and leaving trails of crumbs and toys and clothes, filling up the big emptiness of the house.

Alika examined the leaves of different stalks in the lo'i. When he moved the larger leaves at certain angles, glistening water droplets sparkled and flashed in the sunlight like a signaling mirror. He saw her on the porch and began to come toward her.

He has a nice way of moving, she told herself, quiet, sure and strong, but he doesn't really understand. He'll never understand what it's like to be forced, to have it all forced on you, forced to spawn a race against your will, without your knowledge—to be like a hole, a big gaping hole in the heavens through which thousands of offspring pour, not one or two, not five or six, but thousands. Elements are missing here, vital, aching human elements: motherhood, pleasure, the feel of tiny feet and the closeness of small clinging limbs, the intoxicating smell of your flesh made flesh.

Alika reached the porch and sat. Kahikina poured his tea into the glass. Yes, she saw, genetic manipulation had made everything strong and beautiful, including the children, but Alika, in all his beauty could not touch this dark and wide emptiness, no one could. She sank into the white rattan chair watching the luminous sun in its declination.

Far away, she heard birds singing. Their songs were faint but present, somewhere on the periphery of her thoughts. Then, another sound began to rise quietly, slowly and gradually like water, like punawai, spring water, seeping up from the voice of the man waiting under the tree. It ascended through the lines of space, washed over her, crumbling gently in waves, crisp waves, his kahea, calling out to be answered, calling out for recognition, flooding in the empty space and vibrating the darkness.

Kahikina rose to her feet. She moved slowly, straight through the house, the fire sky behind her and fixed in her mind, warming every visible thing. Throwing open the front doors she faced the east, and her voice returned to the tall figure at the gate, making for him a deep and resonant chant of welcome.

Olo

On this ground the rocks flew
and spears stabbed
at the blood flushing out
heads were split by clubs
cracking bones
their cries at night
sometimes you can hear them
for the one they saw
right before
they were cut off from
those bodies sweating
out the killing death
forever.
See those mounds
raised fortifications
they are the evidence now
they tell us who sleeps underneath
this part of the earth
this ground
our family calls
home.

Over the bones and sites of war
they built the houses
where we listened as our father told
how it was before the roads and
the lights and in the villages
where he walked in the high valleys when
ever man had a tatau or he sat with the women he said
the vao had so many voices you never hear them now
and how he could swim across the bay then it was so clear
all the way he saw his shadow on the bottom
then our mother would kiss us goodnight
in our beds veiled in mosquito nets
as the light went out
I could see them all dancing
the old ones when the moon came
full across the yard

this place didn't need a sign that said
ua sa.

From this theatre my uncle
coaxed up the green things which
flowering called back the birds to where he wrote
all those words that
still make us weep and cry
and long for each other
then sometimes he would
fight with my aunt
who said that divisions
should be official
so she madly paced and counted
and drew out all the boundaries
I swear it was them down there
our subterranean neighbors
they don't wonder why
we all look haunted
they don't wonder why
we have trouble getting along.

And then there was that time
my family brought me home
they thought it was to die
at twenty-two
sick from the world all ready
with the taste of funereal dirt
in the back of my mouth my
blood prepared me for burial
and I was more than willing
to give myself up
I was more than willing
to fall on this ground.

But in the fever dream
they all came calling
a formal visit
with feather edged
fine mats like flags
they sailed up the lawn

all the hundreds shining
they came up shining
each one to embrace me
each one with his warrior arms
each one bearing a mealofa
of love they came
oiled
scented
and finely dressed
for battle.

Samoan words used in this poem: *mealofa* (gift), *olo* (fort, shelter), *tatau* (tattoo), *ua sa* (keep out/sacred), *vao* (forest)

The Bodhisattva Muses

. . . the wild, because of its energy and beauty, is always eyed by somebody or
other . . . the wild always needs a guardian at the gate, or it will be misused.
— CLARISSA PINKOLA ESTES

The compassionate one is grateful to us for another life.
She practices her art, and we return
her roses with poems arising out of nights of clarity.
The tranquil ascension of mind equals the depths to which
she has suffered.
She can rest now unhindered by memory.
She has earned this, we say, mindful of our negligence
when we failed to guard her beauty as she was developing her light.
We miscalculated the effort it would take
for the compassionate one to transform the two into full power.

The compassionate one calls it an act of kindness.
If only she knew we were saving ourselves, resuscitating
those whom we had once long ago chosen for the art,
those capable of obsession or devotion.
The child who draws a thousand pictures in the dirt,
markings that resemble birds or sharks, demons or storms,
is the same child who washes her hands each time she opens a door.
Our visitations had been infrequent, our infusions feeble.
We gave strength to her voice in a house without shelter.
There was no place safe in which to sing.
How could she offer us roses, we cry, when she could barely feed
    herself?

The compassionate one claims she heard our first appeal
one Sunday morning. We were the ladies in the choir
calling to her, singing about the lamb of God.
Knowing what she knew by then led her down the aisle.

She was the lamb whose chance had come to declare herself
someone else's daughter.
The congregation bore witness to her betrayal of the father.
The singing turned rapturous by the time the compassionate one
had placed herself into the fold.
Praise the Lord, the mother cried, nibbling redemption
without effort, like a candy bar, without
betraying complicity in the father's nightly trespasses.
Praise the Lord, the mother cried, and the crumbs fell out of her mouth.

We appear mysteriously in many forms.
Perhaps we were those singing ladies who appealed
to the compassionate one's need for devotion.
She sought shelter and we answered, in retrospect, feebly
—the form of a father
she hungered for, a sheltering god who struck hard
with a crush so deep she began writing
love letters in a diary of imitation leather.
On the cover, embossed in gold, shined the year of her conversion.
Her first poems, congested as the onion skin pages of the black bible
she was given that day, flew out the window, love letters
we should have intercepted
before the arrival of the boy who talked tenderly, more sweetly
than any god or father, who talked her into giving
what we didn't know had already been taken.

Surely she would have burned the pages of her diary
in a fiery display had the boy not given her heaven
in a patch of grass beyond the cemetery, a nest
he cleared of cigarette stems and bottle shards,
what she was running toward when her father's curses
reached her, pelted her ribs, and knocked her down.

Slow to awaken to danger, we still did not intervene.
Even when the boy treated her badly,
we allowed, for the sake of art, the boy to break her heart.
Through suffering she would become her own subject.
Through words she would heal her way back,
become stronger, more interesting—re-made, pieced by hand,
and humanly flawed.

Through that open window came those who said
they loved her knew what was best for her and in laying
those tender claims insisted she relinquish her light.
A poet, one whose failings had yet to turn sour, saw his chance
at beauty.
Pinned under the blade of his windshield
a love letter had fluttered out of that open window.
The girl had promise. He flailed at the light.
The poet, a tinkerer of the third tier, inserted himself between the
    lines.
The girl had promise.
So began the poet's pursuit of the voice
he thought he heard singing in a tree outside his window.
He wanted to bring the voice
into his room, stash it under his pillow,
reduce it to a whisper.
Only then would she sing for him.
The girl had promise.

Light was catching up to beauty.
We had to work quickly.
We vowed to surround the compassionate one
with passionate attention.
We inflicted addiction—writing as an act of existence.
Only when words struck the page did an experience
become manifest.
The interference of her words to brutal experience
a shield others took as insolence, standoffishness.
When she was called selfish by those who said
they loved her knew what was best for her, we breathed
a chorus of exhortation
to defy without heartlessness.
We did not want a heart of stone.
We wanted poems.

We failed to give her our protection
during the time of the gathering of the light.
Those who said they loved her knew
what was best for her grew jealous of her solitude.
We failed to give her our protection
when we did not shelter her in her father's house,

a father who could fuck his own daughter and proudly
show the caseworker his handiwork, his baby—
two hits in one, both daughter and granddaughter—
how do you like that?—
heaven in this godforsaken hellhole,
something to keep him happy in his old age.
There is no place to sing
except somewhere down the road out in the woods,
but by then she is skittish, afraid of any enclosure.

Through that open window came those who said
they loved her knew what was best for her and in laying
those tender claims insisted she be like the rest of them.
These clever ones are no less dangerous
than those who screech to a halt to extinguish
any sign of beauty growing on the side of the road.
They can't stand the sight of it.
The sign of the touched.
Such beauty only makes them feel more gruesome in such light.
So wrong were we to think she could sing
in that house when outside there are men
loitering in the garage
and the party takes a twisted turn into insults,
broken glass, something breaking.
A form of fishing and hunting
done with all those spare parts
scattered around the yard—
what else do you do with heartlessness?—
all those spare parts and all that spare time.

The Sister

The boy did not know the girl had a sister.
This was to cause him great confusion. Years later
he would still wonder which one he had truly possessed.
He chose to turn his ear to the voice of the quietest singing,
a kind of singing the boy himself had known
when he dug the deepest hole in the darkest part of the night.
The voice he thought he heard changed color
at the moment the girl became aware of the boy's intelligent ears.

The boy knew about the loneliness of men.
His father had died of it.
His mother despised it.
She sent the boy to live with his brother.
The boy's brother was also lonely.
The boy knew this about his brother.

One day the boy found something in his brother's drawer
that made him feel lonelier than he had ever felt before.
More lonely than the time his mother had punished him
for fucking her boss's fourteen-year-old daughter.
Maggie—that was her name—cried and cried.
His mother sprayed him with the back yard hose,
threw him out and returned to answering the phone for Maggie's
    father.
She threw a blanket and a pillow into the dead dog's house
and told him to go and live like the dog that he was.
Something about *No son of mine.*
She tossed a bone for effect. The bone nicked his cheek.
A scar grew out of her anger.

Hidden under the mismatched socks the boy found a wad of tinfoil.
Of course he opened it, peeling back the petals to find inside silk
    panties.
The boy sniffed it. His erection was instantaneous.

It became apparent to the boy that his brother
sniffed it often—and between the two of them sneaking into
the flower for a quick sniff, the panties began to lose its scent.
The boy, afraid his brother would send him back to their mother,

tried sprinkling the crotch with water as if a little moisture
would resurrect out of the pinch of crust the scent of a girl
his brother had once known.

The boy could not ask his brother about such things.
They were two lonely men living in two separate rooms
of a poorly ventilated rented house.

Maggie's voice was clear and light
like her eyes that took in nothing that would darken them.
Even when she cried, the boy sensed
she was acting outside herself.

One night Maggie showed up at his dog house drunk.
The boy had a hard time explaining his lack of desire.
He said *exile.* He said *banishment.* She laughed,
unhooked her bra and told him not to be so *serious.*
That's when he said *fleas, no room* and *mother.*
Maggie forgot her shoes as she hurried away.
He wondered what to do with her shoes.
She was always hurrying away after that.
He figured she was trying to forget she had ever left them
outside the dog house.
Forget the strawberry-nippled breasts jiggling toward his mouth.
She looked like a girl who had plenty of shoes.

He hung the shoes from the ceiling of the dog house.
They gave him something to look at,
a mobile of thin buckles, straps and heels.
He would stare at them and think of all the places
he and Maggie would never see.

The boy was ready to go anywhere when his mother sent him to live
with his brother. His mother was tired of trying
not to think of him living in the dog house.
She told him to come back inside.
He refused.
He had staked a corner of the yard as his own.
She felt his eyes on her whenever she settled in for an evening
of television. She stopped drawing the drapes.
She carried the television into her room.

She erected rabbit ears.
And although she felt safe she could never fully enjoy
the jar of pistachio nuts she kept beside her bed.

The boy listened a long time to the voice of the quietest singing
long after he had chased it away by his attention.
He could hear the full possession the voice inhabited.
A voice that was not afraid of the dark.
He turned his ear to the welling that snagged every truth
dragged out of the body's deceit, full-bodied, ragged as
the smoke and the kisses that would be taken joyfully into the body.

The girl liked the way the boy lingered after the bell rang,
the edge of his shadow touching hers.
When his circling brought him to stand beside her,
they were surprised to find she was taller.
The fur on the boy's arms stiffened.
He caught a whiff of the other dwelling.

The voice of the quietest singing pulled on the girl
who strained to the point of snapping in anger
and breaking the chain of flowers pieced together—
shells gathered, sandwiches shared—
the companionable stitches of their life intact.
The feud raged within herself.
The girl did not want to be reminded of her duty to stay close to
    the pack.
She was tired of swimming the same waters,
tired of days spent alone with her own kind.
The voice of the quietest singing retreated as if wounded,
and hid.
The boy remained alert, ready to offer his heart.

The boy began to follow her home
every day after school, at a distance,
a distance his bowels registered with fear
as he approached the girl's street.
It could have been Maggie's neighborhood the way he saw himself
as a trespasser. The houses smelled of mothers who stayed at home,
of clean-shaven fathers who hired women like his mother
to answer their phones.
He felt his words would shatter through his teeth

and make her hurry away.
He could not believe she would find his devotion
good enough.

The voice of the quietest singing cooked for the father,
ironed the newspaper after reading the horoscope
so that when the father came home from work—
a signal to turn off the radio—the newspaper
was as fresh as if it had just been delivered.
The boy, his shadow touching the edge of the patio,
watched through the screen door the evenings
the girl ate quietly beside the father who did not need to speak to
    his daughter.
The sound of chopsticks clicking the air between them
made the boy feel like howling out of that deep hole.

Dreams about the boy the girl was having
made her glad she and her father rarely spoke.
The girl sang recklessly now.
The boy's proximity required this.
The girl wanted to spoil the boy.
She wanted to feed him treats sneaked out of her father's house.
She wanted to give him a good washing, especially
behind the ears. She wanted to stroke his wild hair.
The boy, crouching in the flaming croton, howled.

One night the boy ventured closer.
The girl's dog barked, rattling its chain so loudly
the boy ditched into a hedge.
The dog kept barking, the chain kept rattling.
A light blinked on in a window.
The girl appeared and saw the boy crouching in the flaming croton.
She tapped the glass.
My father is not home.
The boy bounded toward the door, careful
to avoid the dog straining the chain
to the point of snapping its puny neck.
The girl slipped open the latch,
the dog howled
and the boy sprang at her.
The girl fell back onto the livingroom floor
and let herself be covered with kisses.

The voice of the quietest singing said nothing to the father.
She cooked his meals, set aside the newspaper—she no longer
read her horoscope—clicked the chopsticks like knitting needles,
keeping worry to herself. She could no longer be
the guardian to herself.
In this way she remained in hiding.
In this way she lived two lives.
The nights found her running to meet the boy in the spot
they had carved, a diamond in the middle of the baseball field.
She ran to be knocked down on the pitcher's mound,
to feel with each kiss pressing down into her body
a shooting star.
The boy, so hungry with his kisses, lost his way.
The girl became frightened by the loneliness that entered her body.
The boy mistook silence for the quiet singing, so quiet now
he had to dig deeper to hear any sound.

The burden of a baby brought the voice out of hiding.
It brought her forward to speak to the father
who rushed into his daughter's room and tore from the walls
every picture, tore from the shelves
every book, tore from the bureau
every flower from its glass vase, every jewel
from its silken drawstring pouch.
The voice of the quietest singing came out of the shadows,
came out of hiding to console the father.
The girl traced *La Vien Rose* in the tiny figure
of a ballerina twirling across the mirror.
Before the figure reached the other side of the lake,
a hand shut the lid on the music.

Banishment Exile No daughter of mine Don't you ever speak to her again
The words broke through the boy's skull.

Sometimes at night the voice of the quietest singing
stands at the window and senses
he is out there, crouched in the flaming croton,
a boy looking in at a family that would try to forget
the disturbance, the fact that hunger and loneliness
had ever visited, or indeed, had ever existed.

Caldera Illumina

She came to regard the house of rain falling as her muse.
She removed her shoes before entering the house.
She did not want to bring into the house hungry ghosts.
She had seen what happens when the muse is left to die,
roofs collapsing into kitchens, women at windows staring
out of caves.
They hang no curtains, their faces already hidden.
They do not have the strength to muster up
the evil eye.
Still, she runs from them, hiding the roses under her coat,
the roses
she will place in every room of the house,
once she has shut the door behind her.

She wanted nothing in the house to interfere with her work.
She began to work again.

She began to thrash, hauling a body of language into the house,
an assemblage of parts—parts of speech, parts of dreams.
Across the structure of bone she stretched gut,
pulled transparent.
She crouched, spooling what came pouring out,
crude structures that remained
mute as oracles.
She had to go as far as possible.
She had to take the body of language
to near death.

So much of her wanted air.
The claims upon her kept her bound to those who could not live
without her.
Across the structure of bone she stretched gut,
poked holes
for the crude thing to breathe.
She knew the language of smoke,
wrapped breath to link the confluence of wind, rock,
and mist.
Along the crater rim in that hour between night and day,
speech and dreams,

joy and grief,
she walked into a light rain falling.

She had seen the bats gather at dusk beneath the hills.
Clouds of them convening dragging a sprawling
momentum into the sky as ragged as the scrawl of someone
awkward with a pen.

In expectation she left herself open.
She walked into places she should have left
unspoken
without dragging the broken language through groves
built for
worship.

The stone that caught her eye,
the one that called out to her from all the others,
was the one that bewitched,
was the one she brought home.

Across the body of language something clawed
at her breath
so that her breath,
lured like a bat out of the trees,
pursuing the stone's disruption in its blind field,
disintegrated.
A gush of wings broke gravity,
collided with mistaken fruit.
She could not make a sound.
Into her presence it clawed its inarticulate matter.
Into her sleep it flew repeatedly,
like rain battering a windshield.
She howled herself back into night,
moonless and eternal.

Prospering beyond the waking apparent she walked,
talking to the self she came to believe was reliable,
like the one who called her every day
who leaked lies back to her, crowding out with compliments
the other true ally
who walks asks nothing of you

for what you have to tell
says nothing that is not already known.

Calling herself back with the strength of her voice
awakens her.
She begins to fortify herself against that which descends at night
to steal it.
She begins to hide the voice in the rooms of the house,
taking it out of its fur-lined case.

She knows if she can find her—find the girl
who had the sincerity of mind to dig a hole
when it became apparent
she was lost from the others
near nightfall on the high slopes of the volcano,
a hole that sheltered her from the wind, the plummeting temperatures,
and buried herself in it—she can find what is required
to remain alive,
the will
to descend and dig a hole in the earth
with bare hands.

Across the structure of bone she stretches gut,
Bandages
and ropes of skin
spooling at her feet.
She begins to sing,
humming far back in her throat,
a frequency inaudible at the time of construction,
given body
at the recitation of another mouth
surrounding moss, fur, feathers until
it is one mouth speaking one word at a time.

At any moment she can enter the story and find herself
having already entered the room, the house falling with rain.
The clairvoyance of rooms
opens its scent, pressing light upon the temple
so that a dream's fragment
remains throughout the day and all her days
blue with the roses of the sea she leapt from as a child

safe on the high cliff of her father's shoulders,
the blue roses of clouds
pouring rain into her sleep.

The first time she slept in the house the numbers of the clock
dripped like a swollen candle the night blew out.
The hours pooled at her feet.
Out of her throat
came pure lozenges that slipped into the night waters
like tears
the shape of fish.

The secret of the roses
was in the ashes she carried in her hands
to mark the places where blue, vibrant and clear,
was to appear.

Nowhere to go but deeper into the darkest room.
All else is failure, a pile of last year's mail to sort.
She could spend all the days of her waking sifting through
shiny paper and feel she is peeling away toward
the core of something permanent.
She is distraction itself, and into her light
she draws obstacles to keep herself from entering
the last room.

She was the house, the house on fire, flames
leaping from windows inexplicable as the words that illumined
her mind.
She burnished miniature gold leaves
in a fountain of ink.
So the evening's book of hours
unfurled
leaf by leaf,
the ladder's green stem
she climbed to enter the house, the room, the bed
she lay in as a child
watching the torn wallpaper swirl like gray snow from the ceiling.

She left the fire burning in the house.
She left the house glowing in the forest.

She left the forest not knowing
she would return to sift through roses.

What she carried out of the house
was the poultice of smoke and ruin
festering until the moment she entered the last room
fluid, unencumbered.

In the recovery process the patient will begin to doubt
her version of the story.
This is to be expected.
In fact, necessary, given the structure of material.

Somewhere there is the mother whose help you will seek.
And she will not be able to help you.
She cannot help herself.
And the truth of it is painful.

The house, luminous, generous, opened for her an unsettling.
What flew into the window flew out the skylight.
It too was passing through.

Somewhere there is the father whose distance you must keep.
And he will try to exert his will.
He cannot help himself.
And the truth of it is final.

So passing she enters rooms to ignite the familiar
like the stove she lights in the morning.
One day the flame jumps to attention,
simply itself,
a coil of heat to bring water to air—
an act of transformation that will, in fact, occur
without her.

Across the structure of bone she stretches gut,
her senses
hit by years of rot.
In this way she begins to compose the minutiae,
the extraneous, the cluttering, still fluttering, she was, however,
moving inward.

In writing this she knows she is courting danger,
opening herself up
to the black stretch of road.
At every turn distraction
exists to steal her happiness.
She begins to work some kind of wreckage of bone and gut.
She swerves to meet the apparition,
and her eventual arrival.

Two hours left before her return to the world.
The rain keeps falling, the roses weep.
The house has an expectant loneliness of table and chairs.
The wind dwells in the stove, cold with her burning
when she went into the last room.
Two hours left before her return, and still she is gone.
The clock ticks worry.
Two hours left and she has yet
to appear.
The rain gathers years into its falling.
Drink,
rain of childhood,
once you were a cloud.

Out of her window words fly—
candle, cave, church, chair,
breath, bruise, moss, air,
the mind wills the hands—
insect, infinite—
the typist sings one note at a time.
Beyond the light of the kitchen window she steps outside.
She crouches in smoke.
She flicks a match beyond the boundary of the familiar—
insignificant, magnificent—
a juncture between two parts,
speech and dream, bone and gut, two edges of a single crisis—
incision, inscription—and looks up.
The music she hears is what she brings to the night.
The stars appear on schedule.

She approaches sleep like a drug,
night softening the length of her spine,
or a country where attendants greet her, gather her

into a fur of darkness,
feathering her eyelids with the blessings of the blind.
Night takes her hand and walks her down
its corridors, past rooms of gardens of scentless
flowers—no tissue of memory quickens there—
to a room where only sound can reach her.
The human voice requires nothing of space.
The purest note,
fused to a drop of sound—
hovering as if at the edge of sound—
becomes a lake,
cold and blue and vast.

Across the structure she burns the last stick of wood.
Not a shred of combustible material remains.
She has finished her work.
She has burned without regret
what is already done.

The child awakens having suffered a blow to the head
and opens her eyes to a country
where dark plumes of smoke
rise like statues in the fallen air.
Out of the years and the rain she walks toward you,
walks toward you with a certainty
you are somehow known to each other.
You have been there, haven't you—which was your room?
Did we walk past each other, past the garden of scentless
flowers, past the quiet cleanliness of nuns?
Did we swim in the night waters of the lake?
The child gathers the petals
into her small bed—
a place from which no one
had thought to retrieve her—
and in the hour before the sun
feathers the hills, light praising the trees,
longing is matched by beauty
in the singing that carries her to the hospital
balcony
where she opens, let's say, her heart,
to a sound she knew existed
somewhere in this world.

THE QUIETEST SINGING

BIOGRAPHIES AND COMMENTARIES

Eric Chock

Through his work as a poet, as a teacher of poetry writing, and as an editor, Eric Chock has done much to open the eyes of people in Hawai'i to the ways poems can serve as means to understanding and opportunities for expression. Chock has long been interested in making intimate connections between literary endeavor and social concern. In a recent statement, he explained the assumptions that underlie his writings. "I believe that the point of view I write from is born of the local culture which developed in Hawai'i. My work often tries to capture some sense of the various cultural influences which affect individual's lives. I believe in the function that poetry performs in reflecting and shaping the people and culture which give it life, which sustain it. I believe that this social function of poetry is part of the give and take between life and art which ideally makes the two indistingishable, exciting, and mutually beneficial. And I believe that this process is inevitable."

As a teacher and editor, Chock has worked to find avenues for the expression of Hawai'i-based creative writing. As the coordinator and principal teacher in the Hawai'i Poets in the Schools program from 1973 through the present he has introduced many students and teachers to poetry writing. As an editor, his collaboration with Darrell Lum on *Bamboo Ridge: The Hawai'i Writers Quarterly* has created a place for writing by, for, and of Hawai'i.

Chock's poems—which have appeared in two collections, *Ten Thousand Wishes* and *Last Days Here*—are usually concerned with Hawai'i scenes and subjects.

Comments on "For George, Our Neighbor"

"This contemporary age-old saga is quirky and outrageous. Our hero struggles with a seemingly insurmountable foe—the guy next door—eh, we know him, too!—and how things can escalate when we start to catapult catshit over the fence. George, Our Neighbor, becomes archetypal—in every neighborhood there lives that pack rat eccentric, that 'Japanese Einstein,' that mysterious Boo Radley."

—CATHY SONG

"Wonderful all that clutter of mangoes, cats, and mail, the complications of affection and quarrels of close neighbors who can't help living in one another's lives. Anywhere in the world. Lai dat. Equally universal is the sense of loss at the end of the poem which calls up a sadness reminiscent in another language of the snows of years past. I should say that of Chock's poems I like this one the best, this rich characterization of George."

—PHYLLIS HOGE

Phyllis Hoge

Phyllis Hoge writes that "the vivid natural language of poetry expresses with honesty life's truths in a clear verbal music. Deep emotion is not enough. Wisdom, the understanding of experience, however wide and varied is not enough. A poet has to discover his or her own language and find out how to handle it—with love, yes, but also with respect. Poets, who understand how dangerous the medium is, learn only by study and long practice how to master it."

Phyllis Hoge's chief work in Hawai'i, after she joined the University of Hawai'i's Department of English in 1964, was to foster a hospitable milieu for the writing and appreciation of poetry by playing host for eight years to "The Only Established Permanent Floating Poetry Game in Honolulu," an open poetry workshop, which met fortnightly primarily in her home. Later she conceived and initiated Haku Mele o Hawai'i, one of the first poets in the schools programs in the country. In her teaching in the community and at UH she encouraged a focus on ordinary, everyday experience as the material for poems and urged the use of natural language, including dialects such as pidgin. Her understanding of the art of poetry derives from the Irish poet Yeats, whose verse was the subject of her Ph.D. thesis at the University of Wisconsin.

Her volumes of poems include *Artichoke and Other Poems* (1969), *The Creation Frame* (1973), and *The Ghosts of Who We Were* (1986).

Comment on "Letters from Jian Hui"

"The voice of the letters from Jian Hui captures the sometimes humorous, often poignant linguistic surprises a foreign speaker brings to another language—in these poems, a native Mandarin speaker is struggling to express herself in English: 'Usually there is not much to do and I am boring.' I like the way this happens through the series of poems without it being overdone. I especially like the sense of earnestness I hear in Jian Hui, that earnestness and desire to do the very best that she possibly can rings very true to experience with overseas Chinese friends. Nothing is taken for granted and friendships are deeply treasured."

—CATHY SONG

Rubellite Kawena Johnson

Rubellite Kawena Johnson is best known for her scholarly work in the area of traditional Hawaiian literature and folklore. Her extensive research has addressed many important specific and general topics. Her study of traditional Hawaiian literature culminated in the 1981 publication of *Kumulipo: Hawaiian Hymn of Creation*, Volume 1, a major reinterpretation of a crucial example of Hawaiian oral poetry.

Johnson was born and raised in the historic district of Koloa on the island of Kaua'i. She attended the University of Hawai'i at Mānoa in the early 1950s, where Samuel Elbert first encouraged her interest in written Hawaiian tradition. Johnson did graduate work in anthropology and folklore at the University of Indiana. Later, under the tutelage of Kenneth Emory, she conducted research on Hawaiian music and folklore at Bishop Museum. Specializing in the fields of folklore and advanced Hawaiian, she taught for many years as a professor in the Department of Indo-Pacific Languages at UH-Mānoa.

Comment on "A Passage to Nowhere"

"The experience of reading it is something like a voyage on a ship where the voyagers are at first sure of where they are going in terms of what the story is about, and then unsure, as if the ship has taken a turn into waters that were not originally part of the itinerary. Then when the voyage is completed, the reader who thinks creatively has a sort of flash understanding of what was happening all along: this is about human beings and death in two contexts. . . . In a way it shows us something about our smallness in the face of the vastness of oblivion, and about our instinctive will to stare it in the face and endure."

— IAN MACMILLAN

Maxine Hong Kingston

Highly acclaimed for multifaceted books that combine autobiographical material with legendary and fictional elements, Maxine Hong Kingston's breakthrough as a writer came with the 1976 publication of *The Woman Warrior*, a work that received the National Book Critics Circle Award for nonfiction and several other distinguished recognitions. In her second book, *China Men*, Kingston's gallery of fathers', grandfathers', and uncles' strange adventures in the American "gold mountain" add up to a chronicle of the difficult and exciting lives experienced by the first several waves of male Chinese immigrants to America.

Kingston grew up in Stockton, California, but she lived in Hawai'i for many years, working as a teacher at both high school and university levels. She reflects on her Hawai'i experiences in her book of reminiscences, *Hawai'i One Summer* from which "Chinaman's Hat" and "A Sea Worry" are excerpted.

Comment on "Chinaman's Hat"

"Any writing about the ocean automatically captures my interest. Particularly, I am drawn to any writing about the ocean as three-dimensional medium, and I am also, I suppose, hard to please on this matter. When I first came here thirty-four years ago, I surfed, bodysurfed, sailed, and thought these activities were 'fun,' but, when I discovered the ocean as a vast and complex world. . . . I found a subject of interest that never went away and never will. My excuse for entry into this world has always been spearfishing, and after all this time I think I know the ocean as three-dimensional medium. When I read this apparently autobiographical account, I suppose I thought at first that the author, who writes, ". . . I don't swim very well," might not be able to capture the essence of it, but then I was quickly turned around in this doubt by Kingston's careful and very vivid meditation on the ocean as a three-dimensional medium.

> *Sometimes the sun made golden rooms, which we entered from dark hallways. Specks of sand shone like gold and fell like motes, like the lights in California. Sea cucumbers rocked from side to side.*

Yes. There are various similes and metaphorical images here, but how perfect they are in rendering these somewhat minute things you see, and I have seen, all these years. For some reason, the sea cucumbers rocking from side to side was my favorite, because, as a matter of fact, they do, and I suppose you could line up a hundred professional writers and have them write about seeing what's under there, and maybe none of them would remember to include the sea cucumbers rocking from side to side. Specks of sand do float, and the sun creates a golden refraction, and yes, they do drift slowly toward the bottom. And yes, the sun does make golden rooms. The entire piece has imagery of this quality, and again, about a subject that is very difficult to capture. Under the surface it's like a dream.

—IAN MACMILLAN

Victoria Nalani Kneubuhl

Victoria Nalani Kneubuhl has spoken eloquently about the importance of her form of art. "Theatre is a conduit into our everyday world through which mystery and magic may still enter. At the same time, theatre can serve as a powerful platform for examining the social and political issues of our time. I am extremely proud to be part of a craft that is forceful yet transitory and fragile."

Kneubuhl was born in Honolulu and is of Samoan, Hawaiian, and Caucasian ancestry. She feels her work is "inextricably woven together" with her experiences of island life.

She has had ten plays produced in Honolulu, primarily by Kumu Kahua Theatre and the Honolulu Theatre for Youth. Two of her plays, *The Conversion of Ka'ahumanu* and *Ka'iulani*, toured Edinburgh, Washington D.C., and Los Angeles. Her children's play *Tofa Samoa* was an invited production at the Okinawa International Children's Theatre Festival in 1994. In addition to writing for the theatre, she works as a writer and researcher for many historical and cultural programs in the islands. For her historical street pageant *January, 1893*, which was performed at the historical sites where the events actually took place, she was named one of the "10 Who Made a Difference" in the Hawaiian Islands by the *Honolulu Star Bulletin* in 1993. The Hawai'i Heritage Center chose her to receive "The Keeper of the Past" award in 1994 for her contributions toward the cause of preserving and sharing Hawai'i's unique heritage. In 1996 she became one of the first artists to received a fellowship from the State Foundation on Culture and the Arts.

Comments on "Ho'oulu Lāhui"

"The story moves. . . . There are surprising twists. It is a good story and thought-provoking. . . . One sympathizes with Kahikina, through whose viewpoint the story is told."

— MILTON MURAYAMA

"Victoria Kneubuhl's futuristic tale of native Hawaiians is both riveting and haunting. . . . This is masterful storytelling that adds another dimension to local literature."

— EDWARD SAKAMOTO

Comments on "Olo"

". . . the notion of the poet's connection to the land is very powerful, as is the connection to a warrior past and the imagined battles."

— DARRELL H. Y. LUM

"Graphic descriptions of the killings in wars and how the dead affect the living. I like the directness."

— MILTON MURAYAMA

Darrell H. Y. Lum

Darrell H. Y. Lum is a fiction writer and playwright who is one of the pioneering voices of Hawai'i literature. His stories celebrate the everyday lives of island people, growing up "small kid time," and the use of pidgin. Beneath the engaging humor and the good fun "talk story" of his work Lum explores the conflicts and complexities of our lives. Finding one's identity, reconciling family relationships, and discovering those things which draw us together as a community are themes which run though his stories.

He has published two collections of short fiction *Sun: Short Stories and Drama* and *Pass On, No Pass Back*. The latter was awarded the Asian American Studies Book award in 1992. His plays have been produced by Kumu Kahua Theatre and Honolulu Theatre for Youth, and his work has been widely anthologized and frequently used in secondary school and college classes across the state and nation. He received the Hawai'i Award for Literature in 1996, the Cades Award in 1991 and an NEA Fellowship for Fiction in 1990. He, along with Eric Chock, co-founded Bamboo Ridge Press in 1978 and has served as one of its editors for the past 20 years.

Comments on "Encountering Sorrow"

"These are I think Darrell's best pidgin stories. They are a riot of puns and jokes. The dialogue is so real that it's like something you've overheard rather than read. The language is so direct: 'My pants is poked out, shet.' These stories capture the awkwardness and wild kidding among seventh-grade Chinese kids in Honolulu in the 1960s —written by a wordsmith who loves word-play and the coining of phrases. The writing is compact, layered, and serious beneath all the joking. So much of Chinese beliefs and practices are revealed. . . . In looking for prospective mates, you look for 'who got carsick, had mental illness in the family, or bad teeth.' Or how the Father wards off bad luck after attending all the funerals. One learns so much while laughing. The grandfather, father, Fish Uncle, and even Aunt Etto are concisely etched. They're individuals. Even the two-dimensional characters—Russo, Wanda Chu, Pearldean Woo, Mr. Sakamoto—are memorable. Scenes feel like they actually happened—'pa-pa-pa-pa-pa oo mau mau . . .'"

— MILTON MURAYAMA

"Darrell Lum's story of father and son entertains as it informs, switching time sequences, going from pidgin to standard English, and painting a poignant picture of family and recognition, of the ties that bind."

— EDWARD SAKAMOTO

"The intensity of this story snuck up on me. The humor, colorful images, funny situations, sharp characters and wonderful language all distracted me from the momentum of the subtext. Great magic and illusion. By the end I was totally identified with the narrator and able to touch his feelings."

— VICTORIA NALANI KNEUBUHL

"Through the clutter and effusion of sounds, smells, textures, and imagery; the proximity; the humidity; and the humor—Darrell Lum gives us generous portions of the richness of local experience. He contrasts this richness with the stark scene in the hos-

pital where not even a last sip of water for the narrator's father is possible. Only the poignant reference to the mother's unheard song somehow heals us, like lighting the obligatory incense and watching it burn."

—ESTELLE ENOKI

Ian MacMillan

Ian MacMillan once said in an interview that the key to the discipline of creative writing is "the way a writer trains himself to think and perceive." Some of MacMillan's best-known works of fiction concern the horrors of war. Imagining the unthinkable by rendering it remarkably real and movingly understood has often been MacMillan's mission and constant challenge to himself. He sets himself difficult story premises in order to compel his writing to be as good as it can be. He confesses that "I frequently doubt whether a story will work, but I convince myself that it will, push through the doubts and keep at it."

Critics have praised his war novels *Proud Monsters, Orbit of Darkness,* and *Village of a Million Spirits* as "luminous," "ferociously chilling," and "powerfully disturbing." They have been called "dark portraits, yet sublime, ultimately uplifting, in their exploration of the means and capacities of the human spirit." Kurt Vonnegut has dubbed MacMillan "the Stephen Crane of World War II."

A resident of Hawai'i since the mid 1960s, Ian MacMillan is the author of five novels and three short story collections, one of which won the Associated Writing Program's Award for Short Fiction. Three of these books—the novel *The Red Wind* (1998) and the short story collections *Exiles from Time* (1998) and *Squid Eye* (1999) are set in Hawai'i. He teaches fiction writing at the University of Hawai'i at Mānoa.

Comments on "Liar Liar"

"Ian MacMillan's tale of a mother and three young children trying to survive and hold onto to their lives and home in contemporary Windward Oahu by means of various scams—involving begging for 'donations' for various non-existent charities—is touching, off-beat, and as real as the house around the block. The fragility of this courageous, endangered family's situation is symbolized by recurring references to a huge, predatory heron that haunts their yard hoping to feast on baby mynah birds. The tale deftly culminates with the son's discovery that art can be among the greatest (and least criminal!) of scams."

—JOSEPH STANTON

"*Ian MacMillan's story of a struggling Kailua family provides a wry look at art and illusion, subtly challenging our sensibilities about why we create and the relevance of art as both product and process. As a case in point, do we believe the commission for this story encouraged the creative effort of the writer, or was the story conceived to question the value and illusion behind government spending for the arts? The story's viability as an artistic statement makes us wonder about MacMillan's intent, just as the public has speculated for ages about, say,* Mona Lisa's *smile."*

— ESTELLE ENOKI

W. S. Merwin

W. S. Merwin was born in New York City and grew up in New Jersey and Pennsylvania. In the early years of his career he lived in France, Portugal, and Majorca. For a time, he earned most of his income from translations from French, Spanish, Latin, and Portuguese. Since the late 1970s, he has spent much of his time at his home on the island of Maui. Hawai'i-related topics and places have become a major focus of many of his more recent works. His many books of poems, stories, and essays have earned him numerous awards, including the Pulitzer Prize. His collections of poems include *The Drunk in the Furnace, The Carrier of Ladders, Writings to an Unfinished Accompaniment, The Rain in the Trees, Travels,* and *The River Sound.*

The selection included in this anthology is an excerpt from Merwin's 1998 epic poem, *The Folding Cliffs: A Narrative of 19th-Century Hawai'i.*

Comments on *The Folding Cliffs*:

"*This section of* The Folding Cliffs *is very moving, the way it expands and contracts, psychologically, through the images of the wound, the dark, the coals, Ko'olau's face 'crumbling into itself,' and yet there is an undercurrent of healing already underway—memory, the offering of chant, rain falling . . . ancestral sounds.*"

— CATHY SONG

"*Merwin's* The Folding Cliffs, *more decidedly than any of the other selections, defines itself as a story, an epic story. For, although the central characters are not world-renowned heroes but Hawaiian lepers, the structure is epic, the rhythms of the Homeric six-beat long line are epic. The gravity and flexibility of that line adapt as readily to speech as to description, to meditation as to action. As the numbered sections indicate, the story told in the poem is of considerable dimension, epic in scope, and what the story tells matters a great deal in the history of Hawai'i.*

The setting and the tale itself are genuinely Hawaiian. Merwin does not rely on a spattering of Hawaiian words and names to carry the feeling of authenticity. The way nature lives is Hawaiian. The scenery is not passive; it is animated. The rain does not fall, it reaches down, as later the dark arms of the house reach forward. Merwin has recognized the Hawaiian sense of nature's participation in the life of mankind. Not all writers know about this. When I was in college learning to write, I had to be admonished over and over again to 'avoid the pathetic fallacy.' Since I believe that trees can understand me and that winds and stones are alive, I did not do what I was told. Never have. I think that kind of response to nature is what's going on in the assumptions underlying The Folding Cliffs. *When I lived in Hawai'i, I listened hungrily to what people who had lived there all their lives had to say about the behavior of nature, the living spirit in the land and ocean and the plants and creatures thereof. That's what I think Merwin has caught in this poem. As far as I can judge (with the help of my Hawaiian-language-teacher daughter), he conveys in a Greek-like English line the essential spirit of Hawai'i."*

— PHYLLIS HOGE

Milton Murayama

Milton Murayama was born in Lahaina, Maui and grew up in Lahaina and in the nearby plantation camp, Pu'ukoli'i. Both localities would later serve as his subjects when he began writing fictions centered on life in Hawai'i.

During World War II, Murayama trained at a Military Intelligence Language School and served with Army Intelligence in India. He received a B.A. in English and philosophy from the University of Hawai'i in 1947 and an M.A. in Chinese and Japanese from Columbia University in 1950. For many years Murayama worked at jobs that would allow him time and energy to write at night.

One of the manuscripts that resulted from those late night efforts was the novel *All I Asking for Is My Body.* Arnold Hiura has described that work as "the only comprehensive literary treatment of the Hawai'i plantation experience, an experience which directly or indirectly affects a very large segment of Hawai'i's population." Murayama's subsequent novels—*Five Years on a Rock* and *Plantation Boy*—are further explorations of "the real, human situation of the plantation." Murayama's adaptation of a segment from *All I Asking for Is My Body* for the theatre is his contribution to this anthology.

Comments on *All I Asking for Is My Body*:

"Milton Murayama has successfully transformed his classic novel into a play without losing the spirit and vitality of his earlier work. Brothers Kiyo and Tosh come alive again, a welcome addition to the theatre."

— EDWARD SAKAMOTO

"Great characters and a sharp portrait of the plantation world. I admired the complex relationships and the realistic portrayal of working-class hardships and struggles over generational values."

—VICTORIA NALANI KNEUBUHL

". . . Of course, beyond the story of family relationships is the changing nature of the culture and the time in which the story takes place . . . All I Asking is about the passing of an era. The sons' desire to get off the plantation, like their father's, drives the boxing. Tosh's cry, 'All I asking for is my body' becomes the cry of each character in the play as they search for their place in the world."

—DARRELL H. Y. LUM

Leialoha Apo Perkins

Leialoha Apo Perkins was born into a tri-lingual family (Hawaiian, Chinese, English) in Lahaina, Maui. She has received degrees from Boston University, Simmons College, Mt. Holyoke College, University of Pennsylvania. Her Ph.D. in Folklore and Anthropology at the latter launched her into field work in Hawaiian language and literature that has continued to be important to her work in subsequent positions at such institutions as the East-West Center, Atenisi University (in the Kingdom of Tonga), and the University of Hawai'i-West O'ahu.

Her works in poetry, fiction, criticism, social commentary, and translation draw upon the wide array of her experiences, including her early years in Lahaina and Boston, her family life, and her observation and participation in the changing multicultural ecologies of the Pacific. Out of a perceived need of islanders to write independently from mainstream Continental American models, Apo Perkins has been concerned with the need for new dictions, new metaphors formulated from local speech values, the reinvention of genres, and the expression of genuine island social values in literature. She has published seven collections of her poetry and fiction: *Natural and Other Stories about Contemporary Hawaiians* (1979), *Kamaka* (1979), *Kingdoms of the Heart* (1980), *Cyclone Country: Poems from Tonga* (1986), *Other Places in the Turning of the Mind* (1986), and *The Oxbridge Woman* (1998).

Comment on "In Praise of O'ahu"

"Apo Perkins captures in verse a voice that seems at once ancient, immediate, and timeless. She evokes heroic figures and events, singing in eloquent cadences of long-gone histories and myths as if she had recently and very personally experienced

them, giving us a past that seems palpable, on-going, and energized by unresolved urgencies."

—JOSEPH STANTON

Edward Sakamoto

Born and raised in Honolulu. After graduating from the University of Hawai'i, Sakamoto moved to California and worked for thirty years as a journalist for various newspapers, including twenty years at the *Los Angeles Times* as a copy editor.

At the time of his selection for the Hawai'i Award for Literature in 1997 he had written fourteen plays, nine of which have Hawai'i themes. His plays have been produced in Hawai'i, New York City, San Francisco, and in many other cities. He is especially known for performances of his plays by the East West Players of Los Angeles, America's oldest Asian American theatre company. A trilogy of his Hawai'i plays—*The Taste of Kona Coffee, Manoa Valley,* and *The Life of the Land*—was published in 1995 by the University of Hawai'i Press.

Several of his Hawai'i plays dramatize situations in which characters must make difficult choices concerning staying in a familiar, obligation-rich place or heading off toward the risky but tantalizing prospects of the faraway.

Comments on "The Family"

"I found myself quickly interested and engaged by this window into a family. It felt like I started looking at a big family picture, and then, as if using a zoom lens, I was focused on Michiko. I like this character and the fact that we learned about her character through what she did, how she thought, and how she responded to her world. Her relationship with Yuriko was painted with a restrained elegance that made it very touching. I especially like the ending and the vivid images of the last two paragraphs."

—VICTORIA NALANI KNEUBUHL

"Ed has captured in his story a wonderful sense of a particular plantation place and time, which reads like listening to an old-timer take a slow and leisurely ramble through one family's trials. . . . The American tale, the story of the rugged individual, does not play out in this story. Instead, we have a quiet, understated ending; one which is undeniably local. Michiko will strike out on her own and her family and community will support her decision, but she will also carry with her the memory of her sister, family, and community."

—DARRELL H. Y. LUM

"Ed Sakamoto's skill at storytelling through social and cultural commentary is well illustrated in this story. Particularly striking is the concluding image of a rain-drenched Michiko distancing herself from her home by withdrawing to a tree, which affords her little shelter. This seems symbolic of the sense of obligation and duty a Japanese girl on the verge of becoming a woman would feel. That the narrator describes neither her emotions nor her thoughts further emphasizes the cultural constraints she experiences and suggests the inevitability of self denial in the choice she must make."

—ESTELLE ENOKI

Marjorie Sinclair

For Marjorie Sinclair writing is way of coming to understandings. "You must continually press yourself to probe deeper, to find the core, the very root of the emotion or story. Not to let yourself skim over things, over the human situation."

Sinclair came to Hawai'i in the 1930s. Her interests in international developments in poetry led her to the study of languages—including Chinese, Japanese, and Hawaiian. She taught in the English Department of the University of Hawai'i from 1950 until her recent retirement.

She has published poetry, fiction, translations, and a biography of Nahi-'ena'ena, the daughter of King Kamehameha. *The Path of the Ocean*, Sinclair's volume of translations from the Hawaiian was called "a sensual education" by Michael Ondaatje and "a wonderfully comprehensive offering of the rich lyrical literature of Polynesia" by W. S. Merwin. *The Place Your Body Is*, a collection of Sinclair's own poems, appeared in 1984. Her works of fiction include two novels set in Hawai'i of the 1940s, *Kona* and *The Wild Wind*, both recently brought back into print by Mutual Publishing.

Comment on "Secrets"

"For me, something that is 'haunting' achieves that effect by leaving open as much or more than it explains. That is what I like about this story. . . . The skeptic as well as the believer are served, because Kimo could have dreamt the experience with Mr. Kahalewai, could also have really gone through the experience and then failed to find the right house. His wife could have seen some other old man. And what about the three days rather than one? The believer gets the plot completed but with an ambiguity that forces more thought and more looking backward into the story, perhaps even reading it a second time. The theme of secrets kept, and secrets taken to the grave, is managed here with a skill that leaves the reader with a thought-provoking, even 'haunting' series of secrets. As Chekhov would say, theme in fiction is the careful presentation of a question. The answer is up to the reader. . . . About the writing itself:

description of nature is one of the most difficult jobs for writers. In this story the natural description is both rich and precise, and so tangible an evocation of the setting that you'll be sure you can smell the rotten mangoes and the mold. I think this piece stands as a model of how a skilled writer can appeal to the reader's senses."

—IAN MACMILLAN

Cathy Song

Cathy Song exhorts her poetry students to seek their own voices by paying careful attention to the voices around them. In the introduction to *Sister Stew*, Song and her co-editor explain that remembered echoes of the voices of family and friends enable us to write about "the moments when we listened, watched, and understood, as if life, like a piece of music, could be apprehended in all its strangeness."

Song's rapid rise to prominence on the national poetry scene shows that she has found a voice that many want to hear. Her first book, a collection of poems, *Picture Bride*, won her the 1982 Yale Younger Poets Award and publication of the volume by Yale University Press; that much-praised book was nominated for the National Book Critics Circle Award. Her subsequent collections include, *Frameless Windows, Squares of Light* (Norton, 1988), and *School Figures* (Pittsburgh University Press, 1994).

Comments on Song's poems

". . . All three selections are about poetry itself. In 'Caldera Illumina' I keep recognizing my own various approaches to and avoidances of the writing job: the just claims which keep me from it, my need to hide my meaning at the same time as I reveal it, the need to go, 'deeper into the darkest room,' trying to reach 'the core of something permanent,' and what always accompanies that need—'distraction itself . . . obstacles to keep her from entering the last room,' wanting and not wanting to arrive there.

In 'The Bodhisattva Muses' I read how devotion to writing the poem heals the very suffering which makes it come into being. It is as though some force outside ourselves wants poems to be made, and, knowing that they must be made from pain of the open heart . . . through which she would heal her way back.

Of the three poems, 'The Sister,' probably the least metaphorical, provides the fullest narrative. Yet I feel the characters—the boy, his brother, Maggie, the father, the sister, the mother—are all representative aspects of finding the poem—'the voice of the quietest singing' as well as the 'two lives' any poet has to live, and the barriers or obstacles which may 'shut the lid on the music.'

Mysterious 'roses,' sometimes associated with blue, figure in each of these poems—

indeed, they seem to contain the being of the poems. She hides the roses, keeping them safe and secret, yet once the door is closed she'll place them in every room of the house. Houses and the imagery of houses—doors, curtains, kitchens, windows, rooms—are important in Song's work. I am tempted to think this is a natural outcome of a female take on human experience, though maybe it's only my own desire for security and shelter. Perhaps this is the real reason these lines especially appeal to me: 'Women at windows staring out of caves. They hang no curtains, their faces already hidden.'"

—PHYLLIS HOGE

About the Editors

Darrell H. Y. Lum wanted to be a cowboy when he was little but his brother owned the six-shooters. Then he wanted to be a fireman (before they were called firefighters) but his mother told him not to play with the water hose. Then he wanted to race cars until he crumpled the front right fender of his father's 59 Plymouth on the garage wall while learning how to drive a three speed column shift. There was nothing left to do after that but to tell stories.

He received the Hawai'i Award for Literature in 1996, the Cades Award in 1991, and a Fellowship for Fiction from the National Endowment for the Arts in 1990.

* * * * *

Joseph Stanton teaches art history and American studies at the University of Hawai'i at Mānoa. He has published hundreds of poems in *Poetry*, *Poetry East*, *Harvard Review*, and numerous other magazines. His essays on art and literature have appeared in such journals as *American Art*, *Art Criticism*, and *Journal of American Culture*. His recent books include *Imaginary Museum: Poems on Art* (Time Being Books, 1999) and *A Hawai'i Anthology* (SFCA, 1997), the latter in collaboration with Estelle Enoki. In 1997 he received the Cades Award for Literature. He has lived in Hawai'i, primarily in Leeward O'ahu, since 1972.

* * * * *

Estelle Enoki facilitated arts programming in Hawai'i's rural communities as an arts program specialist with the State Foundation on Culture and the Arts. For nearly a decade, she also coordinated the Hawai'i Award for Literature ceremonies and, in partnership with Bamboo Ridge Press and the Hawai'i Literary Arts Council, developed initiatives to further programming in the literary arts. Prior to joining the agency, she worked with arts programs among underserved communities in the East Bay Area of California. Her father is from Honomu and her mother was from Waipi'o Valley.

About the Artist

Nora Yamanoha is a resident of Kailua-Kona. In the print, she finds unlimited expressive possibilities. Yamanoha concentrates on the unique entity of the monotype and has no interest in high-tech replication. Her abstract imagery is derived from her quiet surrounding environment.